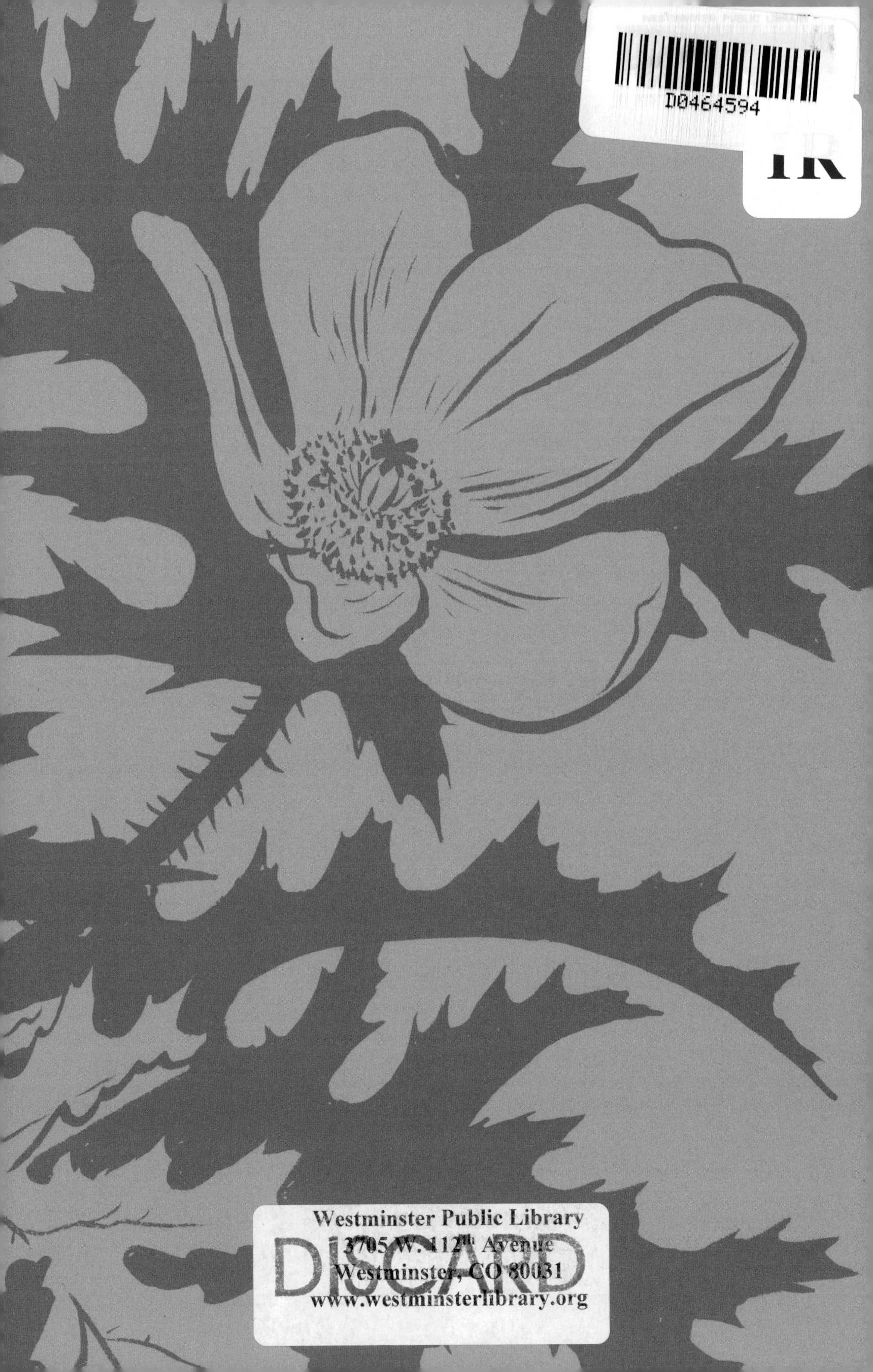

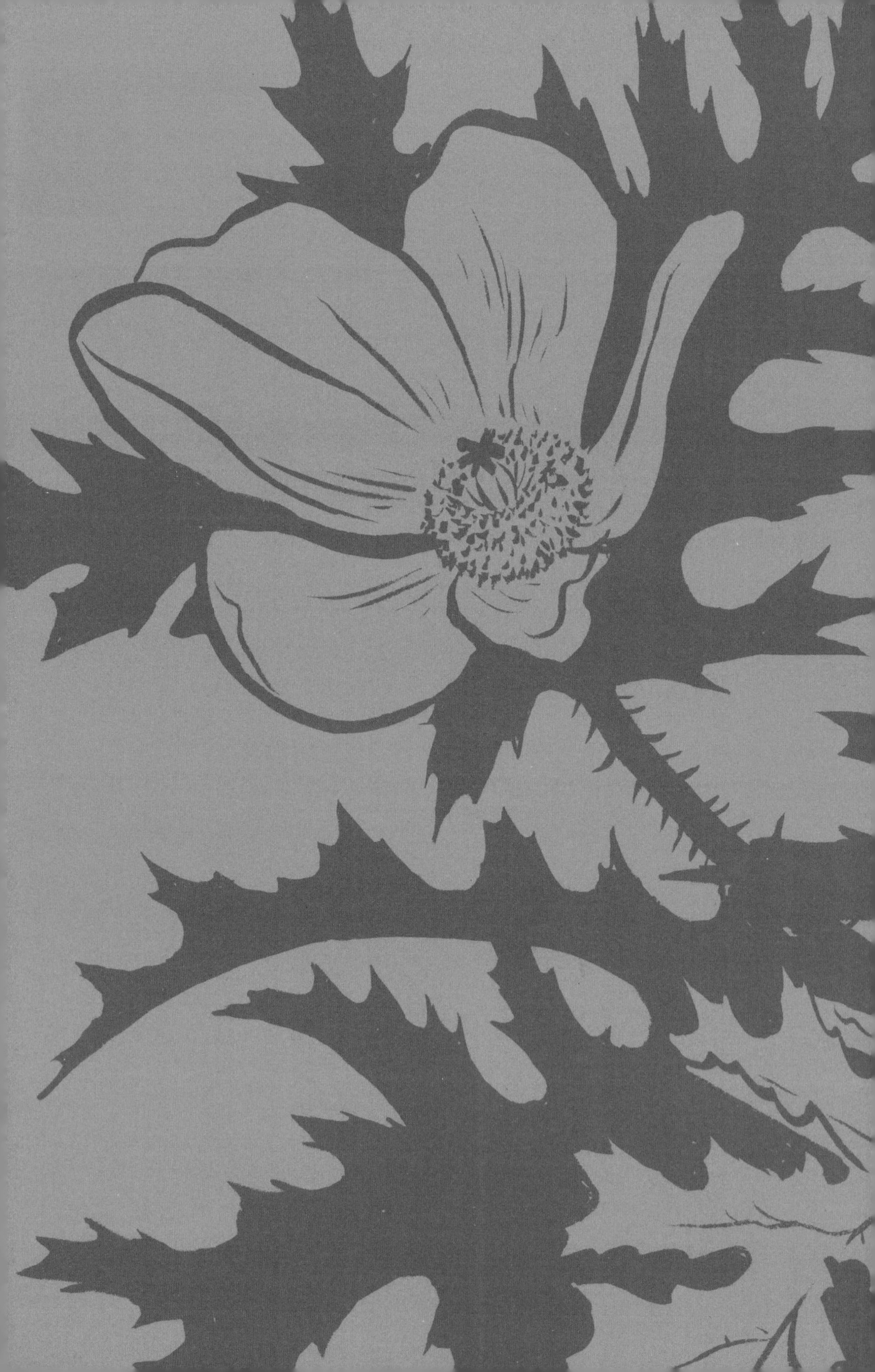

Night
Fisher

MOLOKAI VOLCANO
PACIFIC OCEAN
STAGE 1
EARLY PLEISTOCENE
(1.8-1.6 MILLION YEARS AGO)
WEST MAUI VOLCANO
LANAI VOLCANO
EAST MAUI VOLCANO
KAHOOLAWE VOLCANO
0 5 Miles
40°
30°
20°
10°
156°00′
21° 00
50°
40°
30°
MOLOKAI
STAGE 2
WEST MAUI
LANAI
EAST MAUI
KAHOOLAWE
0 5 Miles
21° 00′
50′
40′
30′

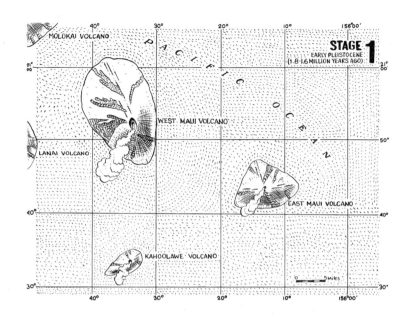

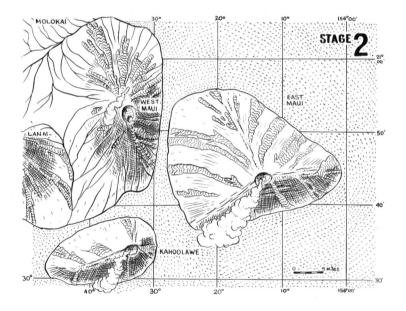

fig 1-7: The formation of the island of Maui, Hawaii as dictated by mounting lava, weather erosion, and a fluctuating sea level which characterizes the *Pleistocene Epoch.*

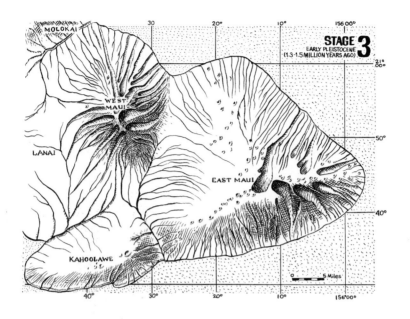

STAGE **3**
EARLY PLEISTOCENE
(1.3-1.5 MILLION YEARS AGO)

MOLOKAI

WEST MAUI

LANAI

EAST MAUI

KAHOOLAWE

0   5 Miles

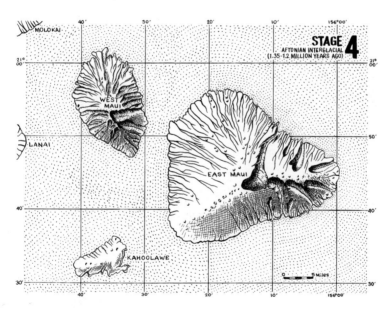

STAGE **4**
AFTONIAN INTERGLACIAL
(1.35-1.2 MILLION YEARS AGO)

MOLOKAI

WEST MAUI

LANAI

EAST MAUI

KAHOOLAWE

0   5 Miles

3

STAGE 5
KANSAN GLACIAL
(900,000-750,000 YEARS AGO)
MOLOKAI
WEST MAUI
EAST MAUI
LANAI
KAHOOLAWE
40′
30′
20′
10′
156°00′
21° 00′
50′
40′
30′
0
5 Miles

STAGE 6
ILLINOIAN GLACIAL
(400,000-250,000 YEARS AGO)
MOLOKAI
WEST MAUI
EAST MAUI
LANAI
KAHOOLAWE
40′
30′
20′
10′
156°00′
21° 00′
50′
40′
30′
0
5 Miles

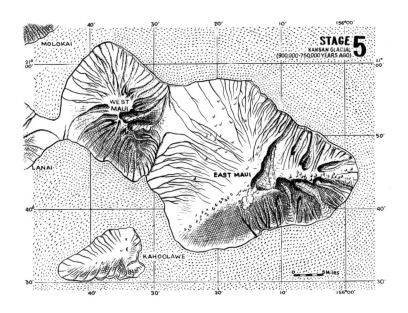

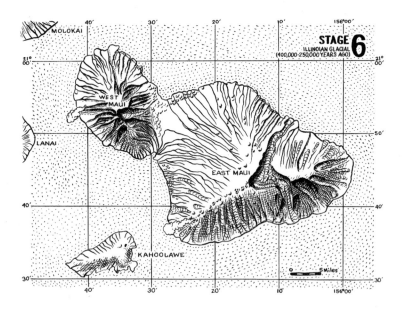

for Mom + Dad

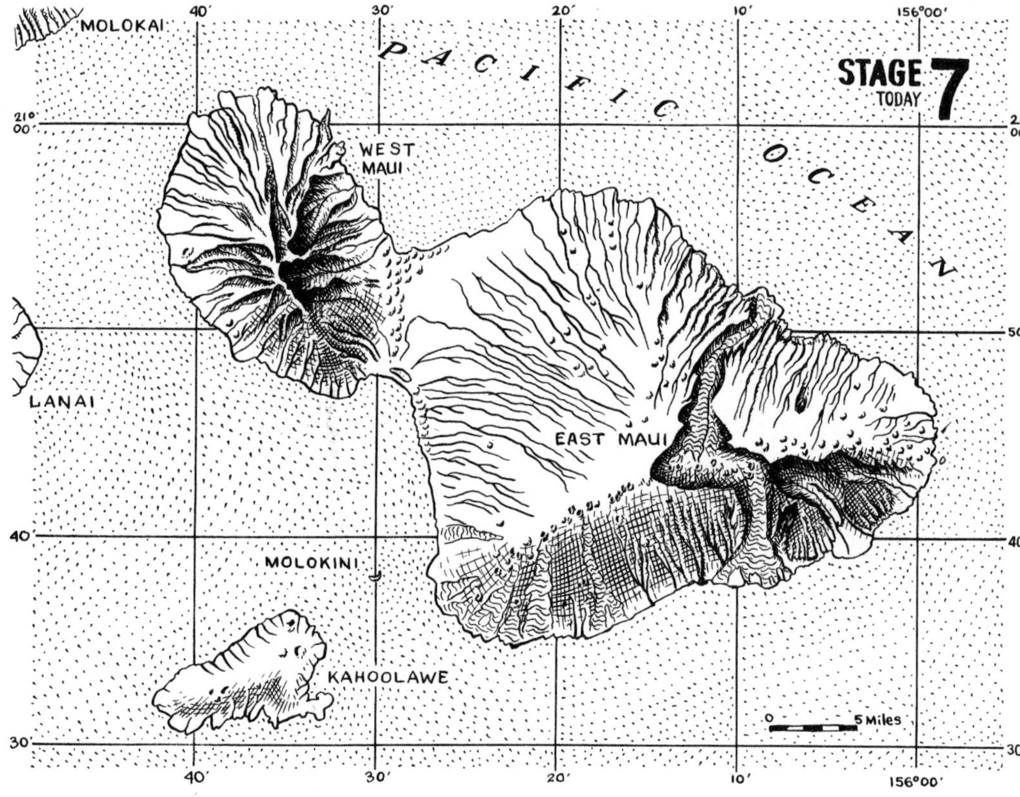
MOLOKAI
PACIFIC
OCEAN
STAGE 7
TODAY
WEST
MAUI
LANAI
EAST MAUI
MOLOKINI
KAHOOLAWE
0
5 Miles
40′
30′
20′
10′
156°00′
21°
00′
50′
40′
30′

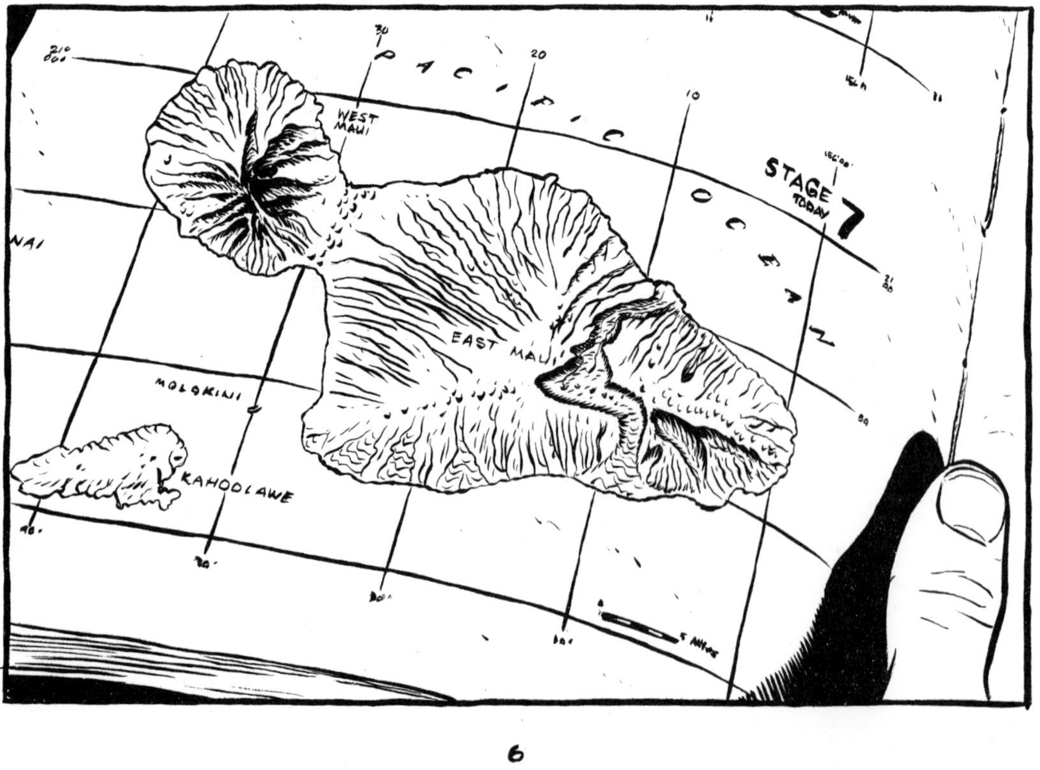
PACIFIC
OCEAN
WEST
MAUI
STAGE
TODAY
7
EAST MAUI
MOLOKINI
KAHOOLAWE

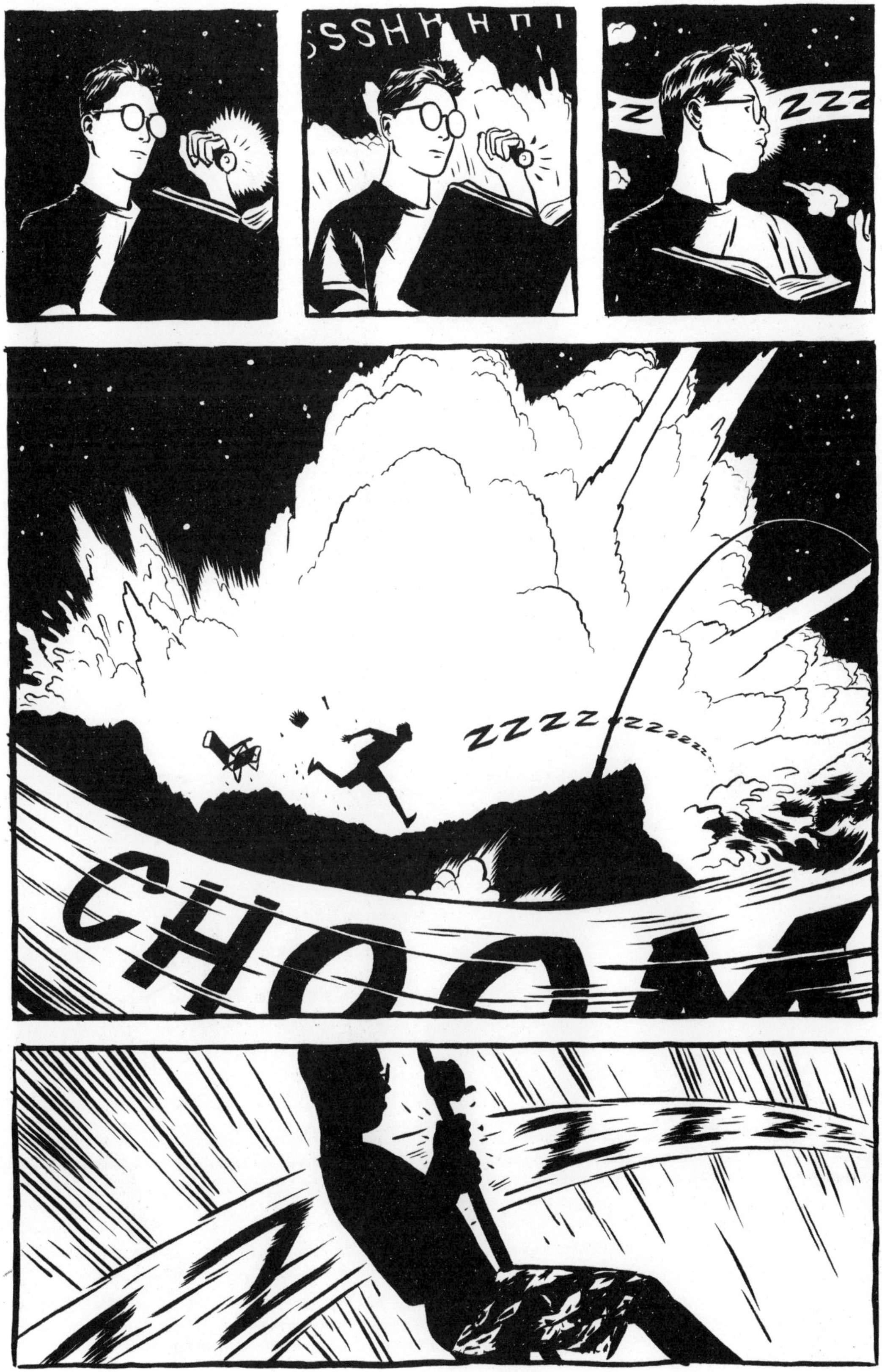
SSHH
ZZZ
ZZZZ
CHOOM
ZZZ

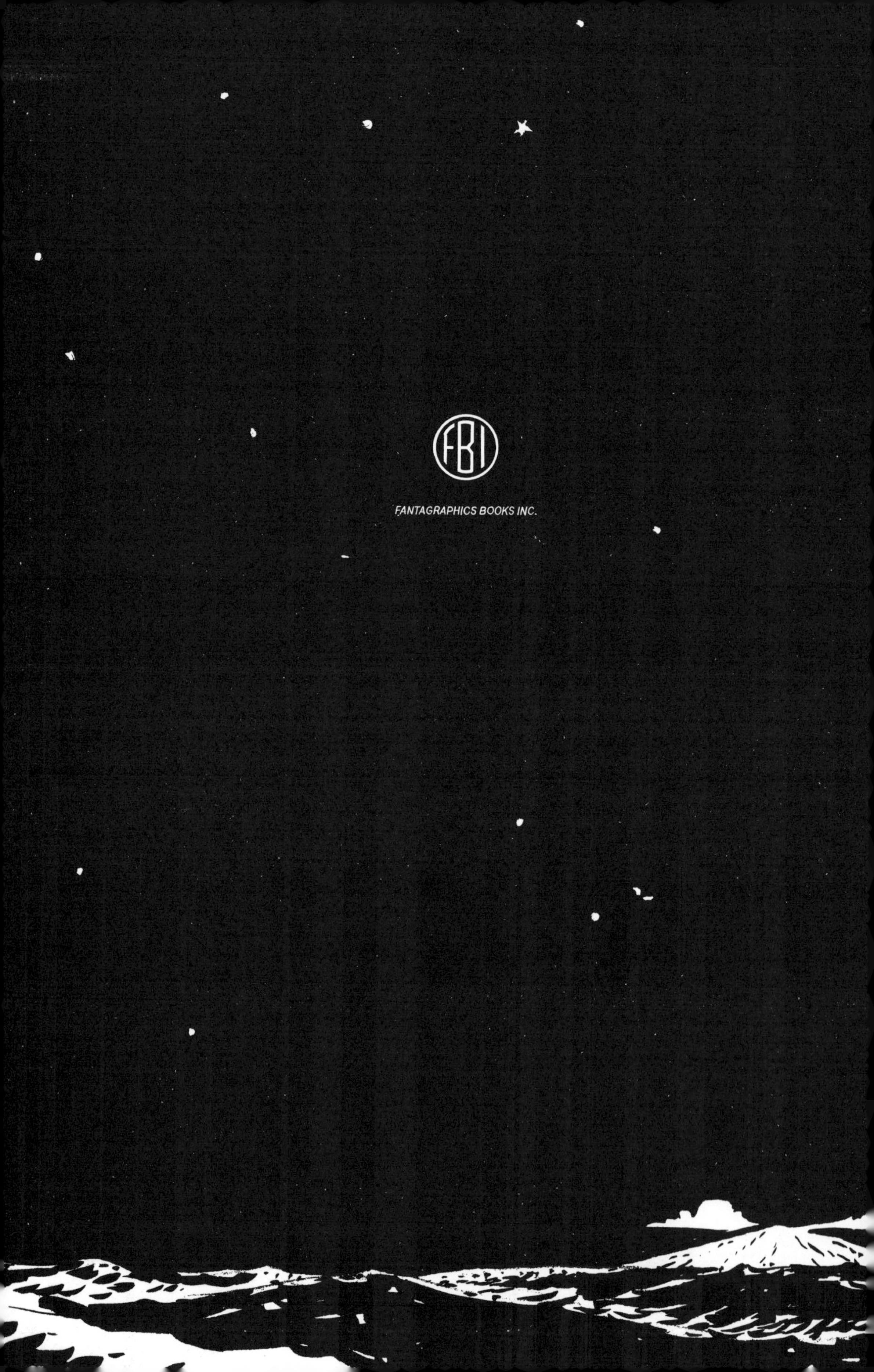

FANTAGRAPHICS BOOKS INC.

NIGHT FISHER

R. KIKUO JOHNSON

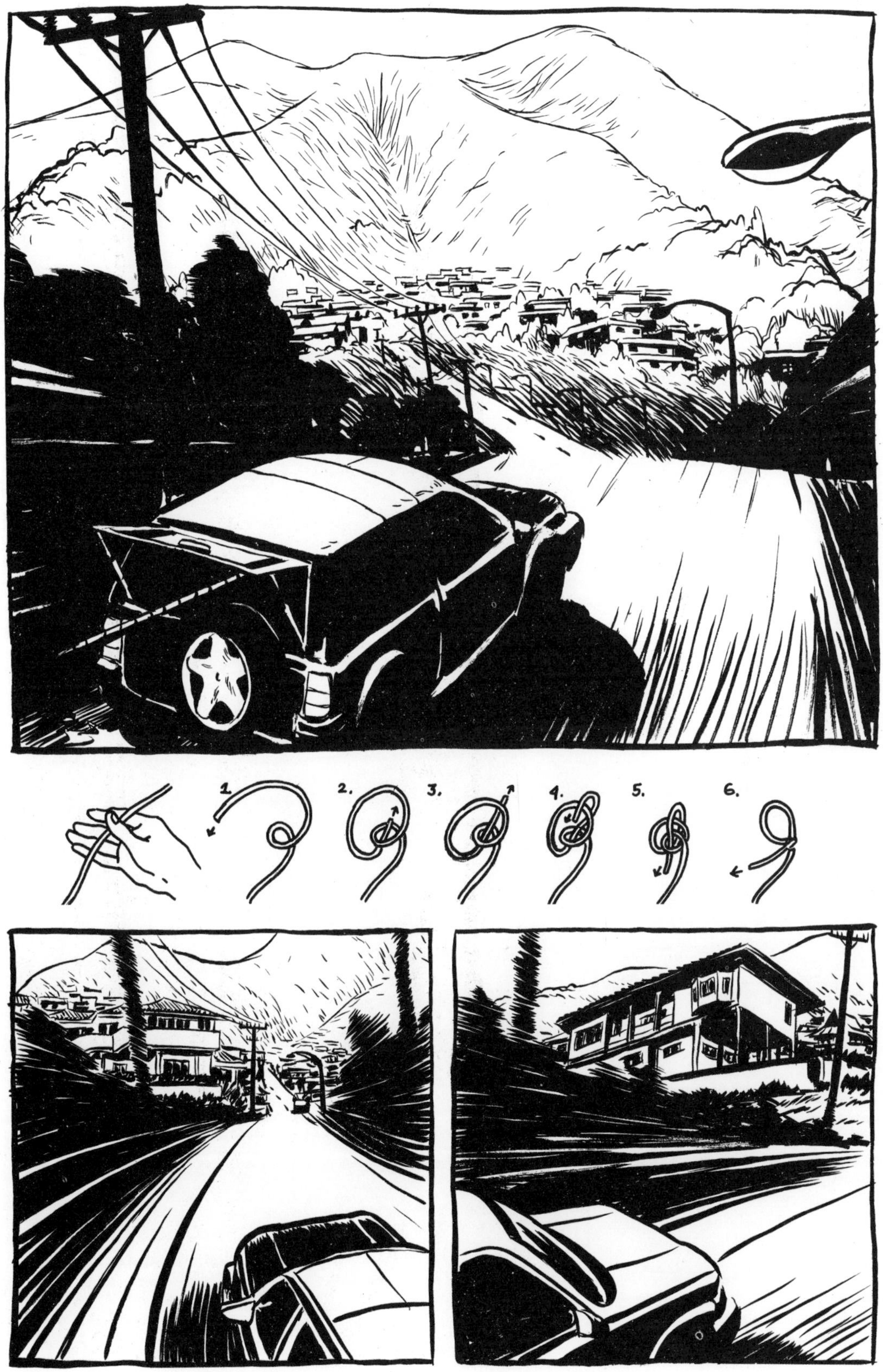
1.
2.
3.
4.
5.
6.

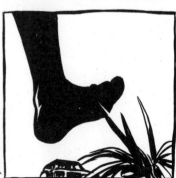

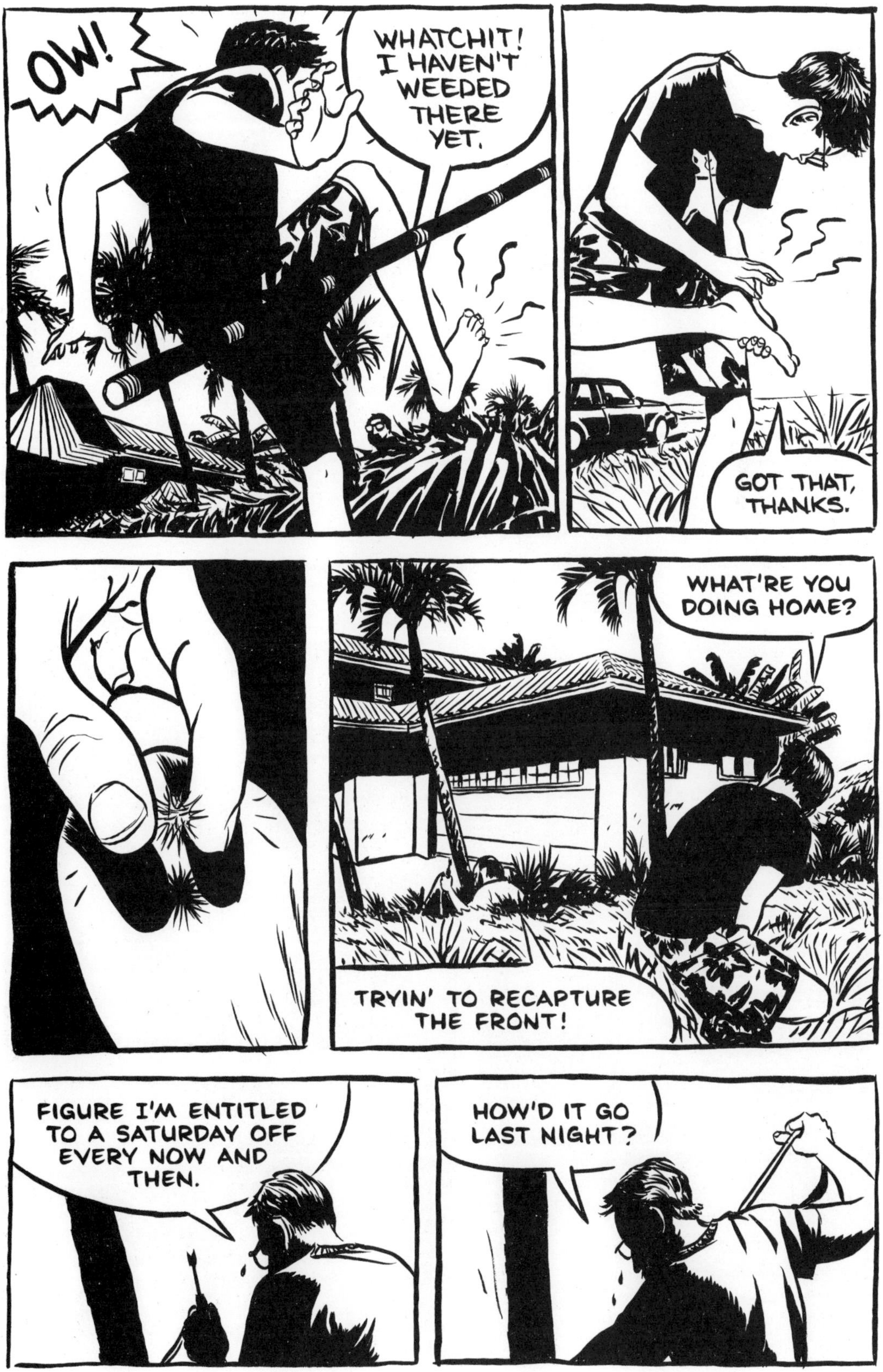
OW!
WHATCHIT! I HAVEN'T WEEDED THERE YET.
GOT THAT, THANKS.
WHAT'RE YOU DOING HOME?
TRYIN' TO RECAPTURE THE FRONT!
FIGURE I'M ENTITLED TO A SATURDAY OFF EVERY NOW AND THEN.
HOW'D IT GO LAST NIGHT?

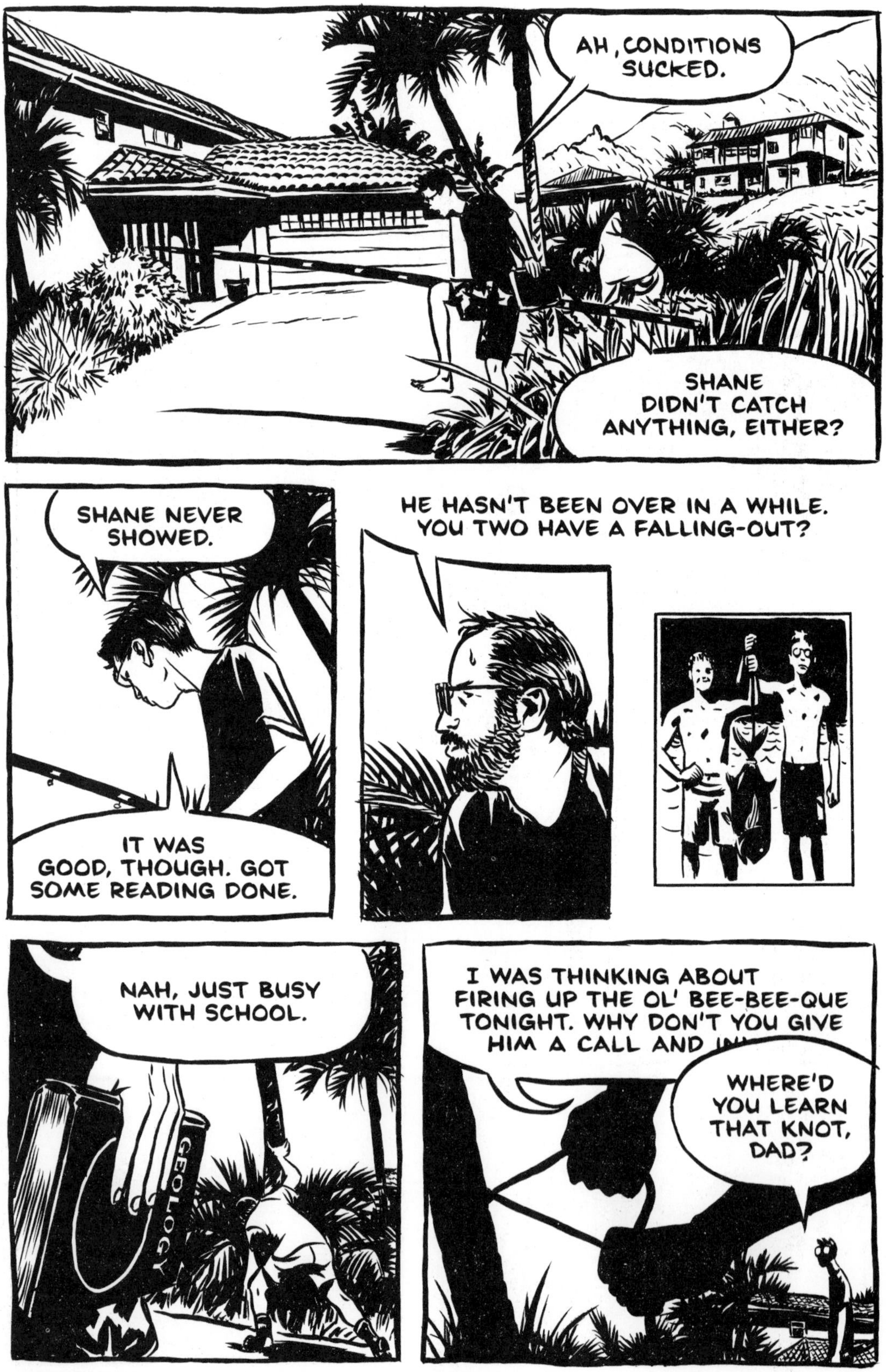
AH, CONDITIONS SUCKED.
SHANE DIDN'T CATCH ANYTHING, EITHER?
SHANE NEVER SHOWED.
IT WAS GOOD, THOUGH. GOT SOME READING DONE.
HE HASN'T BEEN OVER IN A WHILE. YOU TWO HAVE A FALLING-OUT?
NAH, JUST BUSY WITH SCHOOL.
GEOLOGY
I WAS THINKING ABOUT FIRING UP THE OL' BEE-BEE-QUE TONIGHT. WHY DON'T YOU GIVE HIM A CALL AND IN
WHERE'D YOU LEARN THAT KNOT, DAD?

THIS? LEARNED IT ON THE BOATS WHEN I WAS YOUR AGE.

I'M TRYING TO STRAIGHTEN THIS TREE, BUT THIS IS AS FAR AS SHE'LL GO.

>HEH<

GUESS IT'S A BIT LIKE PUTTING BRACES ON

"...PUTTING BRACES ON A SMILE FULL OF CAVITIES." YES, DAD, I *KNOW.*

MY DAD'S A DENTIST, AND THIS IS HIS FAVORITE JOKE. HE'S NEVER MISSED A CHANCE TO DEMONSTRATE ITS VERSATILTY.

SMILE FULL OF CAVITIES!

HE APPLIES IT TO HIS GOLF GAME, TO THE STOCK MARKET, AND MOST OFTEN TO THE JUNGLE IN FRONT OF OUR HOUSE.

15

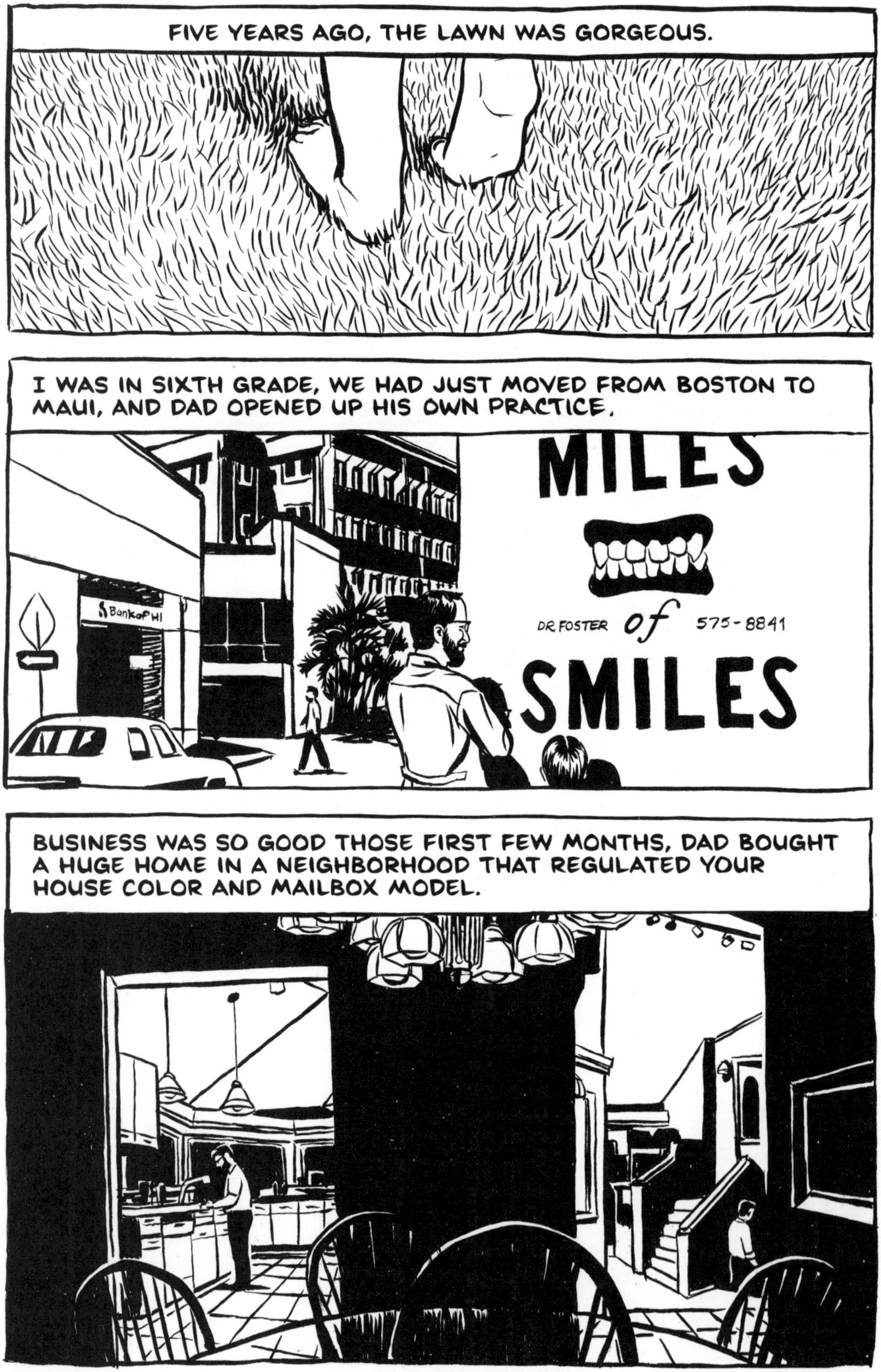
FIVE YEARS AGO, THE LAWN WAS GORGEOUS.
I WAS IN SIXTH GRADE, WE HAD JUST MOVED FROM BOSTON TO MAUI, AND DAD OPENED UP HIS OWN PRACTICE.
Bank of HI
MILES
DR. FOSTER
of
575-8841
SMILES
BUSINESS WAS SO GOOD THOSE FIRST FEW MONTHS, DAD BOUGHT A HUGE HOME IN A NEIGHBORHOOD THAT REGULATED YOUR HOUSE COLOR AND MAILBOX MODEL.

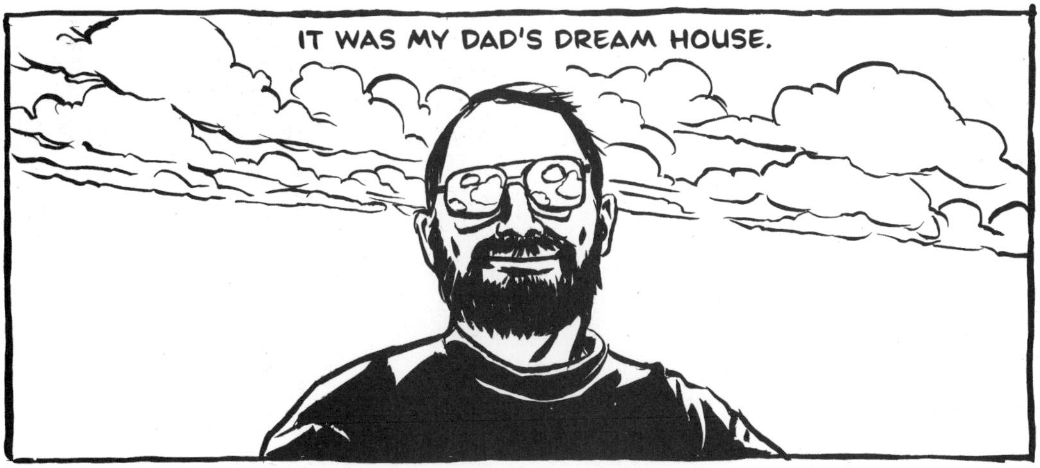
IT WAS MY DAD'S DREAM HOUSE.

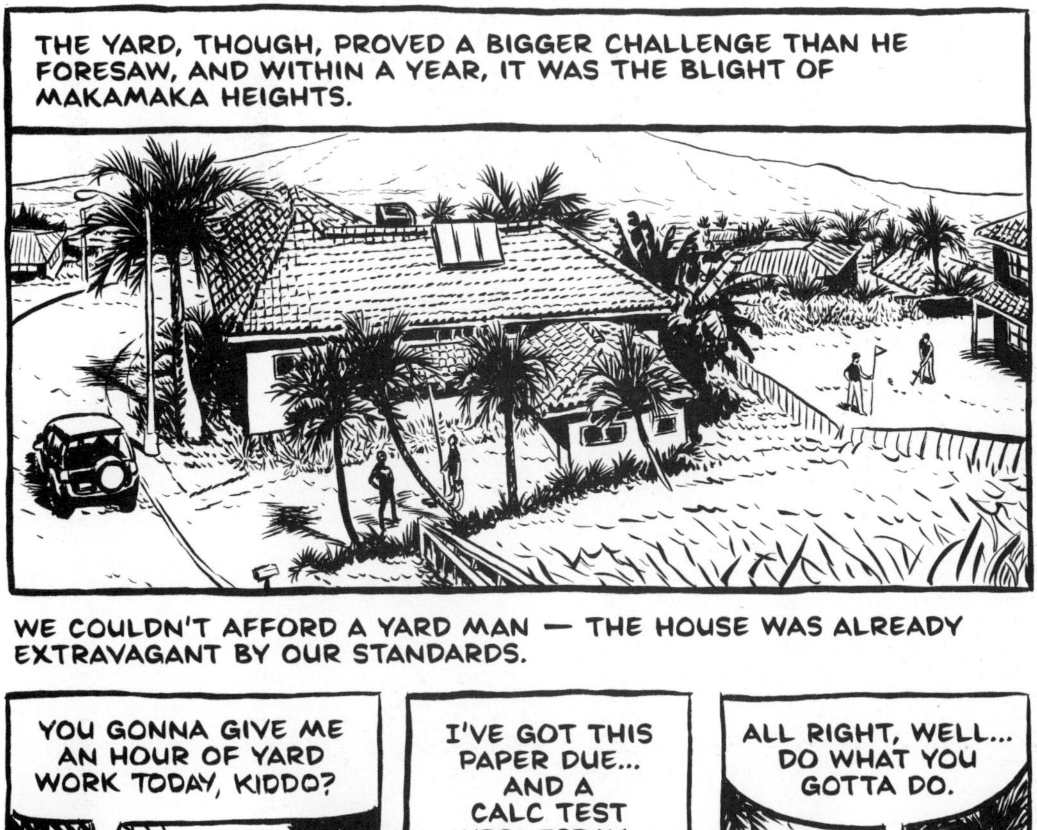
THE YARD, THOUGH, PROVED A BIGGER CHALLENGE THAN HE FORESAW, AND WITHIN A YEAR, IT WAS THE BLIGHT OF MAKAMAKA HEIGHTS.

WE COULDN'T AFFORD A YARD MAN — THE HOUSE WAS ALREADY EXTRAVAGANT BY OUR STANDARDS.

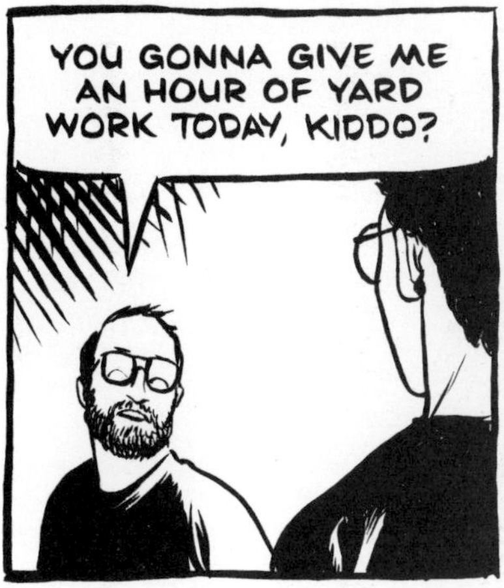
YOU GONNA GIVE ME AN HOUR OF YARD WORK TODAY, KIDDO?

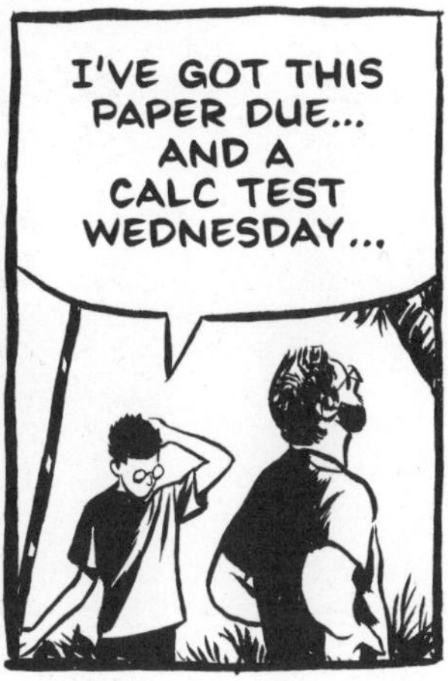
I'VE GOT THIS PAPER DUE... AND A CALC TEST WEDNESDAY...

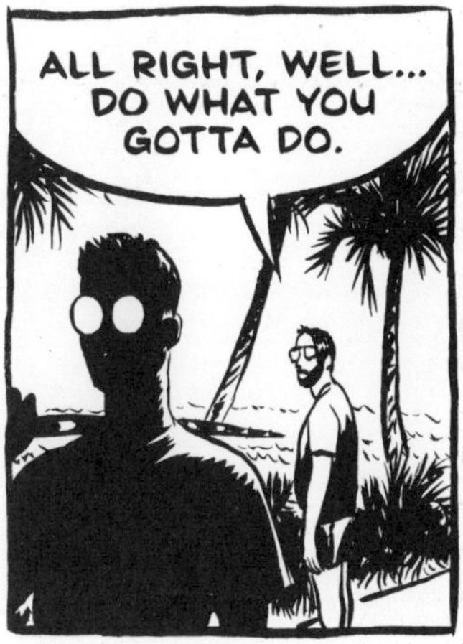
ALL RIGHT, WELL... DO WHAT YOU GOTTA DO.

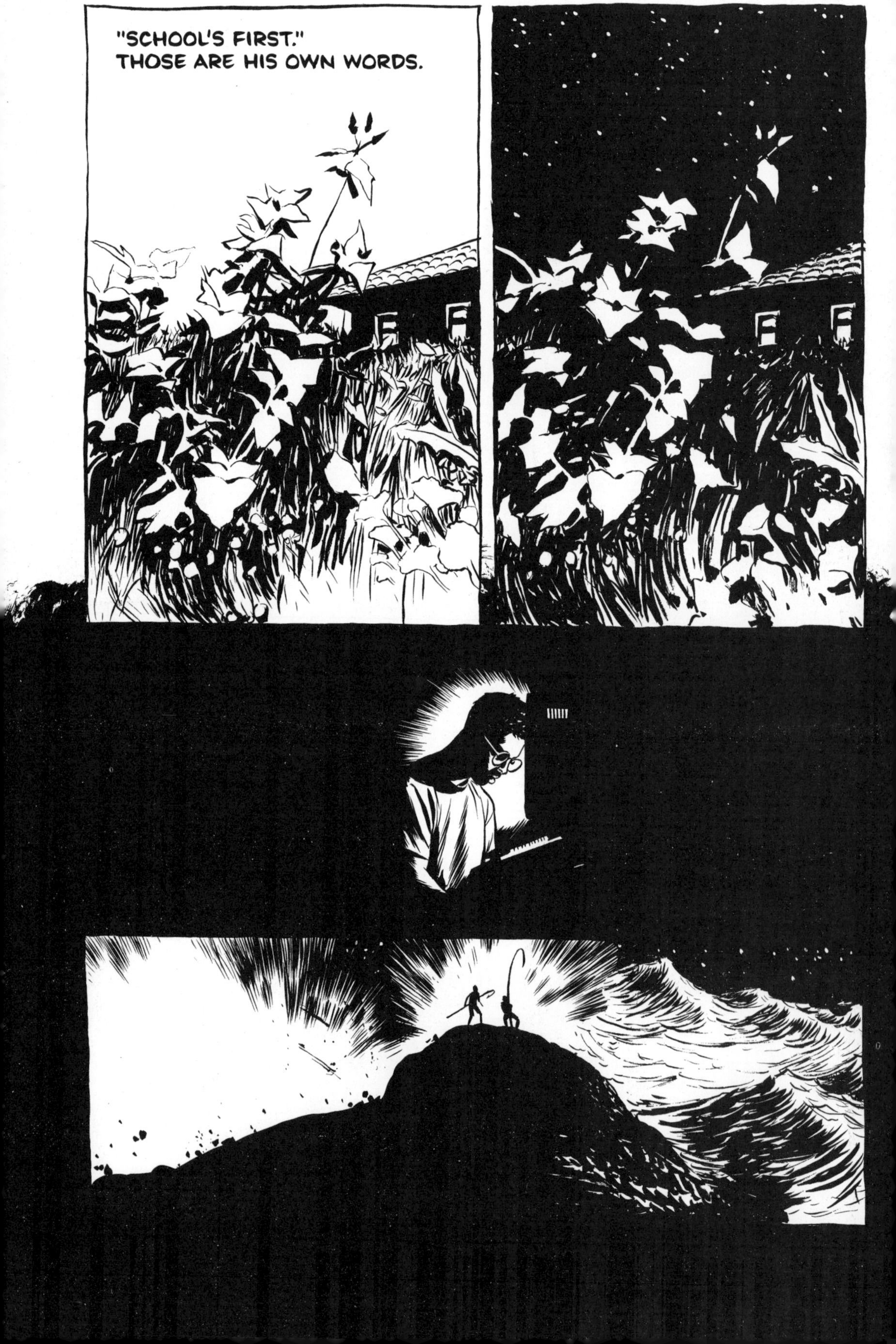
"SCHOOL'S FIRST."
THOSE ARE HIS OWN WORDS.

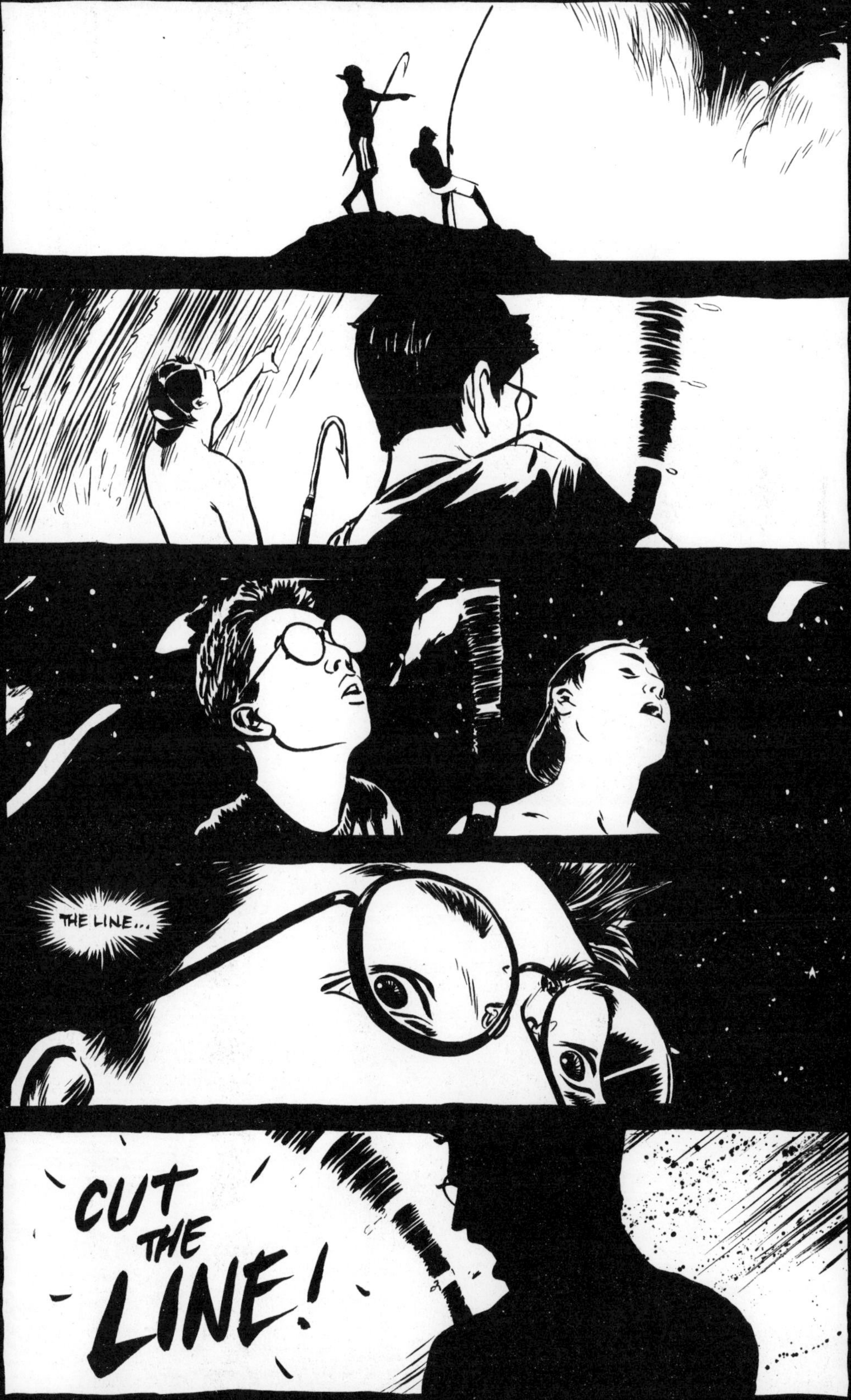
THE LINE...
CUT THE LINE!

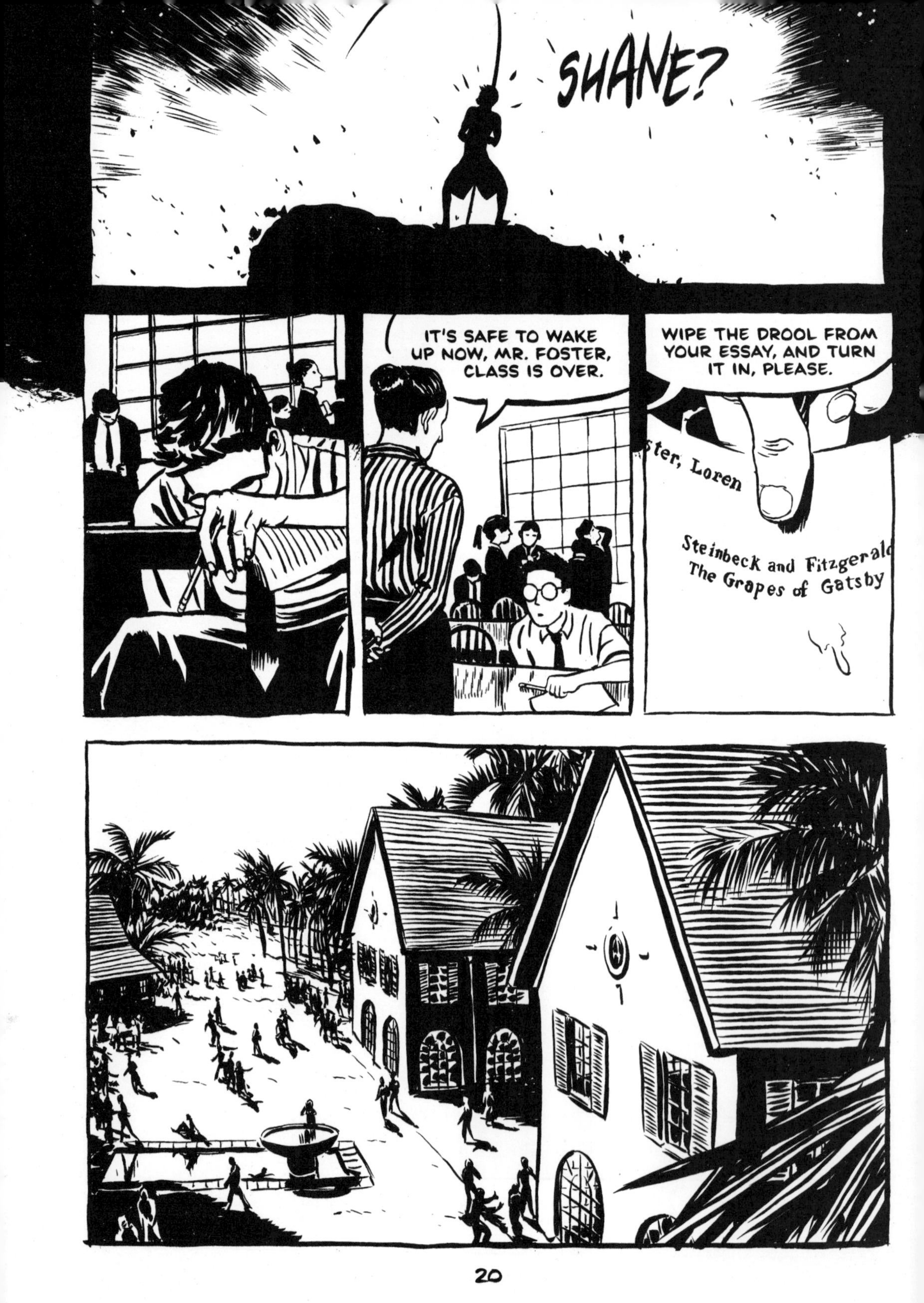
SHANE?
IT'S SAFE TO WAKE UP NOW, MR. FOSTER, CLASS IS OVER.
WIPE THE DROOL FROM YOUR ESSAY, AND TURN IT IN, PLEASE.
ster, Loren
Steinbeck and Fitzgerald
The Grapes of Gatsby

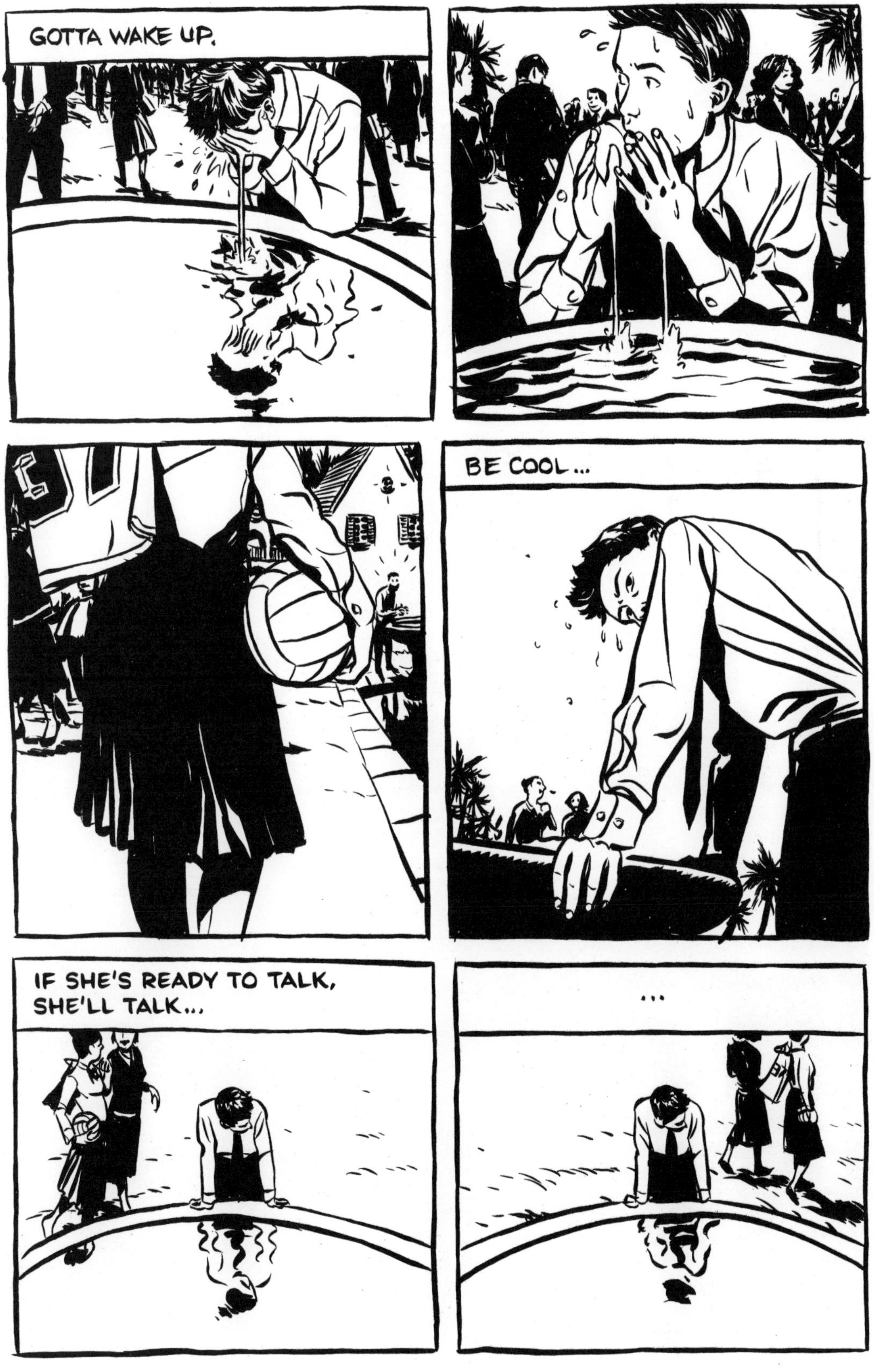
GOTTA WAKE UP.
BE COOL...
IF SHE'S READY TO TALK, SHE'LL TALK...
...

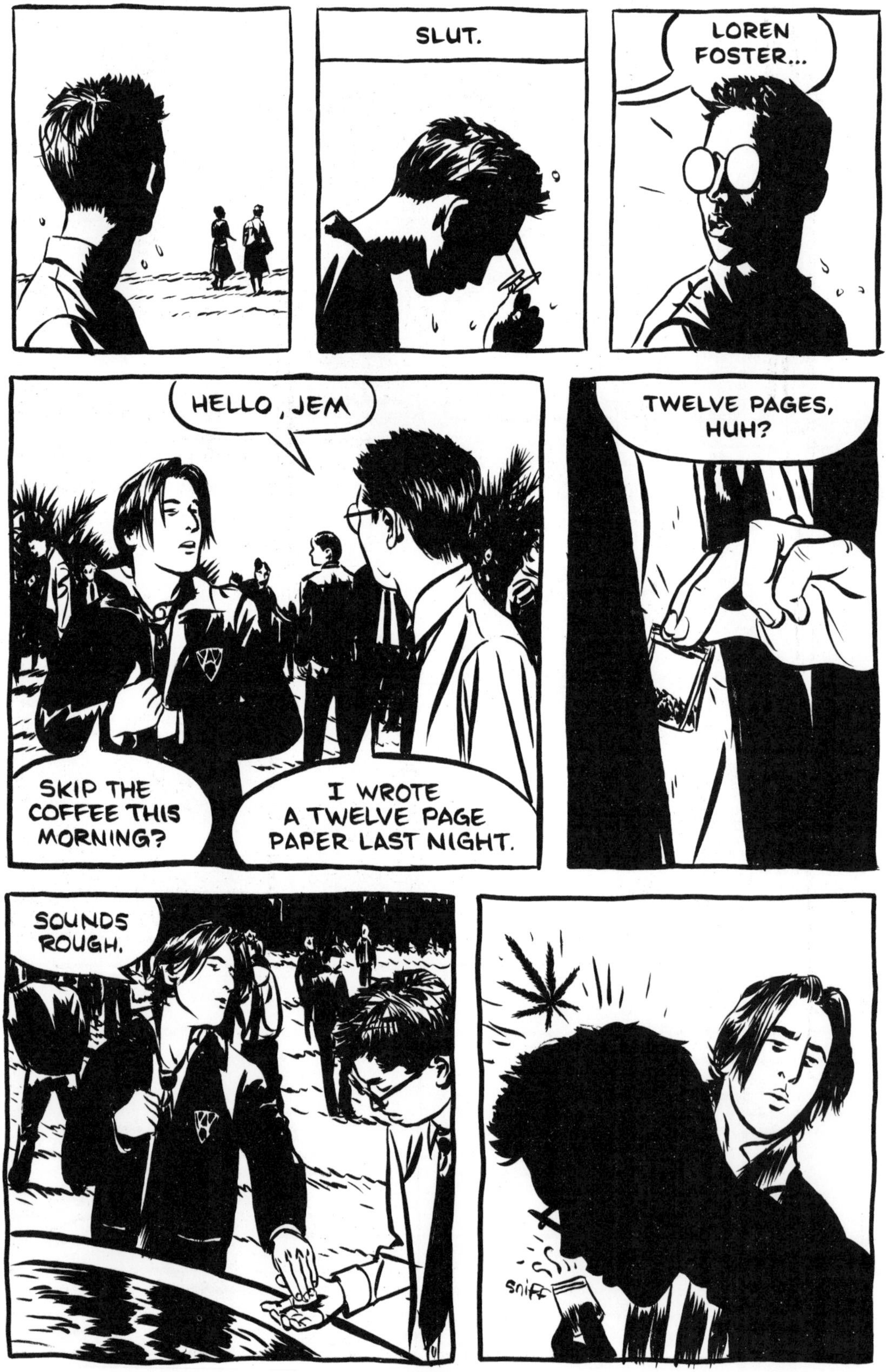
SLUT.
LOREN FOSTER...
HELLO, JEM
SKIP THE COFFEE THIS MORNING?
I WROTE A TWELVE PAGE PAPER LAST NIGHT.
TWELVE PAGES, HUH?
SOUNDS ROUGH.
sniff

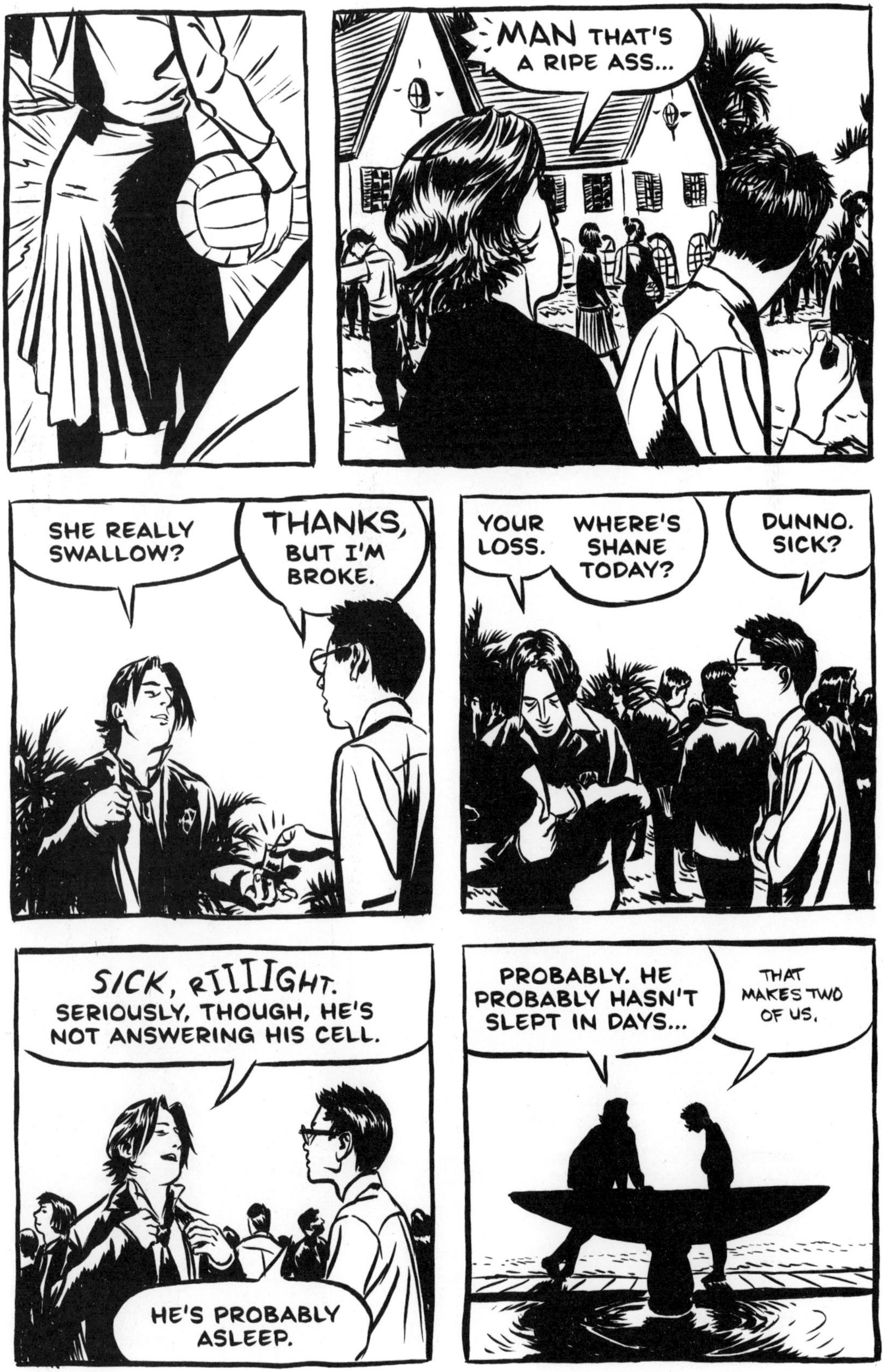
MAN THAT'S A RIPE ASS...
SHE REALLY SWALLOW?
THANKS, BUT I'M BROKE.
YOUR LOSS.
WHERE'S SHANE TODAY?
DUNNO. SICK?
SICK, RIIIIGHT. SERIOUSLY, THOUGH, HE'S NOT ANSWERING HIS CELL.
HE'S PROBABLY ASLEEP.
PROBABLY. HE PROBABLY HASN'T SLEPT IN DAYS...
THAT MAKES TWO OF US.

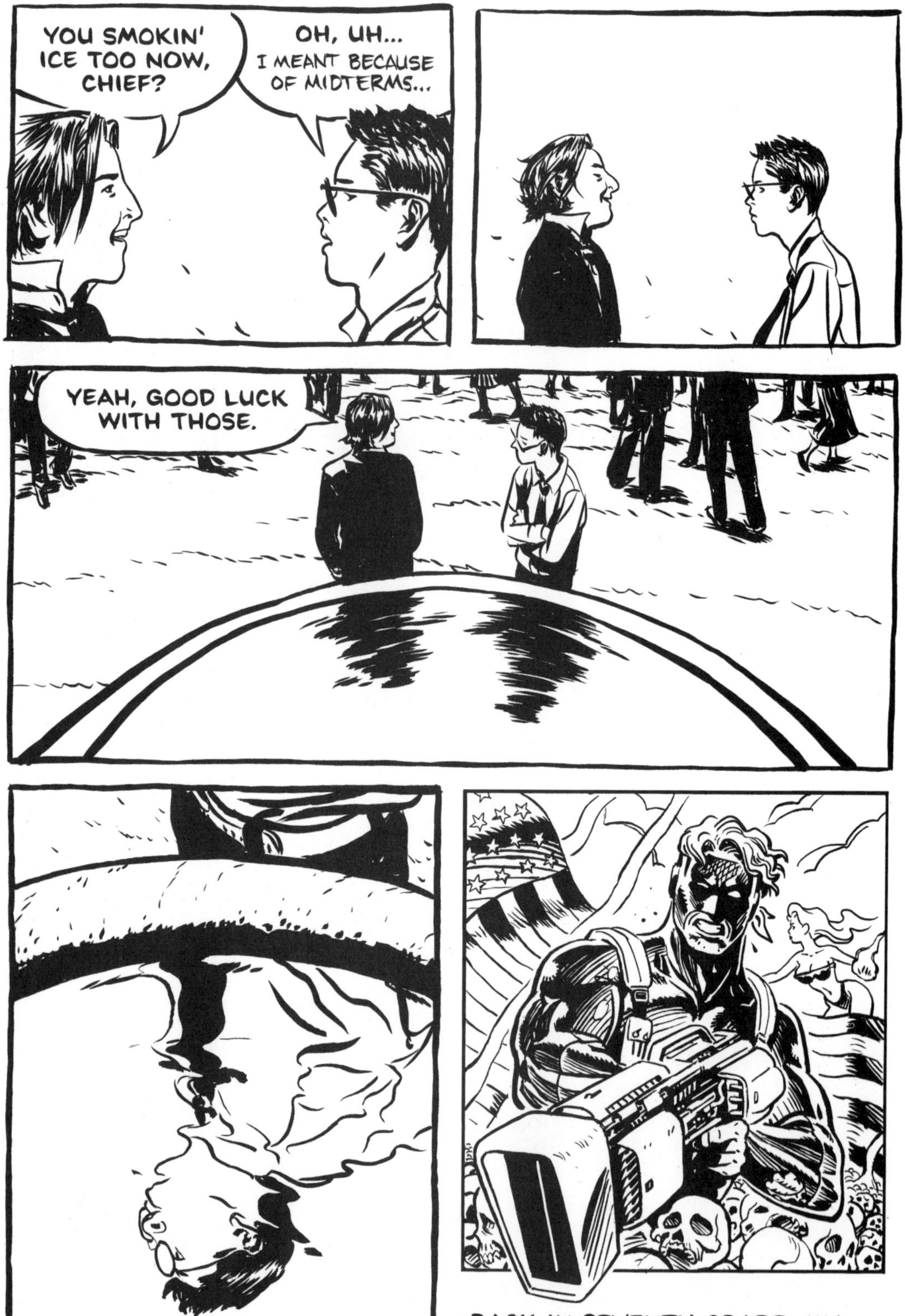
YOU SMOKIN' ICE TOO NOW, CHIEF?
OH, UH... I MEANT BECAUSE OF MIDTERMS...
YEAH, GOOD LUCK WITH THOSE.

BACK IN SEVENTH GRADE, MY BEST FRIEND, SHANE, DECIDED TO TRY SMOKING POT.

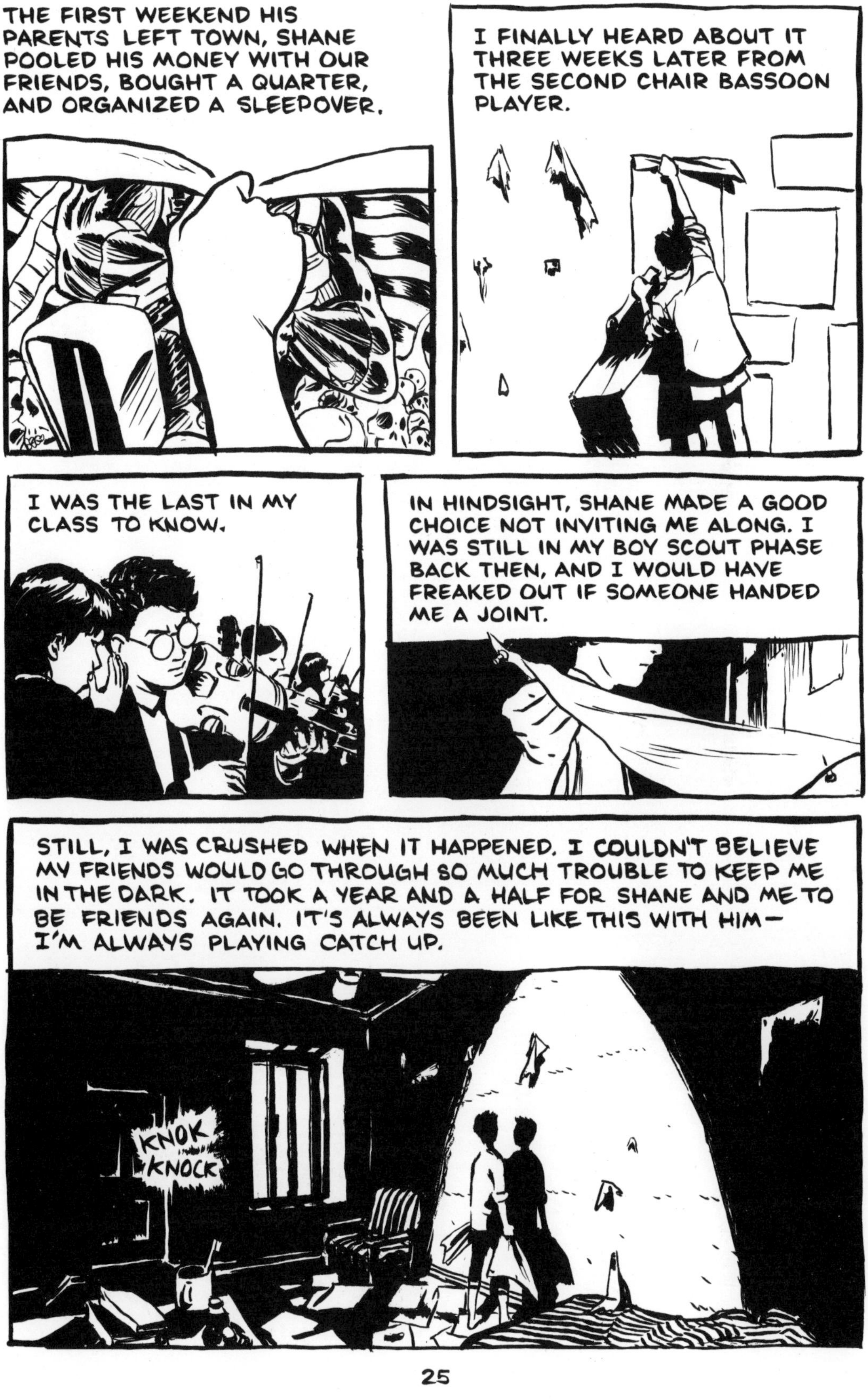
THE FIRST WEEKEND HIS PARENTS LEFT TOWN, SHANE POOLED HIS MONEY WITH OUR FRIENDS, BOUGHT A QUARTER, AND ORGANIZED A SLEEPOVER.
I FINALLY HEARD ABOUT IT THREE WEEKS LATER FROM THE SECOND CHAIR BASSOON PLAYER.
I WAS THE LAST IN MY CLASS TO KNOW.
IN HINDSIGHT, SHANE MADE A GOOD CHOICE NOT INVITING ME ALONG. I WAS STILL IN MY BOY SCOUT PHASE BACK THEN, AND I WOULD HAVE FREAKED OUT IF SOMEONE HANDED ME A JOINT.
STILL, I WAS CRUSHED WHEN IT HAPPENED. I COULDN'T BELIEVE MY FRIENDS WOULD GO THROUGH SO MUCH TROUBLE TO KEEP ME IN THE DARK. IT TOOK A YEAR AND A HALF FOR SHANE AND ME TO BE FRIENDS AGAIN. IT'S ALWAYS BEEN LIKE THIS WITH HIM— I'M ALWAYS PLAYING CATCH UP.
KNOK KNOCK

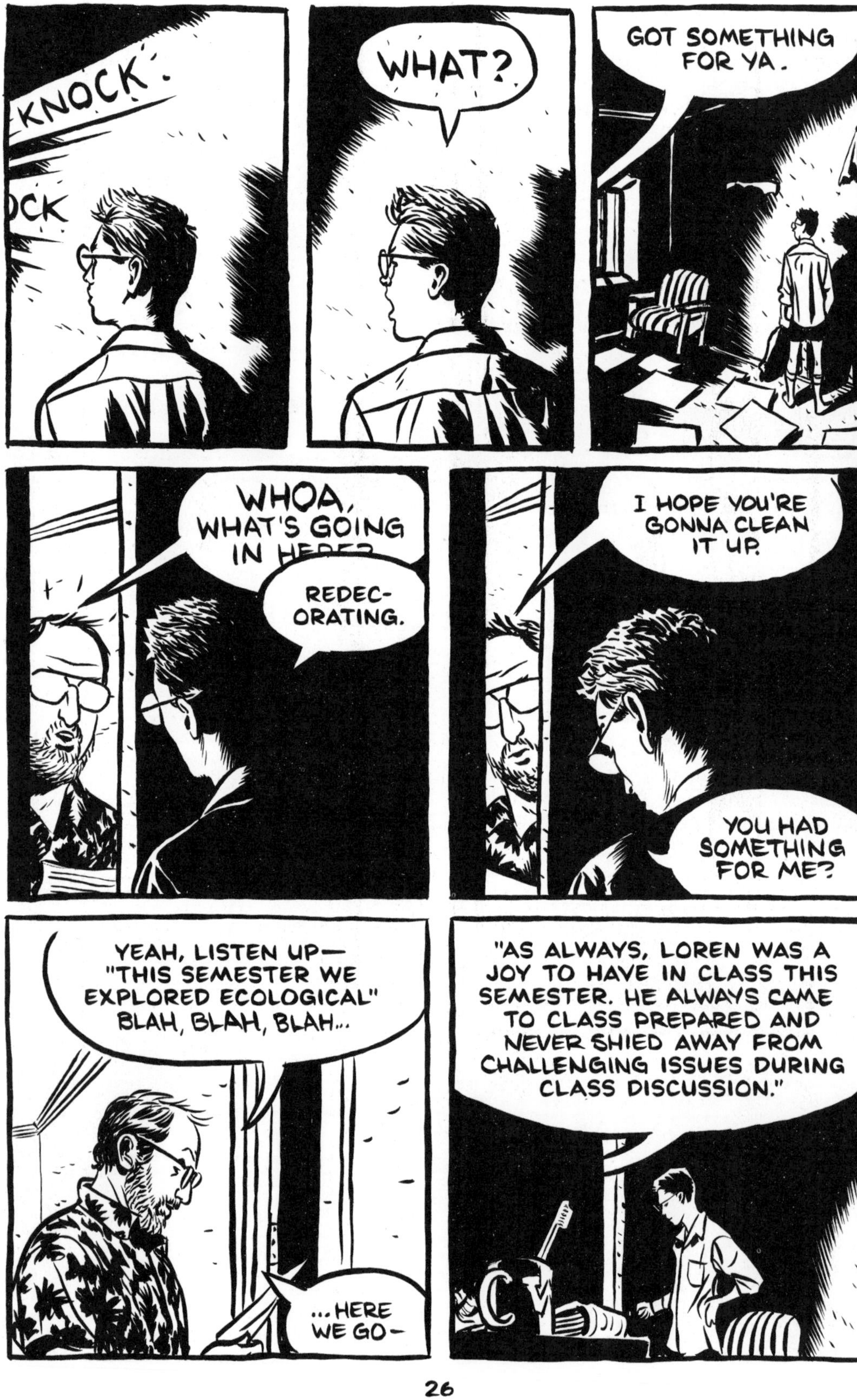
KNOCK
OCK
WHAT?
GOT SOMETHING FOR YA.
WHOA, WHAT'S GOING IN HERE?
REDECORATING.
I HOPE YOU'RE GONNA CLEAN IT UP.
YOU HAD SOMETHING FOR ME?
YEAH, LISTEN UP— "THIS SEMESTER WE EXPLORED ECOLOGICAL" BLAH, BLAH, BLAH...
...HERE WE GO-
"AS ALWAYS, LOREN WAS A JOY TO HAVE IN CLASS THIS SEMESTER. HE ALWAYS CAME TO CLASS PREPARED AND NEVER SHIED AWAY FROM CHALLENGING ISSUES DURING CLASS DISCUSSION."

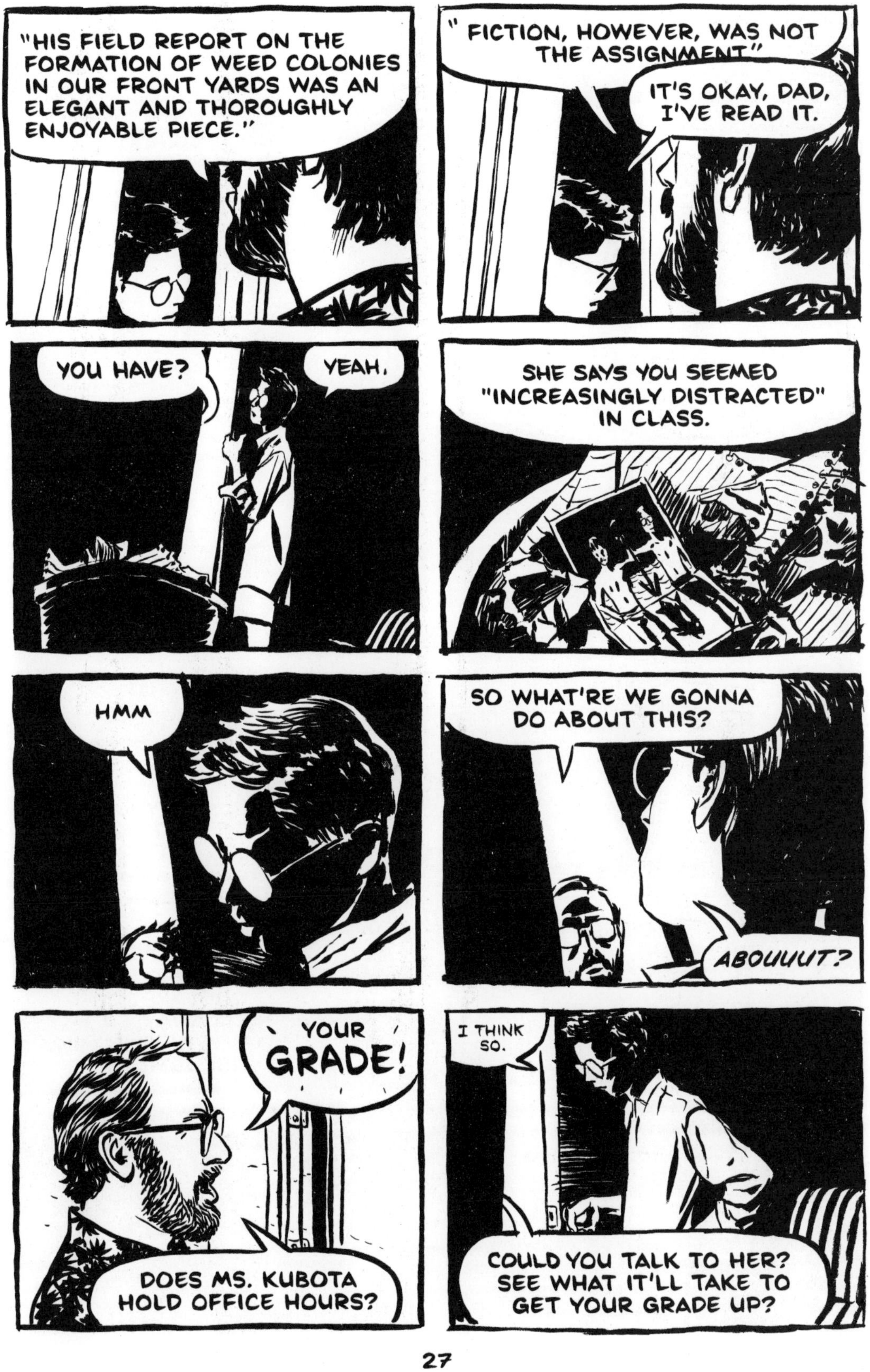
"HIS FIELD REPORT ON THE FORMATION OF WEED COLONIES IN OUR FRONT YARDS WAS AN ELEGANT AND THOROUGHLY ENJOYABLE PIECE."
"FICTION, HOWEVER, WAS NOT THE ASSIGNMENT."
IT'S OKAY, DAD, I'VE READ IT.
YOU HAVE?
YEAH.
SHE SAYS YOU SEEMED "INCREASINGLY DISTRACTED" IN CLASS.
HMM
SO WHAT'RE WE GONNA DO ABOUT THIS?
ABOUUUT?
YOUR GRADE!
DOES MS. KUBOTA HOLD OFFICE HOURS?
I THINK SO.
COULD YOU TALK TO HER? SEE WHAT IT'LL TAKE TO GET YOUR GRADE UP?

I GUESS...

...BUT I DIDN'T THINK A **B** WAS THAT BAD A GRADE...

Rodriges	ster, Loren		
ubota	English lit		
lfour	A.P. Bio	A	A
	A.P. Calculus	A	B
amoto	Japanese 4	A	A
itas	A.P. Euro Hist	A	A
iams	Year		

IT'S NOT A **BAD** GRADE, BUT YOU CAN DO BETTER, RIGHT?

C'MON LOREN, I CAN'T REMEMBER THE LAST TIME YOU GOT LESS THAN A NINETY-TWO!

JUST GO TALK TO HER-- I'M SURE S-- RING **RING**

RING RING

SIGH

HELLO?

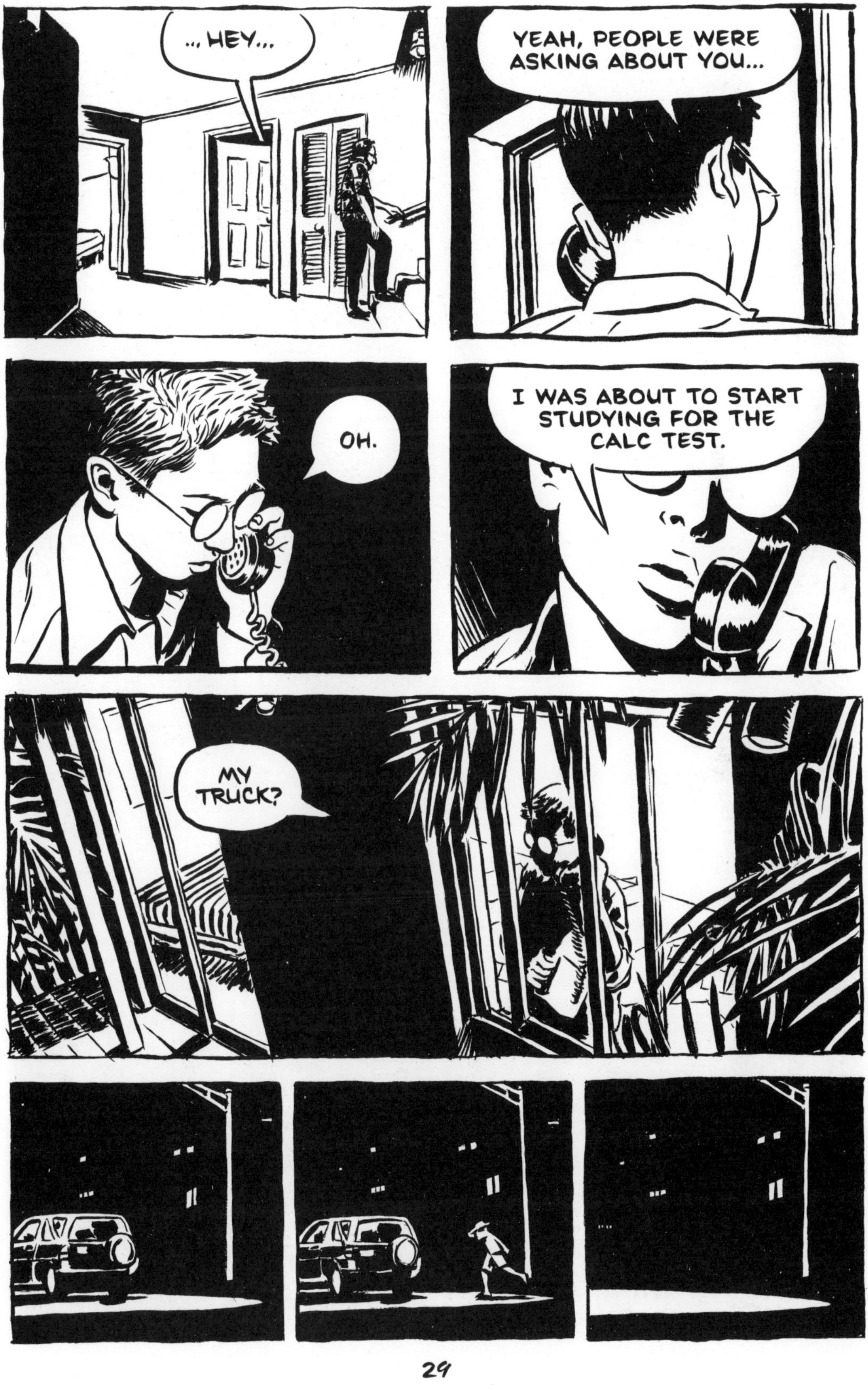
... HEY...
YEAH, PEOPLE WERE ASKING ABOUT YOU...
OH.
I WAS ABOUT TO START STUDYING FOR THE CALC TEST.
MY TRUCK?

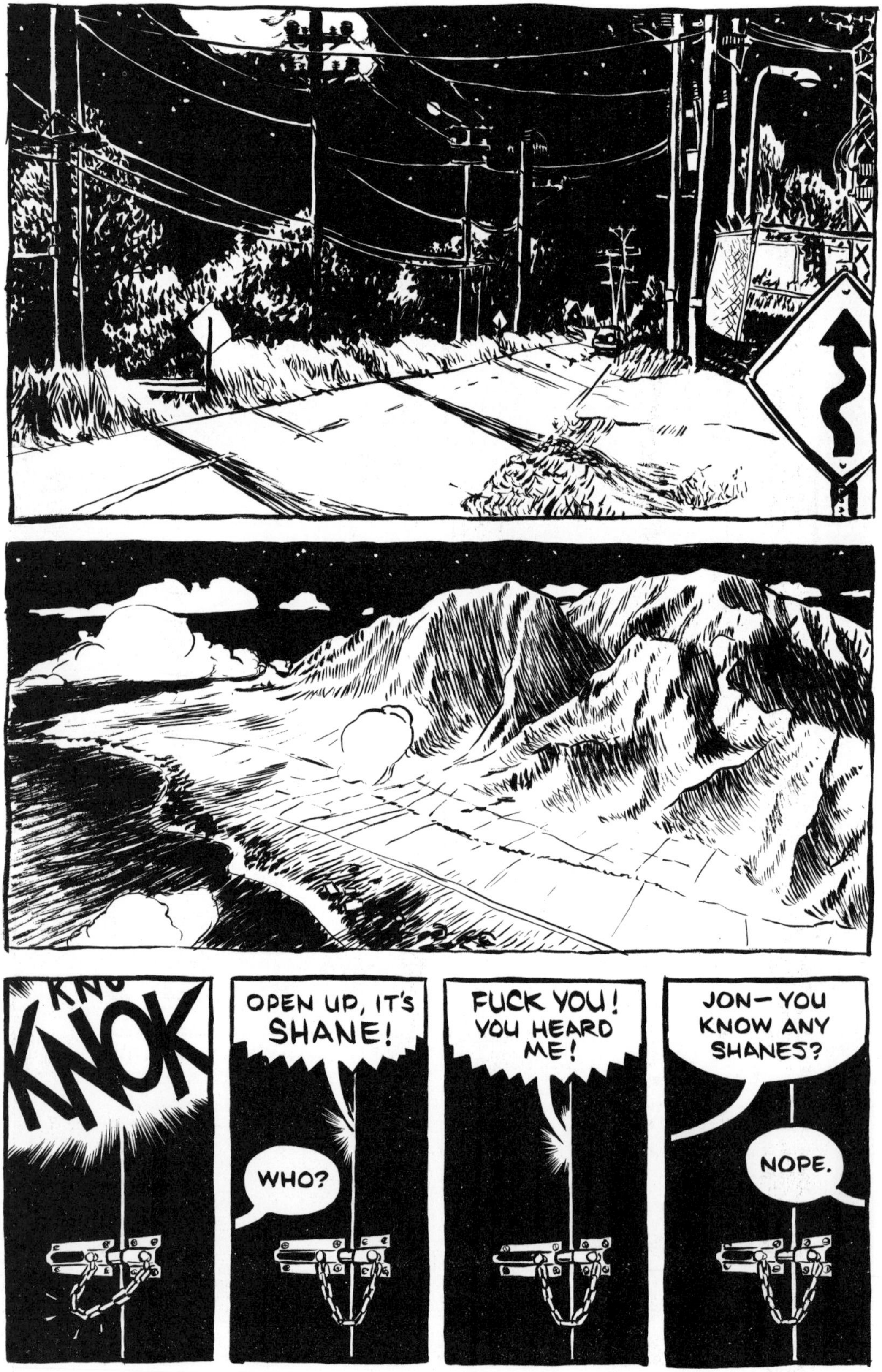
KNOK
OPEN UP, IT'S SHANE!
WHO?
FUCK YOU! YOU HEARD ME!
JON— YOU KNOW ANY SHANES?
NOPE.

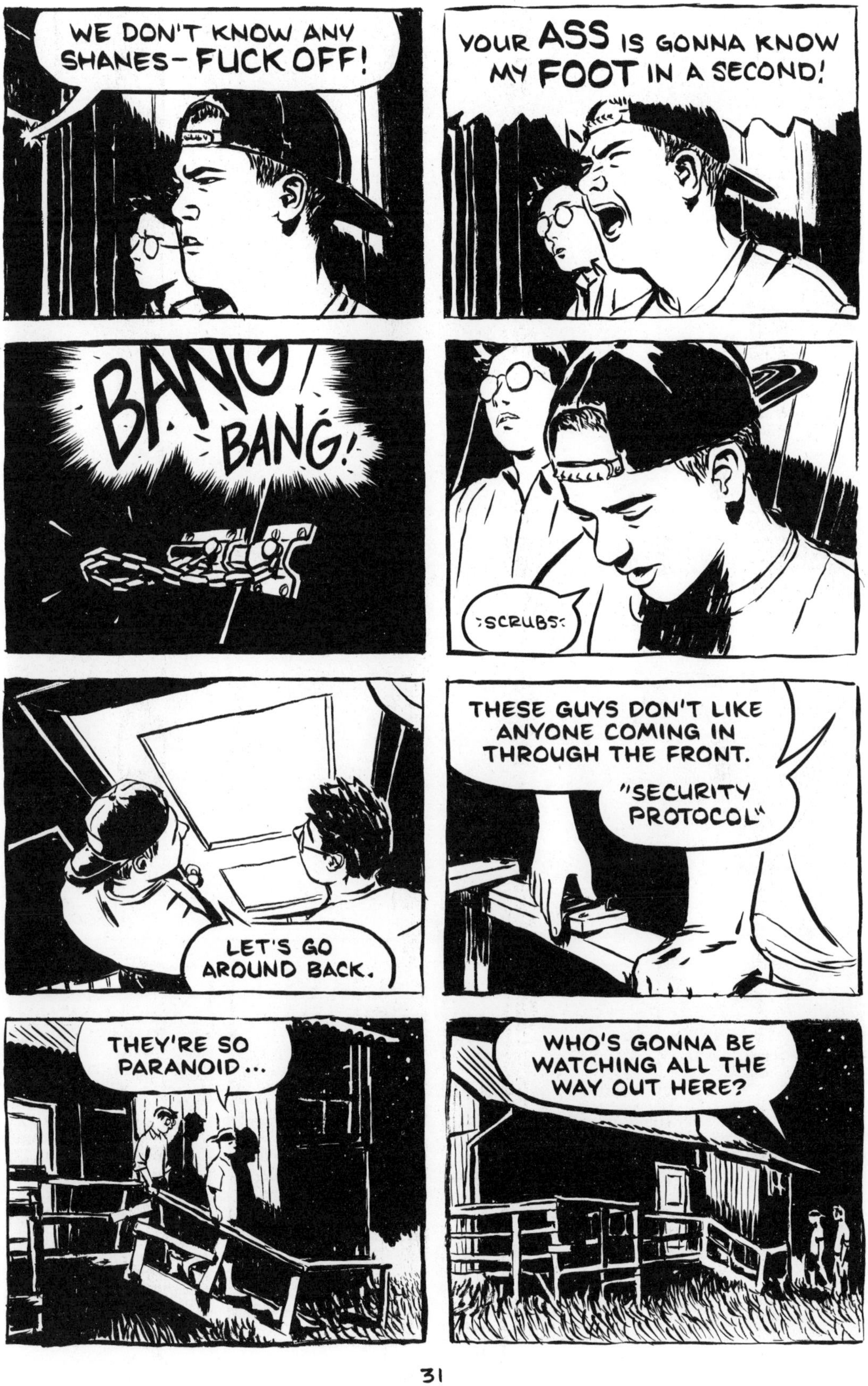

WE DON'T KNOW ANY SHANES– FUCK OFF!
YOUR ASS IS GONNA KNOW MY FOOT IN A SECOND!
BANG
BANG!
SCRUBS
LET'S GO AROUND BACK.
THESE GUYS DON'T LIKE ANYONE COMING IN THROUGH THE FRONT.
"SECURITY PROTOCOL"
THEY'RE SO PARANOID...
WHO'S GONNA BE WATCHING ALL THE WAY OUT HERE?

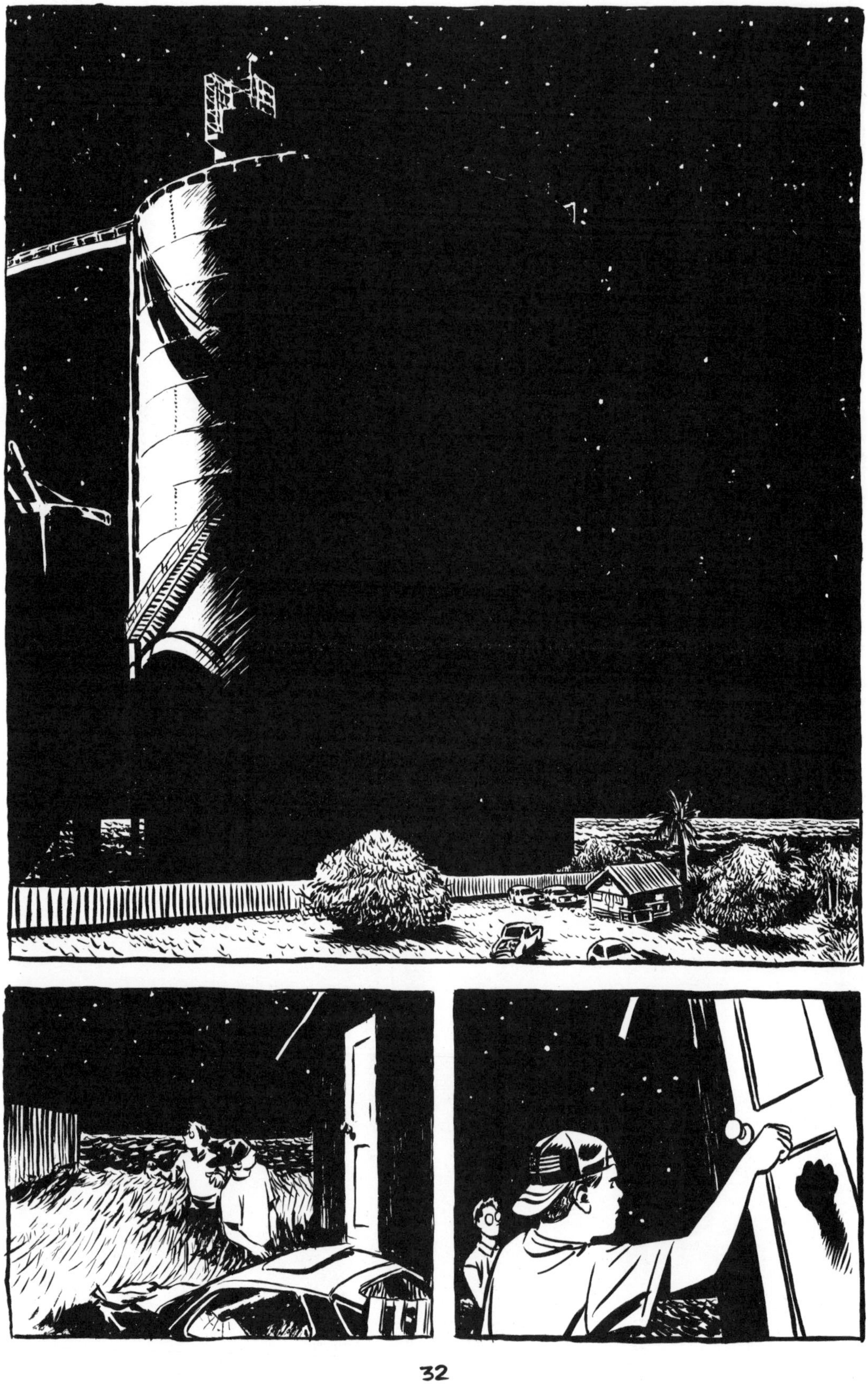

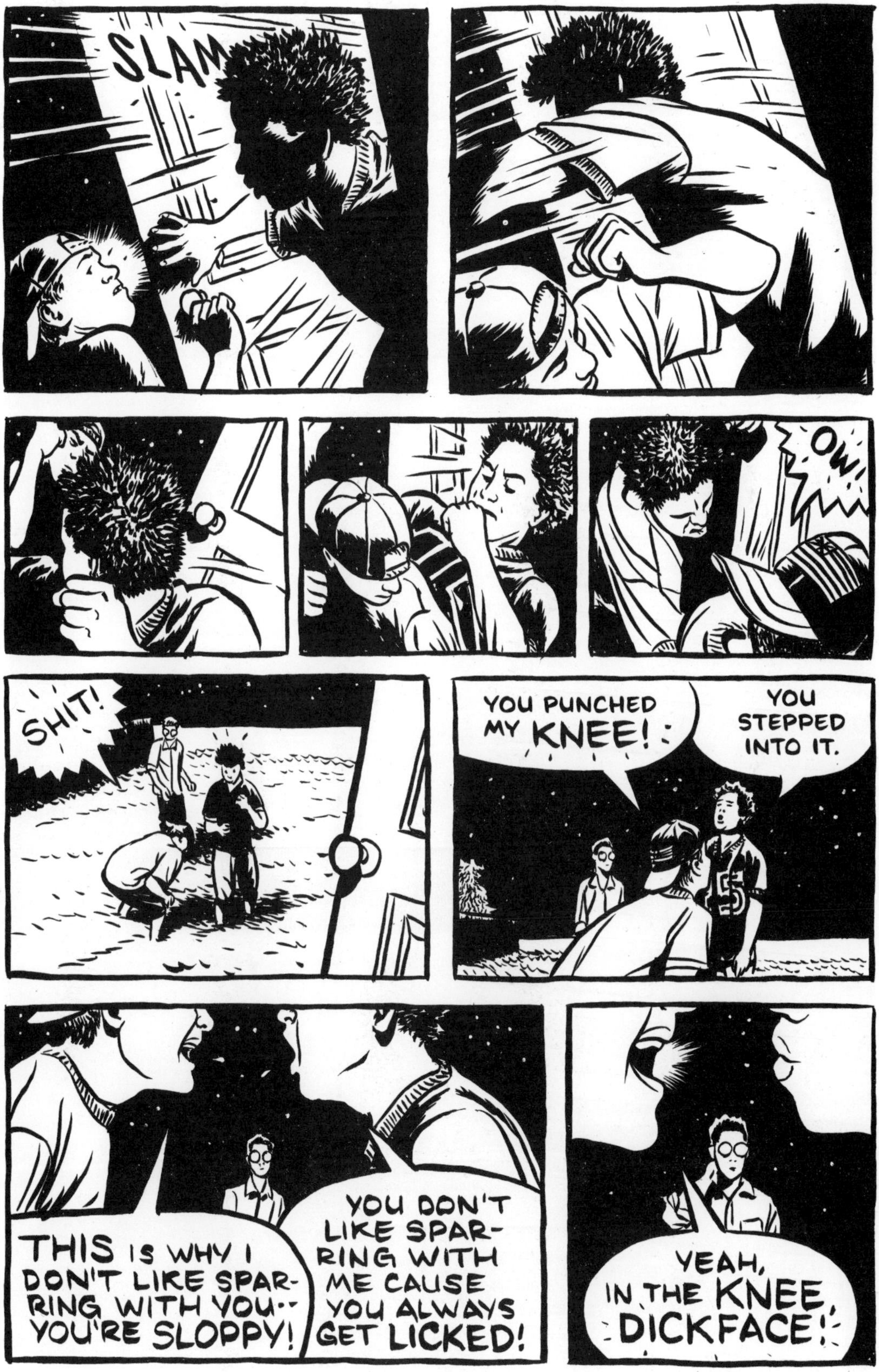
SLAM
OW!
SHIT!
YOU PUNCHED MY KNEE!
YOU STEPPED INTO IT.
THIS IS WHY I DON'T LIKE SPAR-RING WITH YOU·· YOU'RE SLOPPY!
YOU DON'T LIKE SPAR-RING WITH ME CAUSE YOU ALWAYS GET LICKED!
YEAH, IN THE KNEE, DICKFACE!

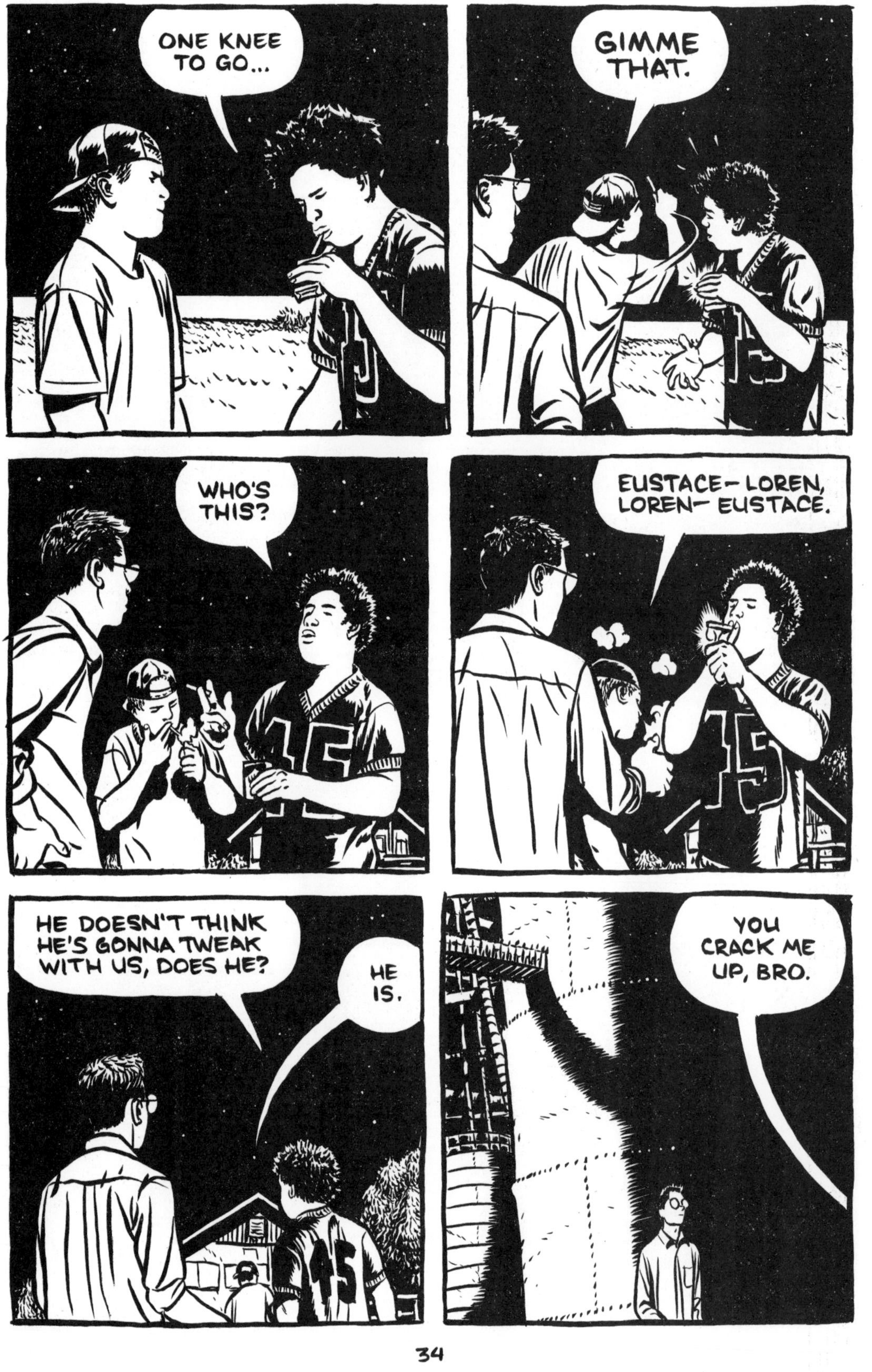
ONE KNEE TO GO...
GIMME THAT.
WHO'S THIS?
EUSTACE– LOREN, LOREN– EUSTACE.
HE DOESN'T THINK HE'S GONNA TWEAK WITH US, DOES HE?
HE IS.
YOU CRACK ME UP, BRO.

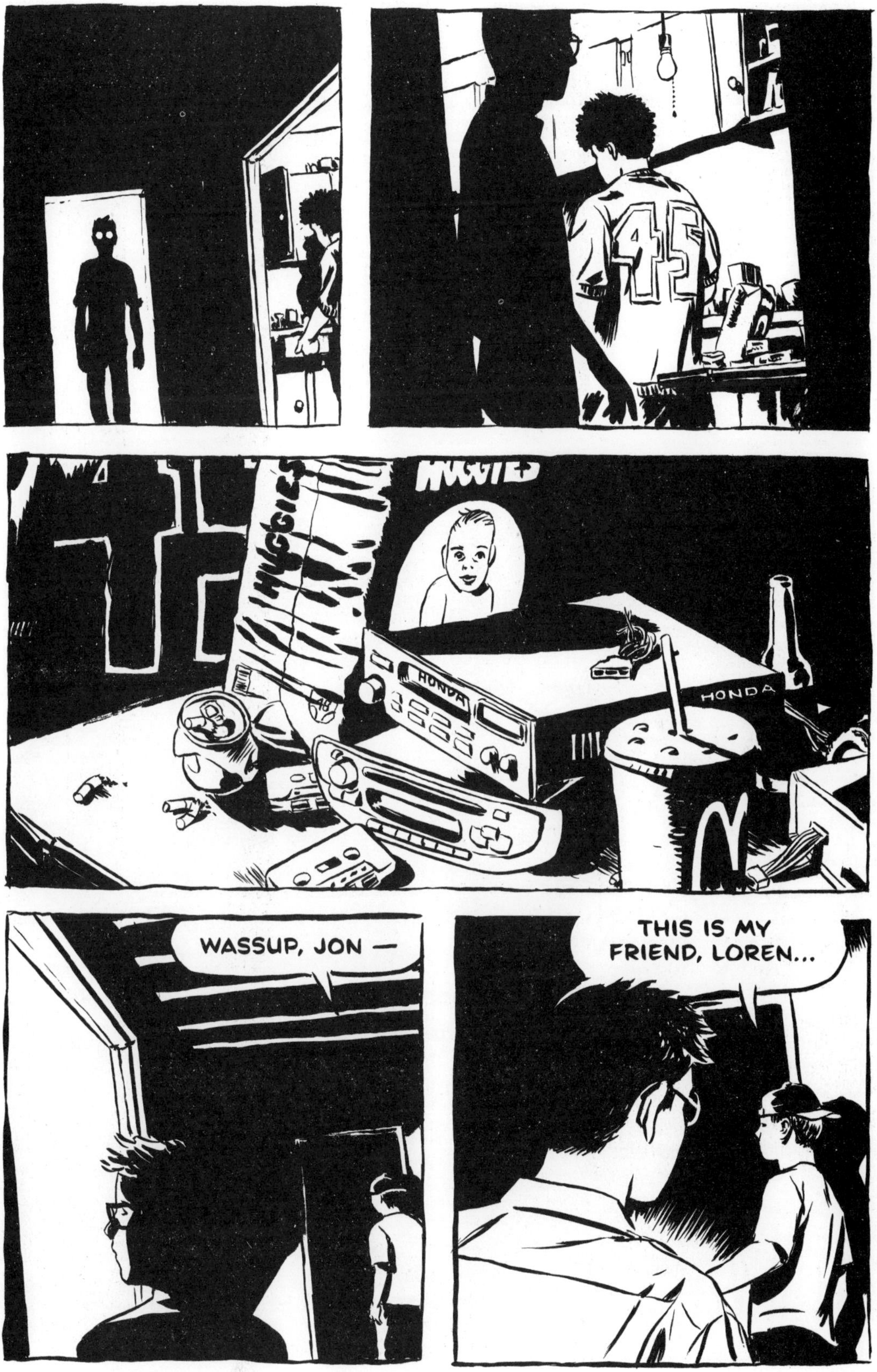
HUGGIES
HONDA
HONDA
WASSUP, JON —
THIS IS MY FRIEND, LOREN...

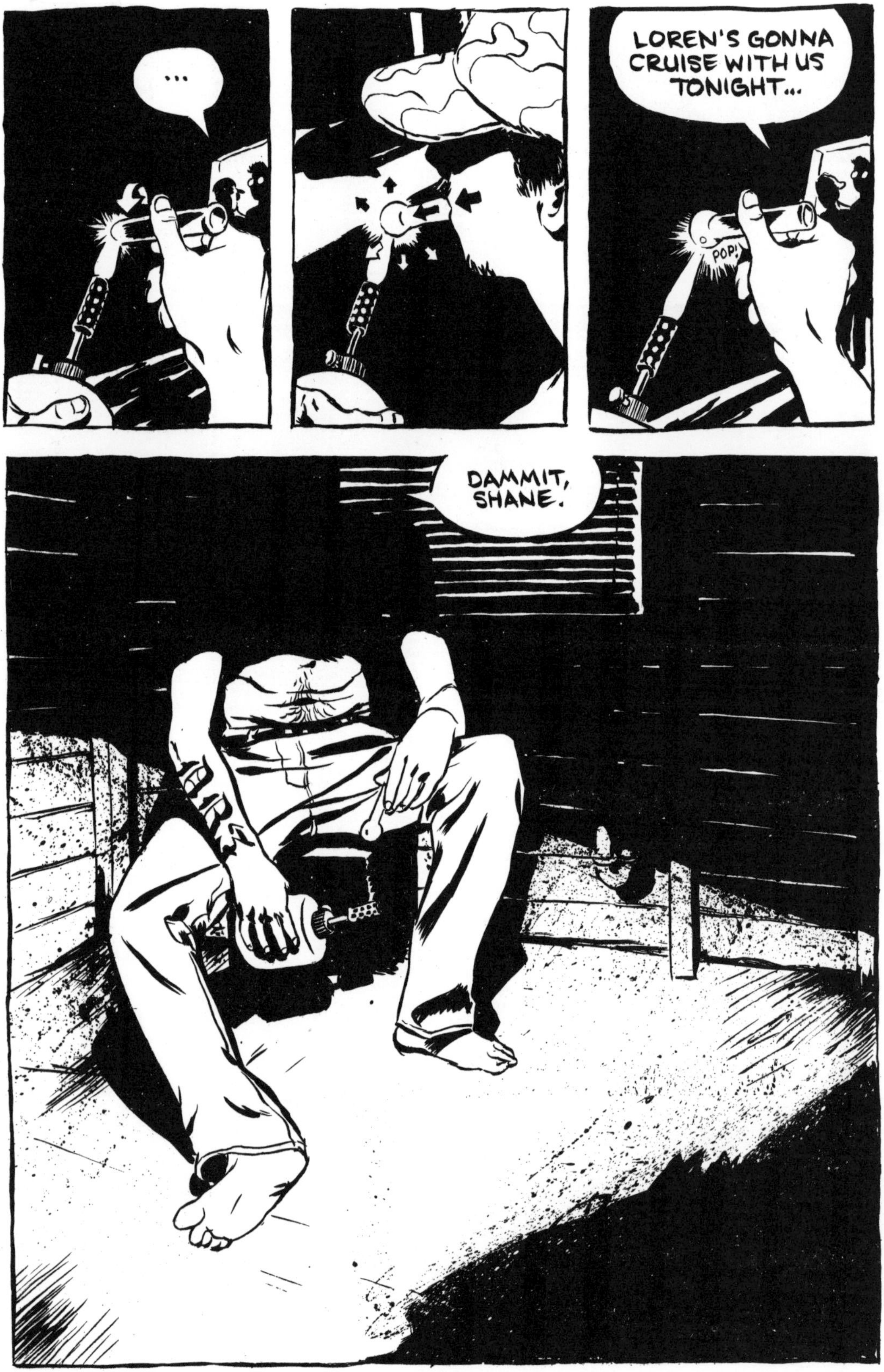
...
POP!
LOREN'S GONNA CRUISE WITH US TONIGHT...
DAMMIT, SHANE!

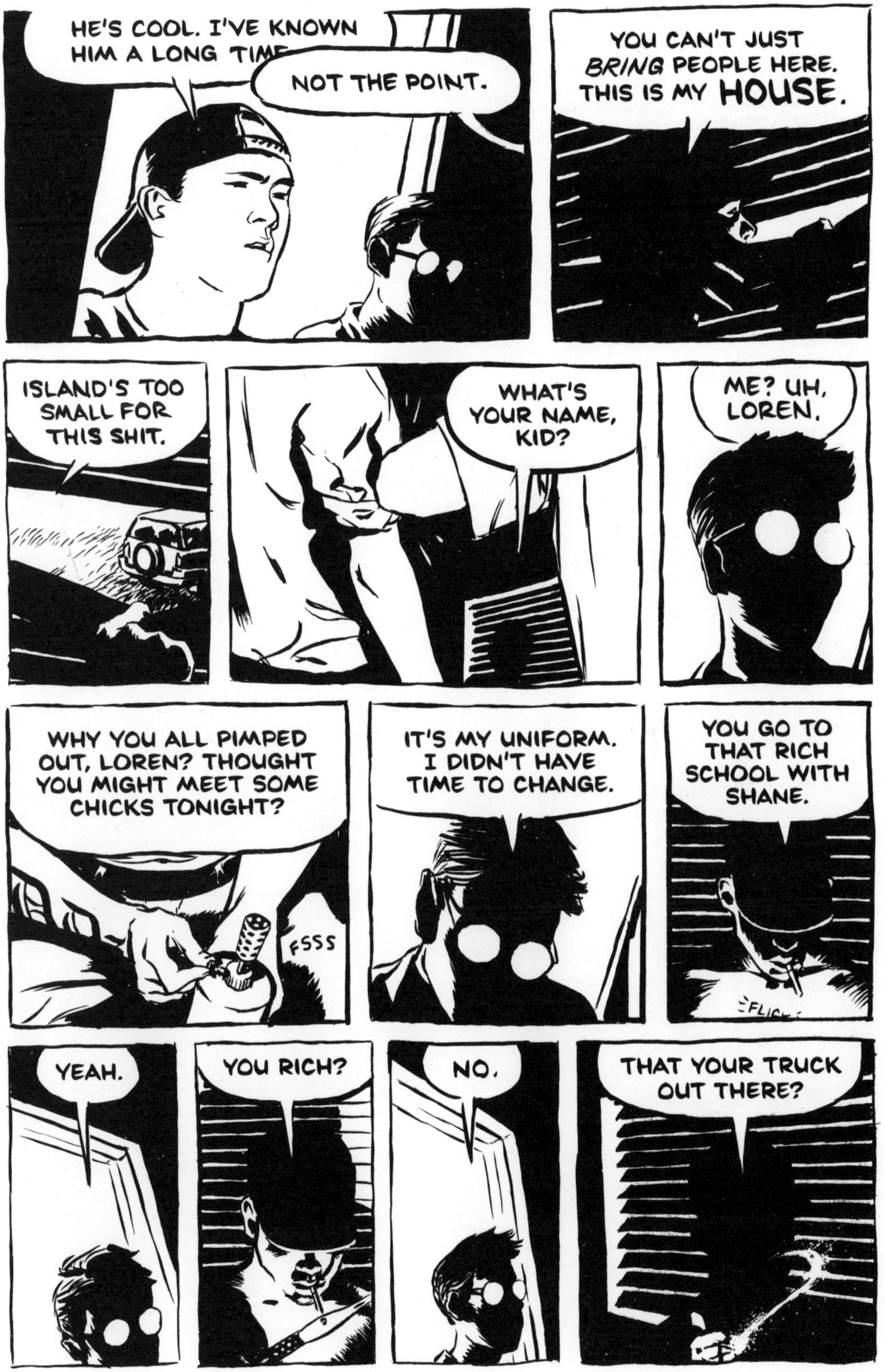

HE'S COOL. I'VE KNOWN HIM A LONG TIME
NOT THE POINT.
YOU CAN'T JUST *BRING* PEOPLE HERE. THIS IS MY **HOUSE**.
ISLAND'S TOO SMALL FOR THIS SHIT.
WHAT'S YOUR NAME, KID?
ME? UH, LOREN.
WHY YOU ALL PIMPED OUT, LOREN? THOUGHT YOU MIGHT MEET SOME CHICKS TONIGHT?
FSSS
IT'S MY UNIFORM. I DIDN'T HAVE TIME TO CHANGE.
YOU GO TO THAT RICH SCHOOL WITH SHANE.
YEAH.
YOU RICH?
NO.
THAT YOUR TRUCK OUT THERE?

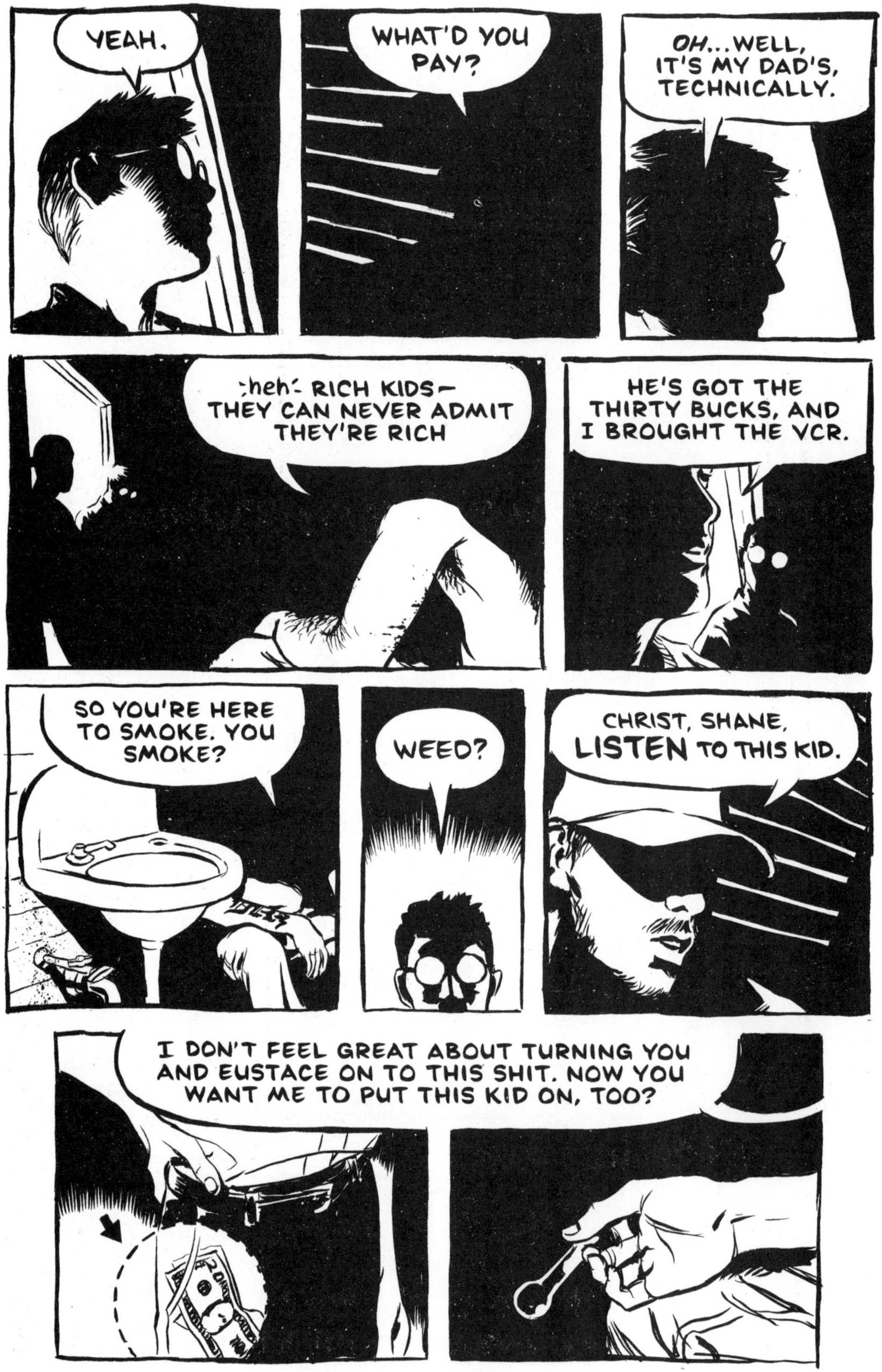
YEAH.
WHAT'D YOU PAY?
OH... WELL, IT'S MY DAD'S, TECHNICALLY.
:heh: RICH KIDS— THEY CAN NEVER ADMIT THEY'RE RICH
HE'S GOT THE THIRTY BUCKS, AND I BROUGHT THE VCR.
SO YOU'RE HERE TO SMOKE. YOU SMOKE?
WEED?
CHRIST, SHANE, LISTEN TO THIS KID.
I DON'T FEEL GREAT ABOUT TURNING YOU AND EUSTACE ON TO THIS SHIT. NOW YOU WANT ME TO PUT THIS KID ON, TOO?

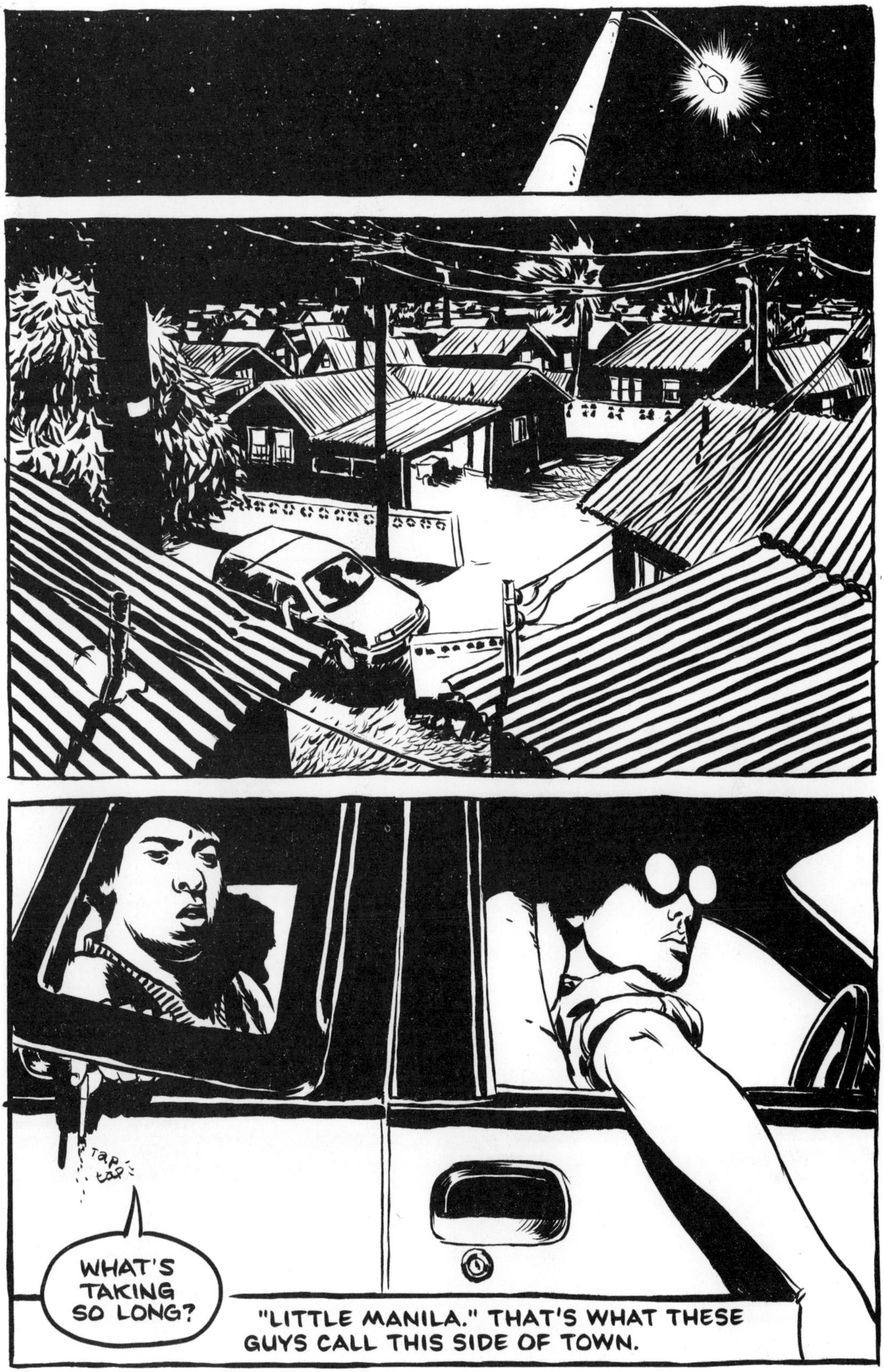
tap tap
WHAT'S TAKING SO LONG?
"LITTLE MANILA." THAT'S WHAT THESE GUYS CALL THIS SIDE OF TOWN.

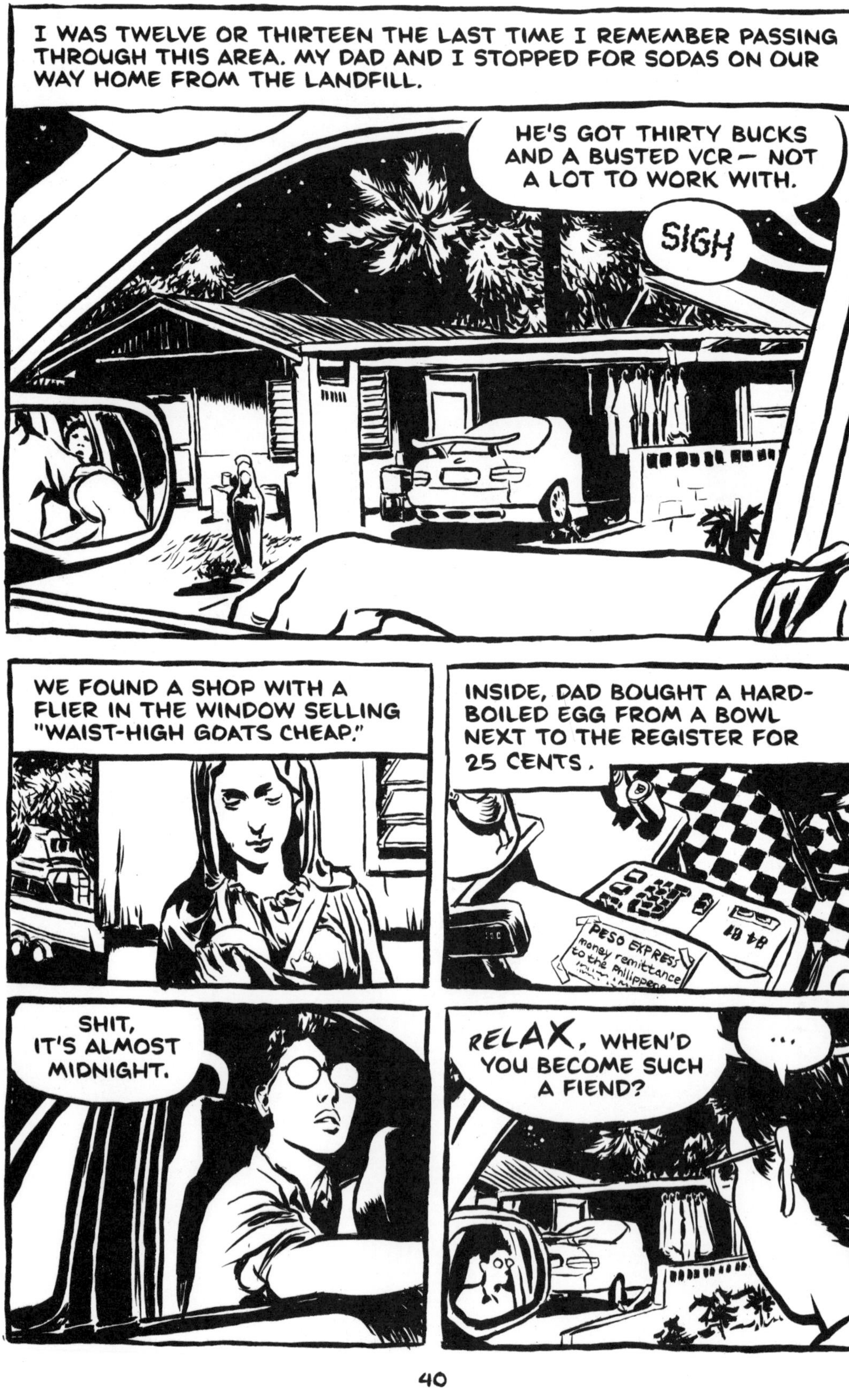
I WAS TWELVE OR THIRTEEN THE LAST TIME I REMEMBER PASSING THROUGH THIS AREA. MY DAD AND I STOPPED FOR SODAS ON OUR WAY HOME FROM THE LANDFILL.
HE'S GOT THIRTY BUCKS AND A BUSTED VCR— NOT A LOT TO WORK WITH.
SIGH
WE FOUND A SHOP WITH A FLIER IN THE WINDOW SELLING "WAIST-HIGH GOATS CHEAP."
INSIDE, DAD BOUGHT A HARD-BOILED EGG FROM A BOWL NEXT TO THE REGISTER FOR 25 CENTS.
PESO EXPRESS
money remittance
SHIT, IT'S ALMOST MIDNIGHT.
RELAX, WHEN'D YOU BECOME SUCH A FIEND?
...

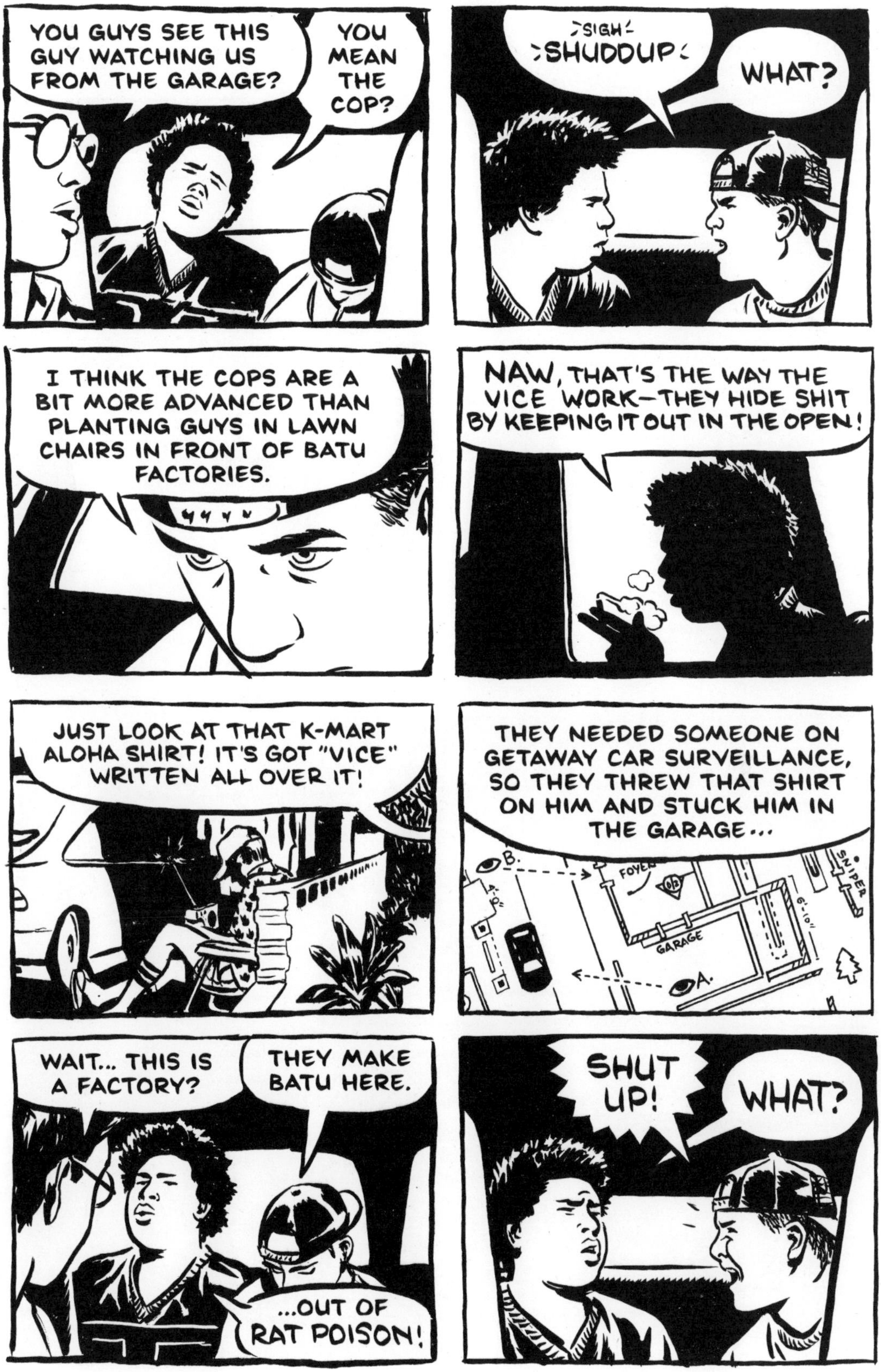
YOU GUYS SEE THIS GUY WATCHING US FROM THE GARAGE?
YOU MEAN THE COP?
SIGH
SHUDDUP
WHAT?
I THINK THE COPS ARE A BIT MORE ADVANCED THAN PLANTING GUYS IN LAWN CHAIRS IN FRONT OF BATU FACTORIES.
NAW, THAT'S THE WAY THE VICE WORK—THEY HIDE SHIT BY KEEPING IT OUT IN THE OPEN!
JUST LOOK AT THAT K-MART ALOHA SHIRT! IT'S GOT "VICE" WRITTEN ALL OVER IT!
THEY NEEDED SOMEONE ON GETAWAY CAR SURVEILLANCE, SO THEY THREW THAT SHIRT ON HIM AND STUCK HIM IN THE GARAGE...
B.
FOYER
SNIPER
GARAGE
A.
WAIT... THIS IS A FACTORY?
THEY MAKE BATU HERE.
...OUT OF RAT POISON!
SHUT UP!
WHAT?

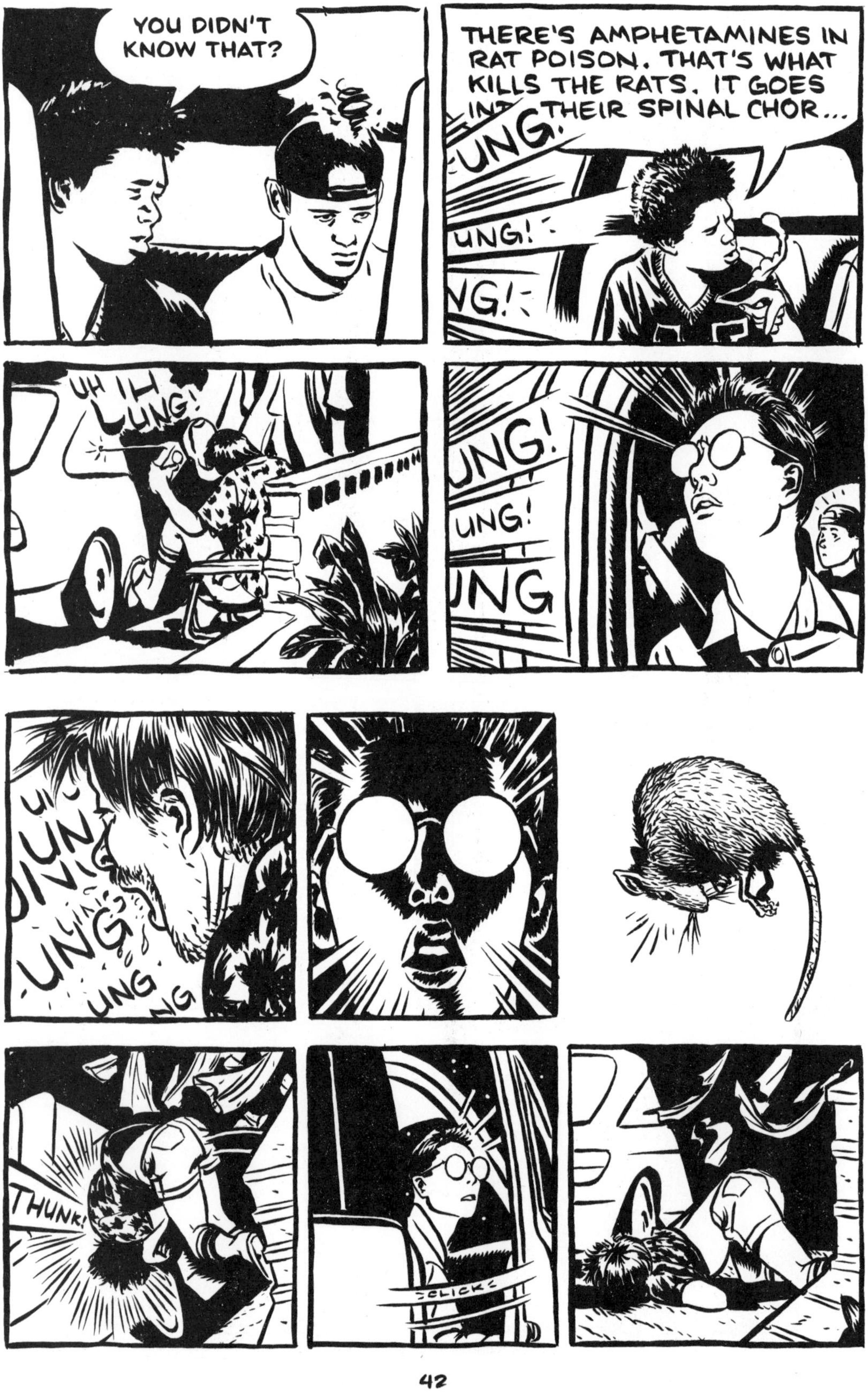
YOU DIDN'T KNOW THAT?
THERE'S AMPHETAMINES IN RAT POISON. THAT'S WHAT KILLS THE RATS. IT GOES IN THEIR SPINAL CHOR...
UNG!
UNG!
NG!
UH IH UNG!
UNG!
UNG!
UNG
UNG
UNG
UNG
THUNK!
CLICK

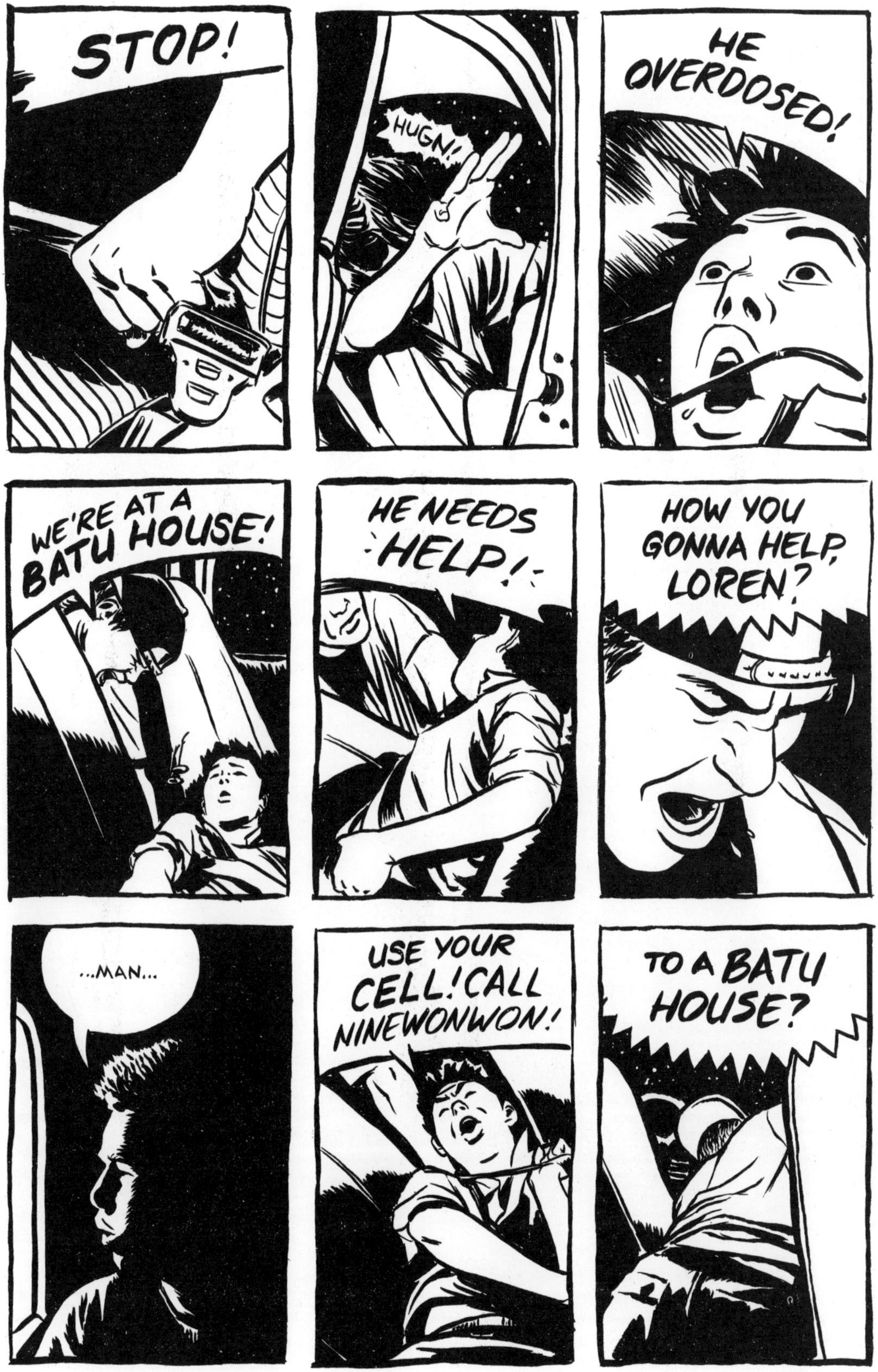
STOP!
HUGN!
HE OVERDOSED!
WE'RE AT A BATU HOUSE!
HE NEEDS HELP!
HOW YOU GONNA HELP, LOREN?
...MAN...
USE YOUR CELL! CALL NINEWONWON!
TO A BATU HOUSE?

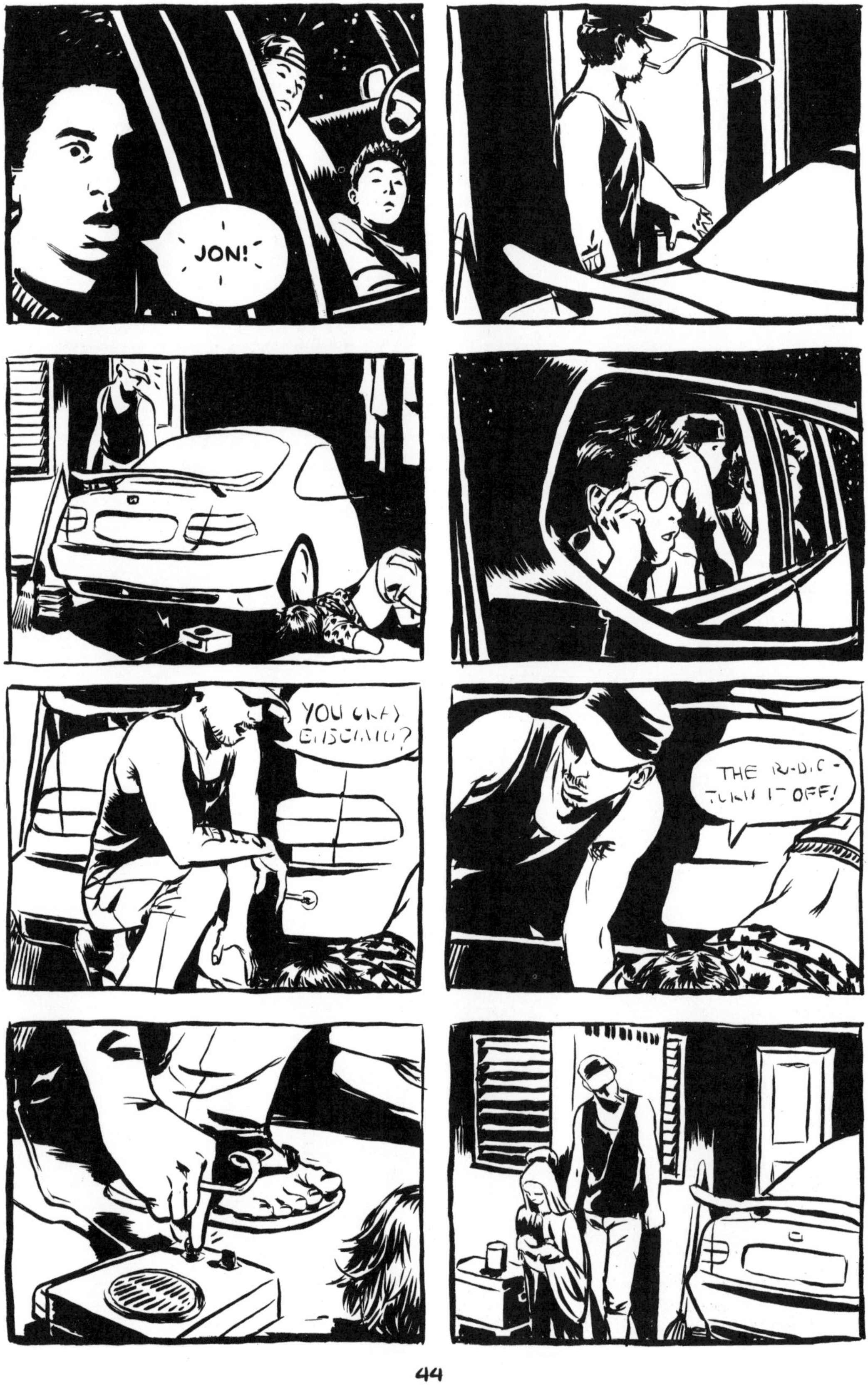
JON!
YOU OKAY
THE RA-DIO-
TURN IT OFF!

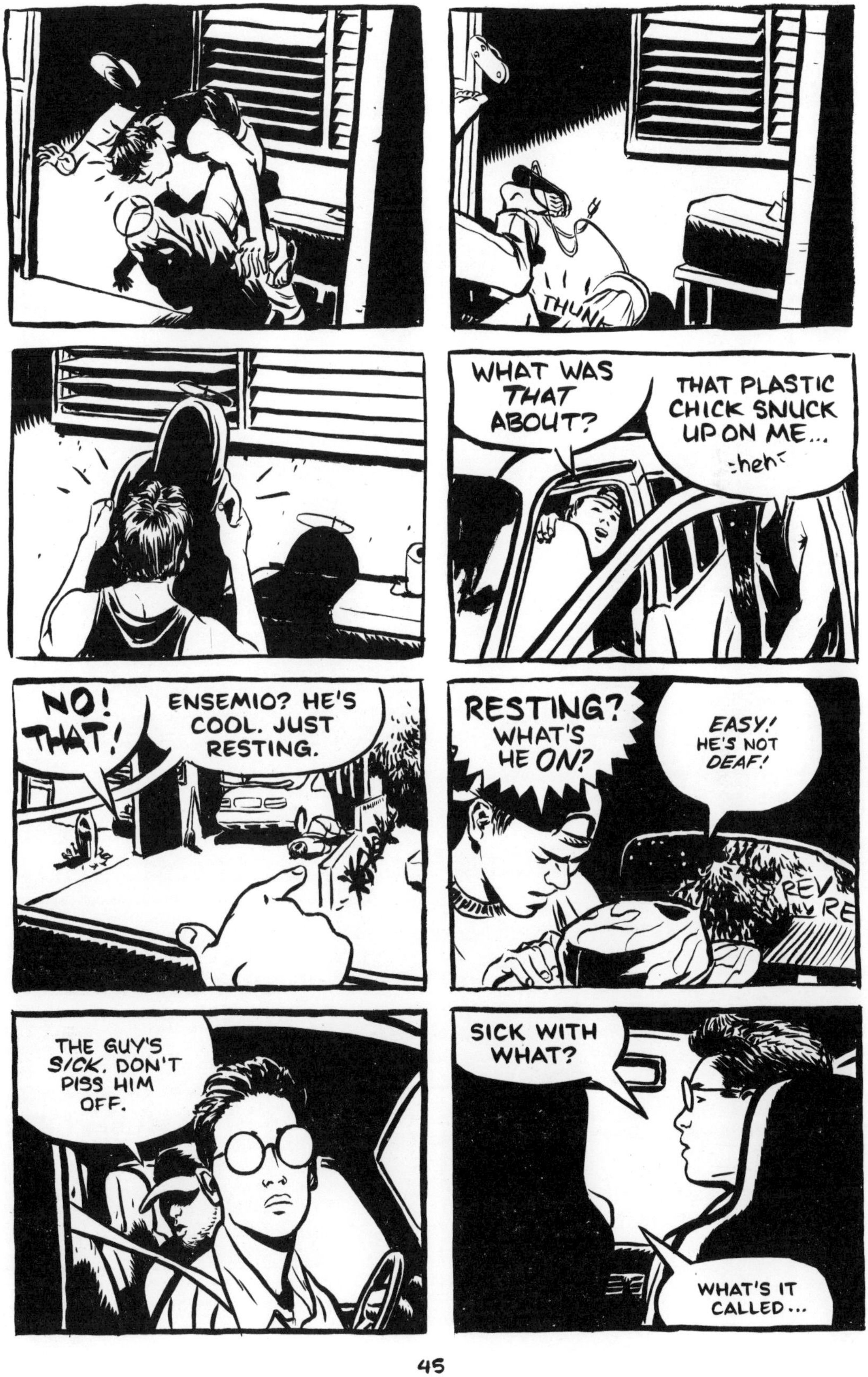
THUNK
WHAT WAS THAT ABOUT?
THAT PLASTIC CHICK SNUCK UP ON ME... heh
NO! THAT!
ENSEMIO? HE'S COOL. JUST RESTING.
RESTING? WHAT'S HE ON?
EASY! HE'S NOT DEAF!
THE GUY'S SICK. DON'T PISS HIM OFF.
SICK WITH WHAT?
WHAT'S IT CALLED...

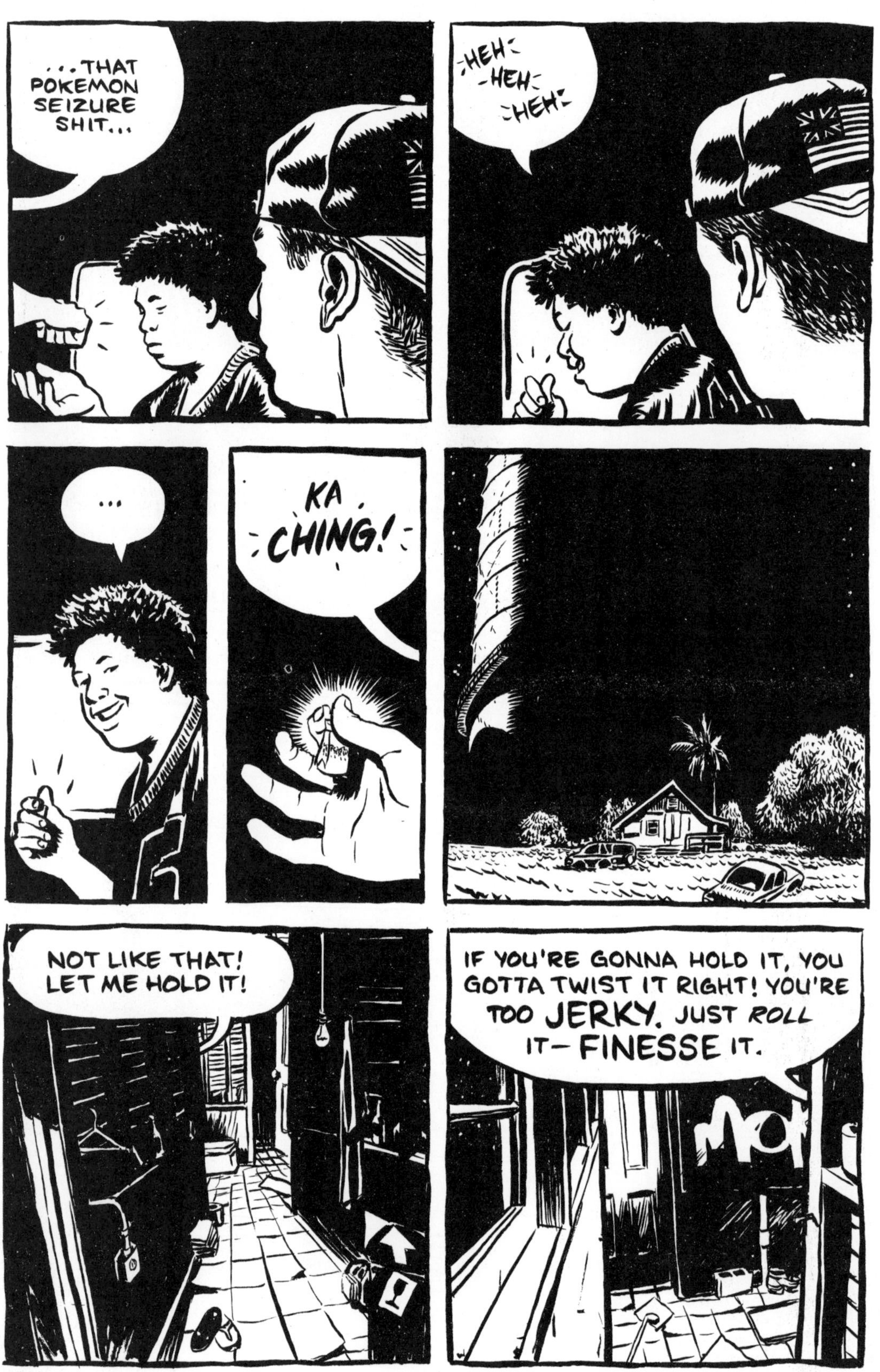
...THAT POKEMON SEIZURE SHIT...
HEH HEH HEH
...
KA CHING!
NOT LIKE THAT! LET ME HOLD IT!
IF YOU'RE GONNA HOLD IT, YOU GOTTA TWIST IT RIGHT! YOU'RE TOO JERKY. JUST ROLL IT— FINESSE IT.
MO

HOW AM I SUPPOSED TO *FINESSE* IT WITH THE FLAME SO CLOSE?

IT'S NOT EVEN MELTED YET, *RELAX!* LOREN—JUST WHEN YOU SEE THE CRYSTALS MELT, SUCK LIGHTLY...

NOT ONE LONG PUFF, THOUGH—SHORT LITTLE PUFFS...

ONE LITTLE PUFF WITH EACH ROCK BACK AND FOURTH.

LIKE RAISINS AND BURNING PLASTIC...

T TOO CLOSE, SHANE! IT'S R BOILING! YOU'RE GONN

DEA HOW MUCH LUNGS! JUST A

bzz zz

bzzz zz

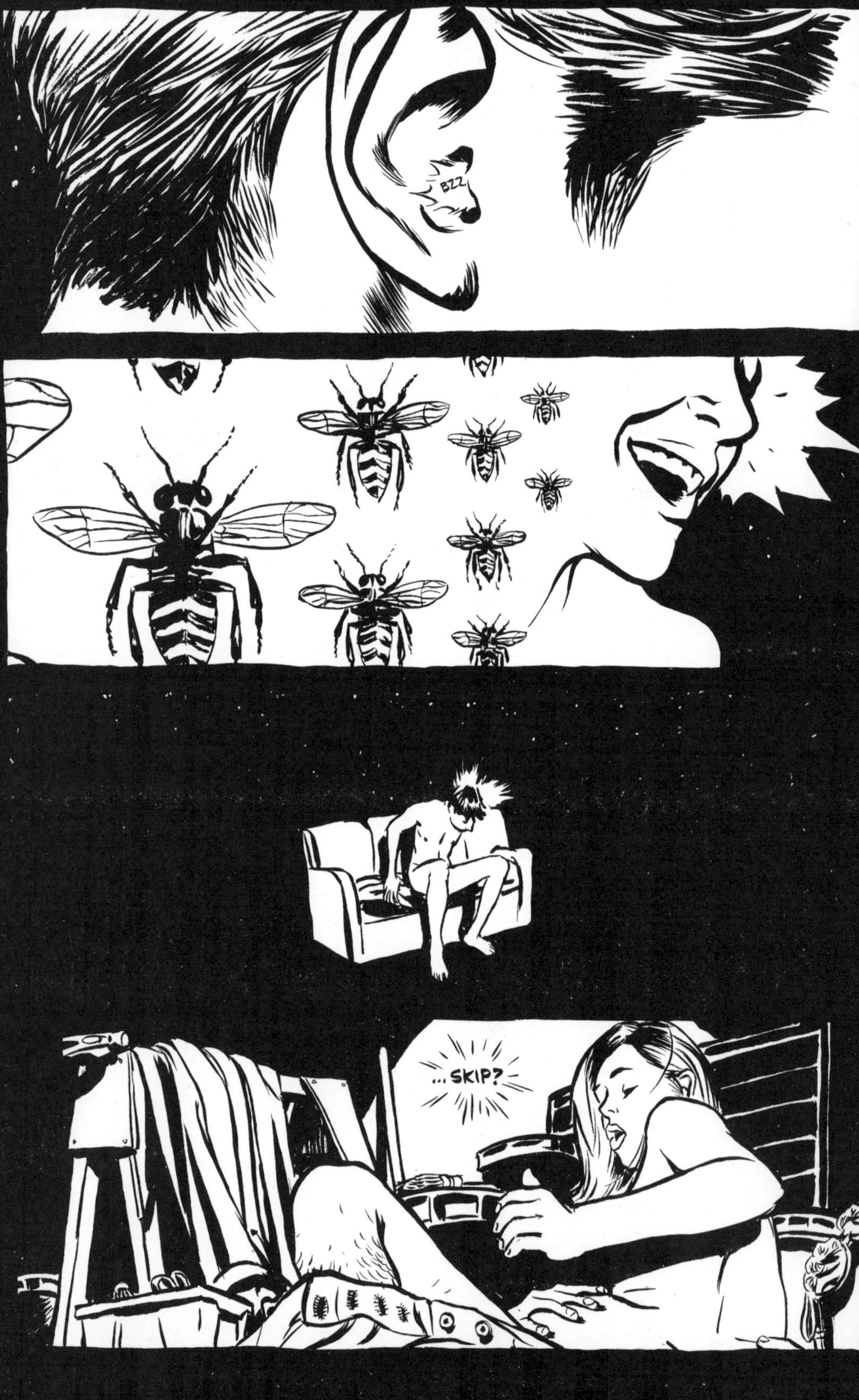
BZZ
... SKIP?

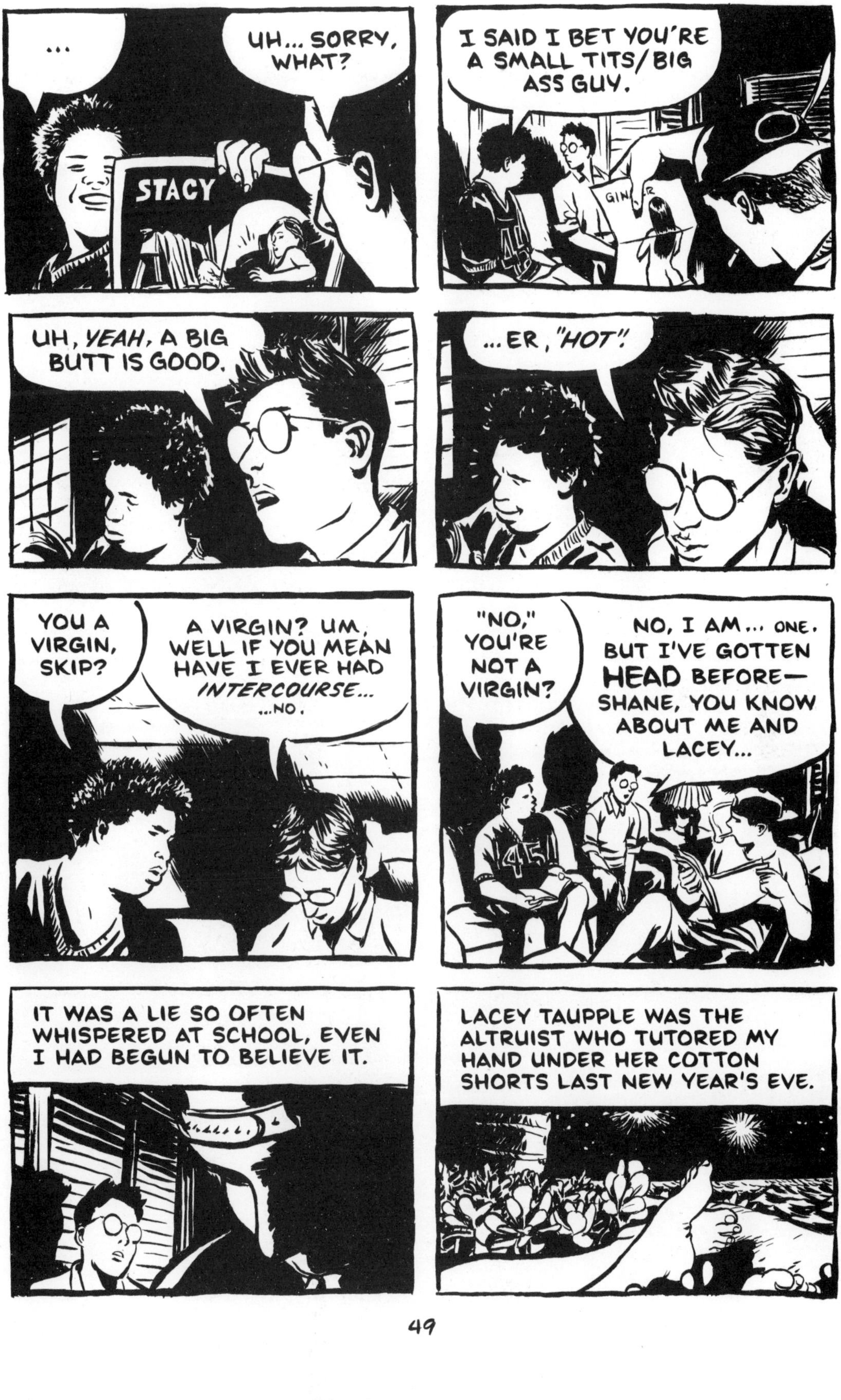
...
UH... SORRY, WHAT?
STACY
I SAID I BET YOU'RE A SMALL TITS/BIG ASS GUY.
UH, *YEAH*, A BIG BUTT IS GOOD.
...ER, *"HOT"*.
YOU A VIRGIN, SKIP?
A VIRGIN? UM, WELL IF YOU MEAN HAVE I EVER HAD *INTERCOURSE*... ...NO.
"NO," YOU'RE NOT A VIRGIN?
NO, I AM... ONE. BUT I'VE GOTTEN **HEAD** BEFORE— SHANE, YOU KNOW ABOUT ME AND LACEY...
IT WAS A LIE SO OFTEN WHISPERED AT SCHOOL, EVEN I HAD BEGUN TO BELIEVE IT.
LACEY TAUPPLE WAS THE ALTRUIST WHO TUTORED MY HAND UNDER HER COTTON SHORTS LAST NEW YEAR'S EVE.

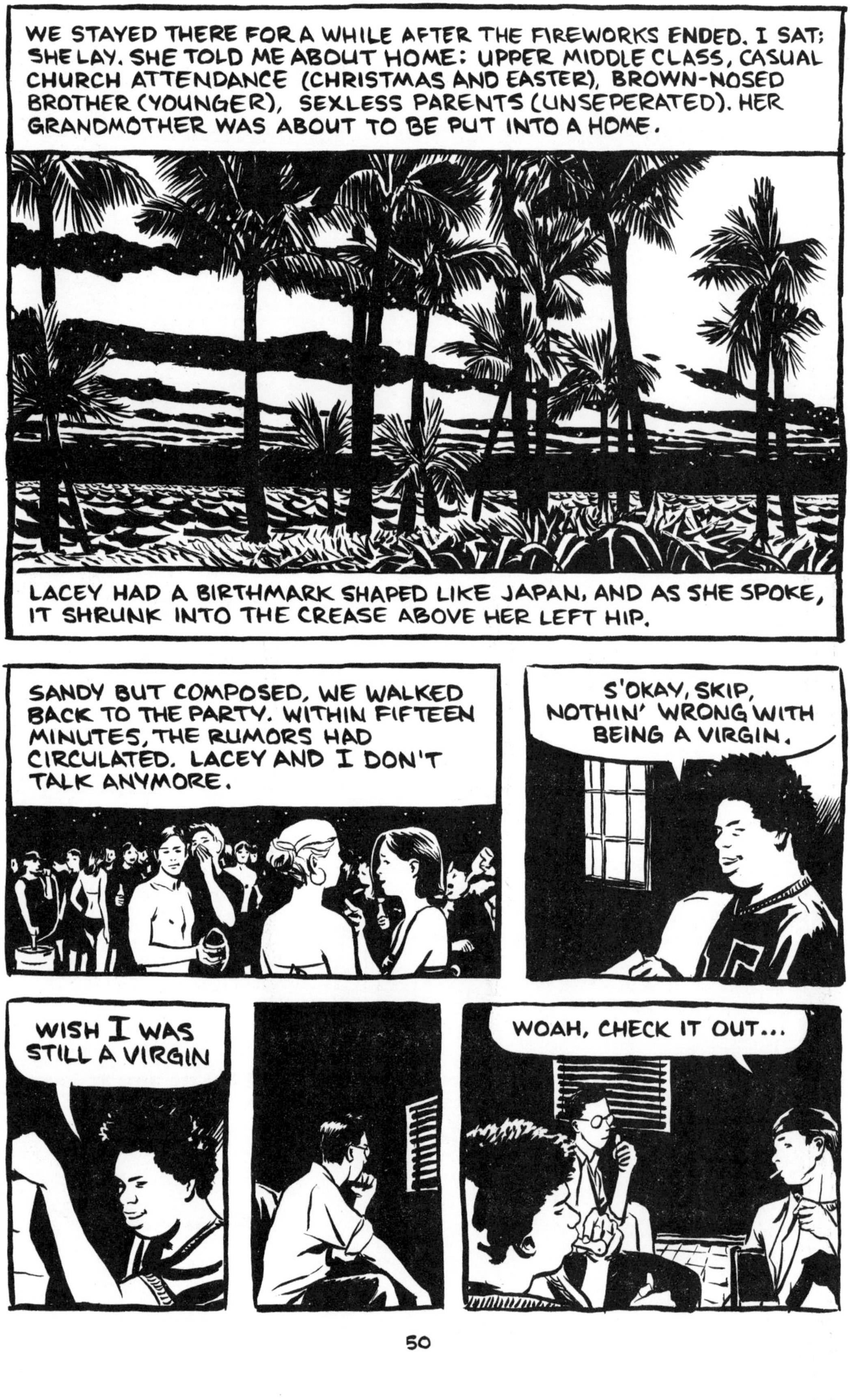
WE STAYED THERE FOR A WHILE AFTER THE FIREWORKS ENDED. I SAT; SHE LAY. SHE TOLD ME ABOUT HOME: UPPER MIDDLE CLASS, CASUAL CHURCH ATTENDANCE (CHRISTMAS AND EASTER), BROWN-NOSED BROTHER (YOUNGER), SEXLESS PARENTS (UNSEPERATED). HER GRANDMOTHER WAS ABOUT TO BE PUT INTO A HOME.
LACEY HAD A BIRTHMARK SHAPED LIKE JAPAN, AND AS SHE SPOKE, IT SHRUNK INTO THE CREASE ABOVE HER LEFT HIP.
SANDY BUT COMPOSED, WE WALKED BACK TO THE PARTY. WITHIN FIFTEEN MINUTES, THE RUMORS HAD CIRCULATED. LACEY AND I DON'T TALK ANYMORE.
S'OKAY, SKIP, NOTHIN' WRONG WITH BEING A VIRGIN.
WISH I WAS STILL A VIRGIN
WOAH, CHECK IT OUT...

ROYAL PATENT,

UPON CONFIRMATION OF THE LAND COMMISSION.

Whereas, the Board of Commissioners to Quiet Land Titles have by their decision awarded unto *Kanahele* claim N° 2/915 B.

an estate of Freehold less than Allodial. in and to the land hereafter described, and whereas *the said Kanahele has commuted the title as awarded for the fee simple title by the payment of six dollars into the Royal Exchequer.*

Therefore, Kamehameha, by the grace of God, King of the Hawaiian Islands, by this Royal Patent, makes known unto all men, that he has, for himself and his successors in office, this day granted and given absolutely, in Fee Simple, unto *Kanahele*

all that contain piece of land situate at *Kanaha Kahului* in the island of *Maui* ,and described as follows:

Commencing at the North angle & Running
S. 5T°E 35 7/12 feet along Umala
S 44°W 25 " " Capt. Maughian's land
N 40 W 23 3/4 " " Wakea
N 61° E 30 ½ " " Ala huina to the place of Beginning

containing *0.621*   acres

more or less; excepting and reserving to the Hawaiian Government all mineral or metallic mines of every description.

To have and to hold the above granted land in Fee Simple unto the said *Kanahele his* heirs and assigns forever, subject to the taxes to be from time to time imposed by the Legislative Council equally upon all landed property held in fee simple.

In witness whereof I have hereunto set my hand and caused the Great Seal of the Hawaiian Islands to be affixed, this *fourteenth* day of *August* 18*53*

Moa REX

Moa
Kamehameha

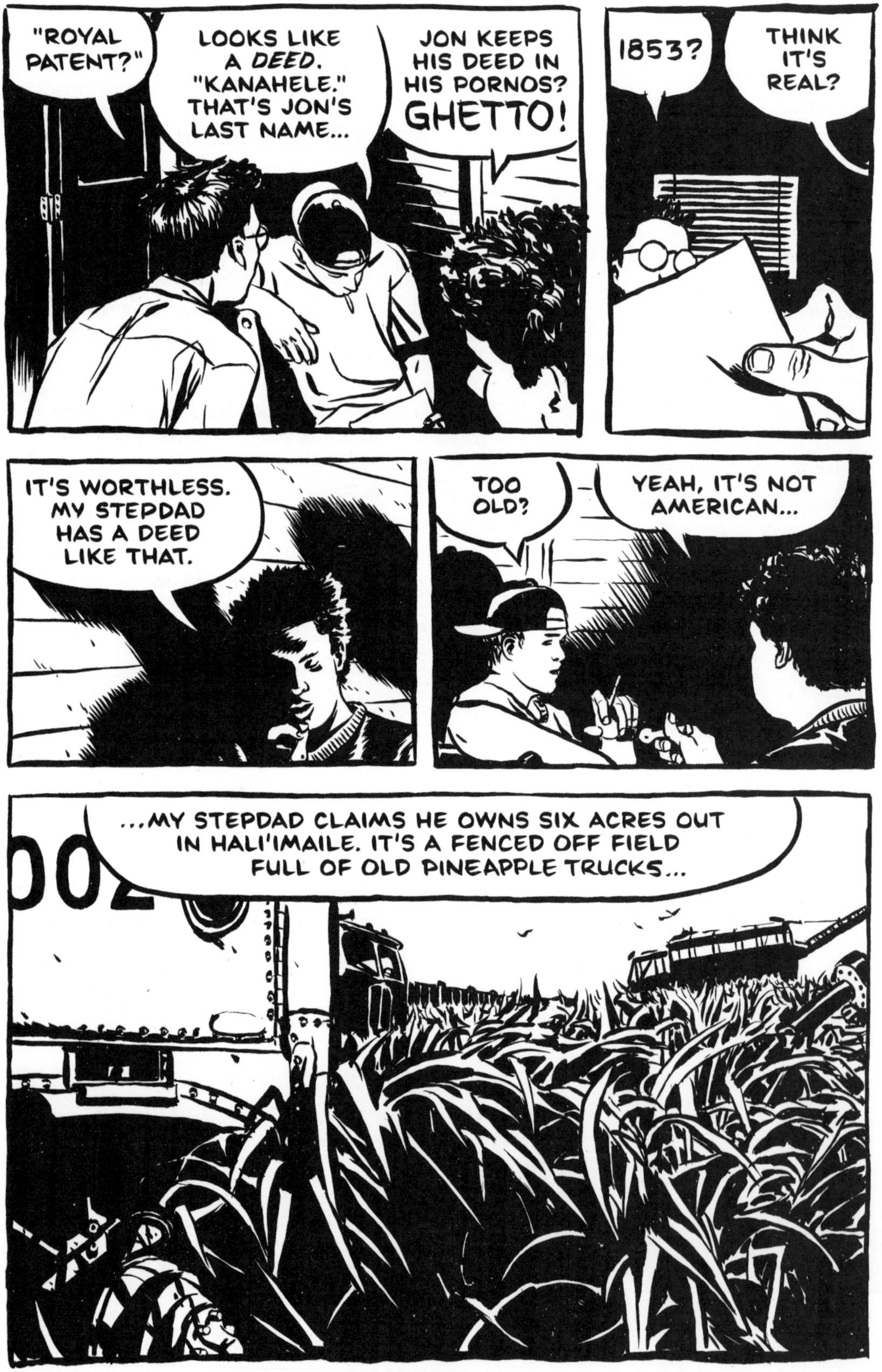
"ROYAL PATENT?"
LOOKS LIKE A *DEED*. "KANAHELE." THAT'S JON'S LAST NAME...
JON KEEPS HIS DEED IN HIS PORNOS? GHETTO!
1853?
THINK IT'S REAL?
IT'S WORTHLESS. MY STEPDAD HAS A DEED LIKE THAT.
TOO OLD?
YEAH, IT'S NOT AMERICAN...
...MY STEPDAD CLAIMS HE OWNS SIX ACRES OUT IN HALI'IMAILE. IT'S A FENCED OFF FIELD FULL OF OLD PINEAPPLE TRUCKS...
002

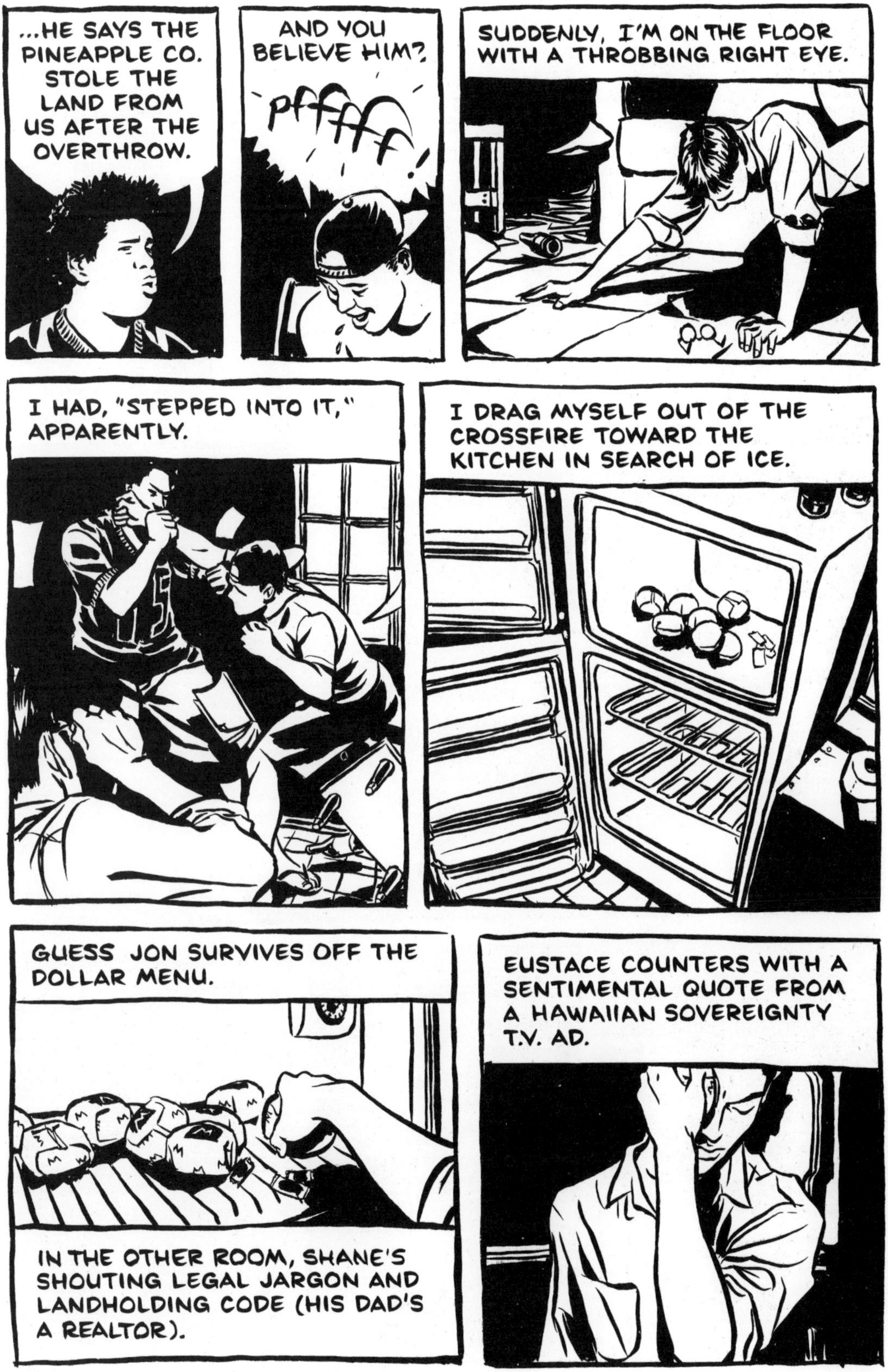
...HE SAYS THE PINEAPPLE CO. STOLE THE LAND FROM US AFTER THE OVERTHROW.
AND YOU BELIEVE HIM?
PFFFFF!
SUDDENLY, I'M ON THE FLOOR WITH A THROBBING RIGHT EYE.
I HAD, "STEPPED INTO IT," APPARENTLY.
I DRAG MYSELF OUT OF THE CROSSFIRE TOWARD THE KITCHEN IN SEARCH OF ICE.
GUESS JON SURVIVES OFF THE DOLLAR MENU.
IN THE OTHER ROOM, SHANE'S SHOUTING LEGAL JARGON AND LANDHOLDING CODE (HIS DAD'S A REALTOR).
EUSTACE COUNTERS WITH A SENTIMENTAL QUOTE FROM A HAWAIIAN SOVEREIGNTY T.V. AD.

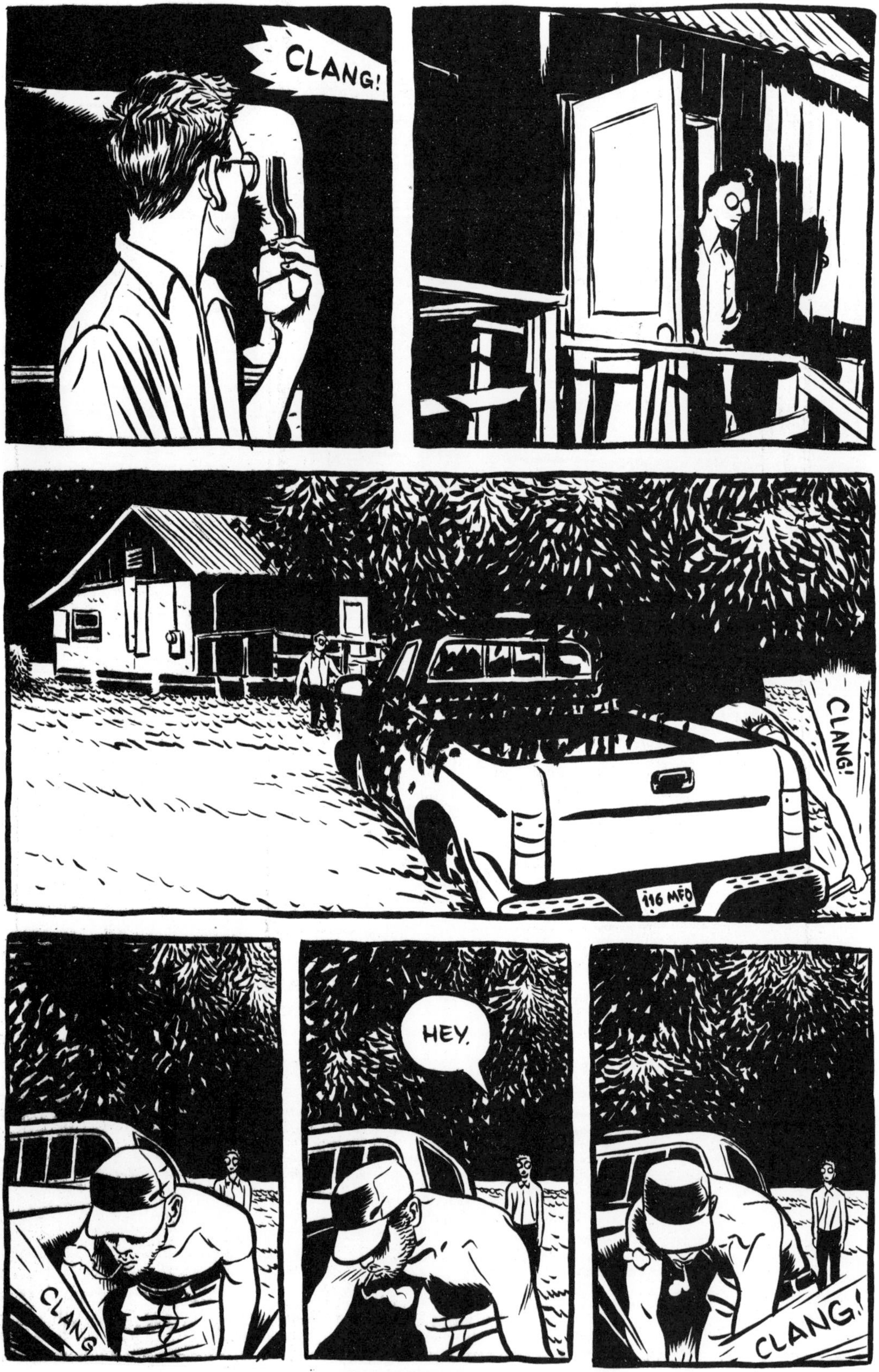
CLANG!
CLANG!
116 MFD
CLANG
HEY.
CLANG!

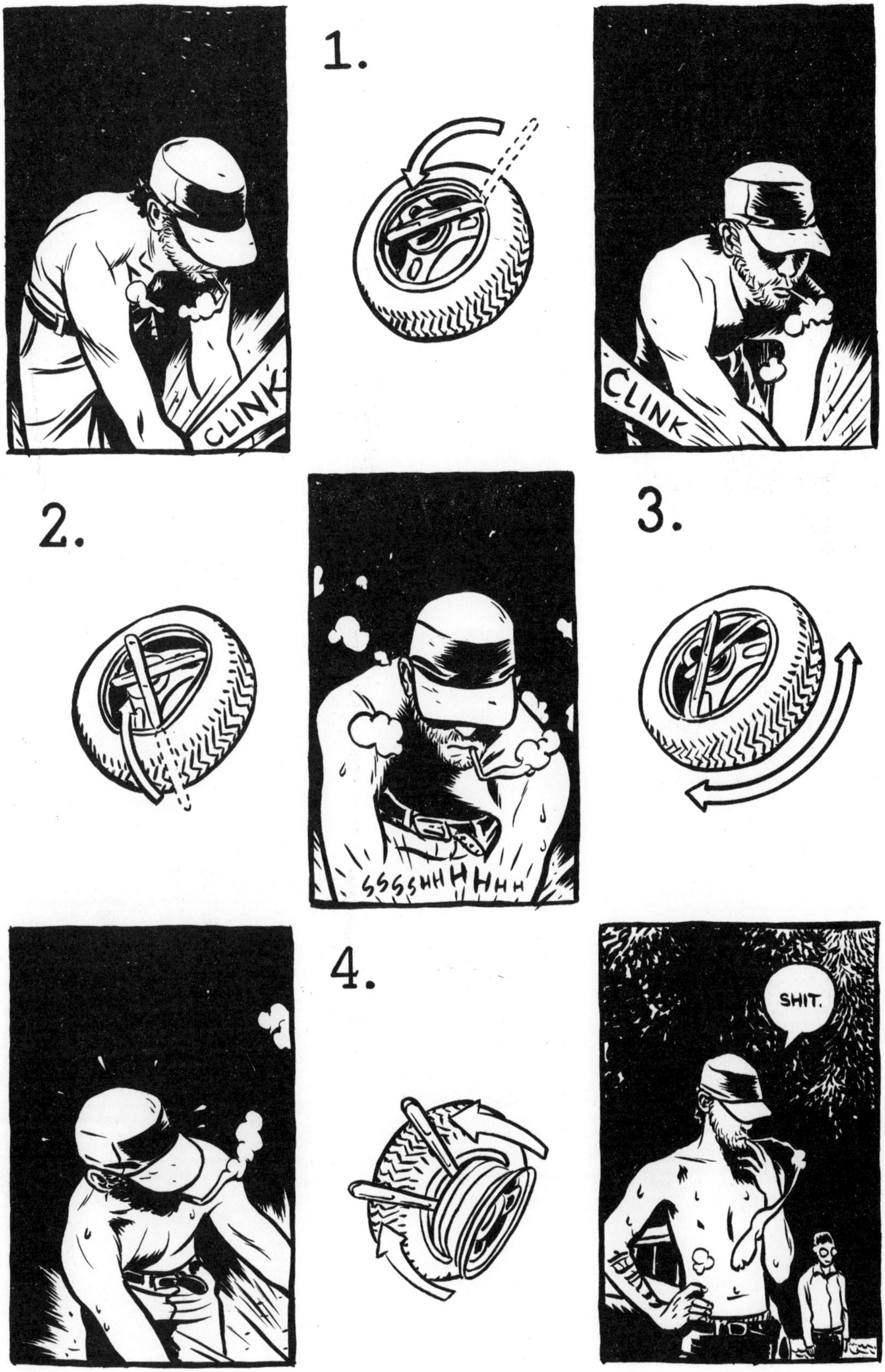
CLINK
1.
CLINK
2.
SSSSHHHHHHH
3.
4.
SHIT.

MOVE THAT LIGHT HIGHER.

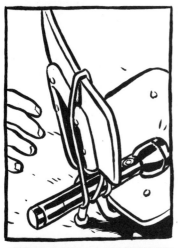

HOW'S THAT?

TIE IT.

CLANG

CLANG

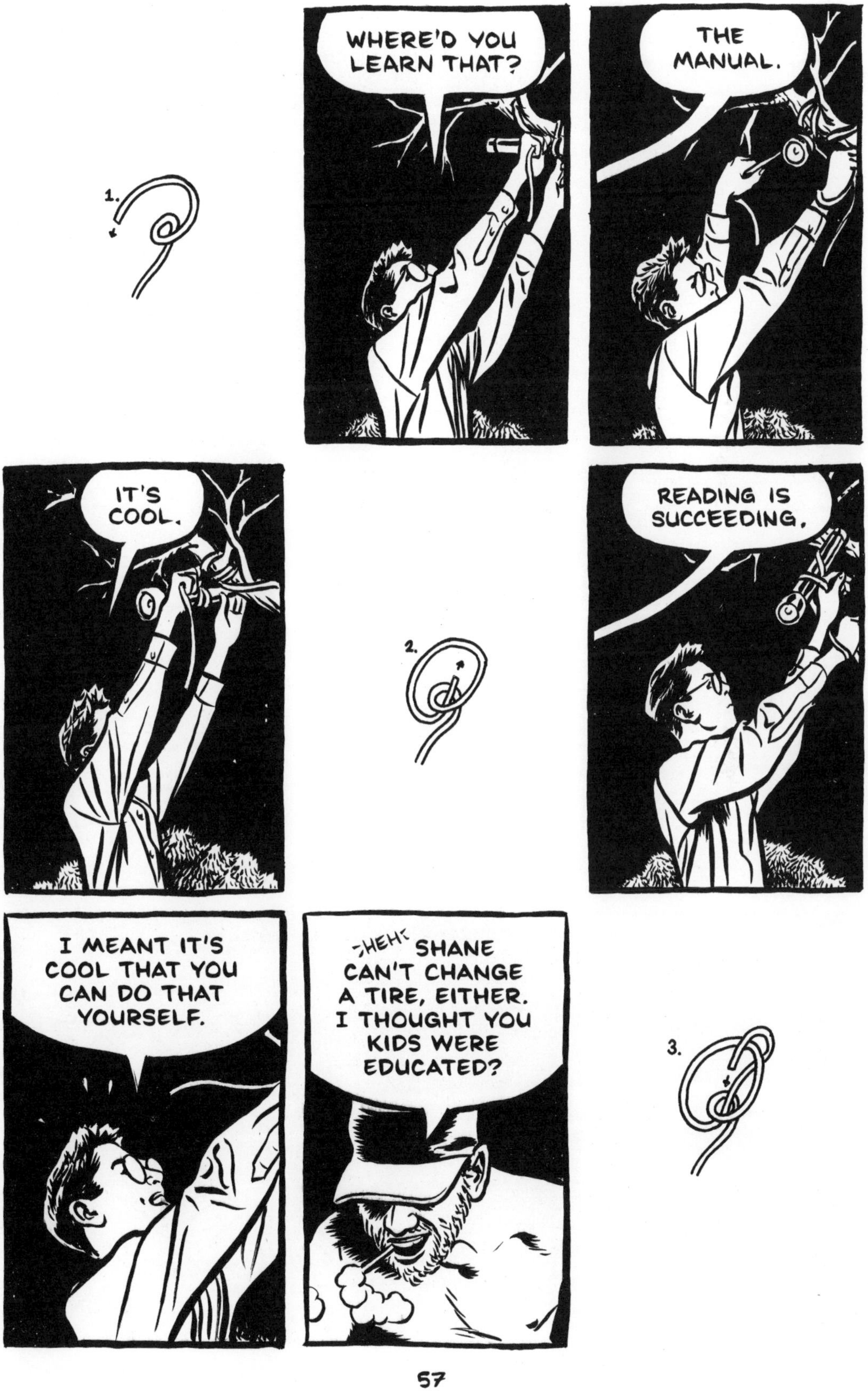
1.
WHERE'D YOU LEARN THAT?
THE MANUAL.
IT'S COOL.
2.
READING IS SUCCEEDING.
I MEANT IT'S COOL THAT YOU CAN DO THAT YOURSELF.
HEH
SHANE CAN'T CHANGE A TIRE, EITHER. I THOUGHT YOU KIDS WERE EDUCATED?
3.

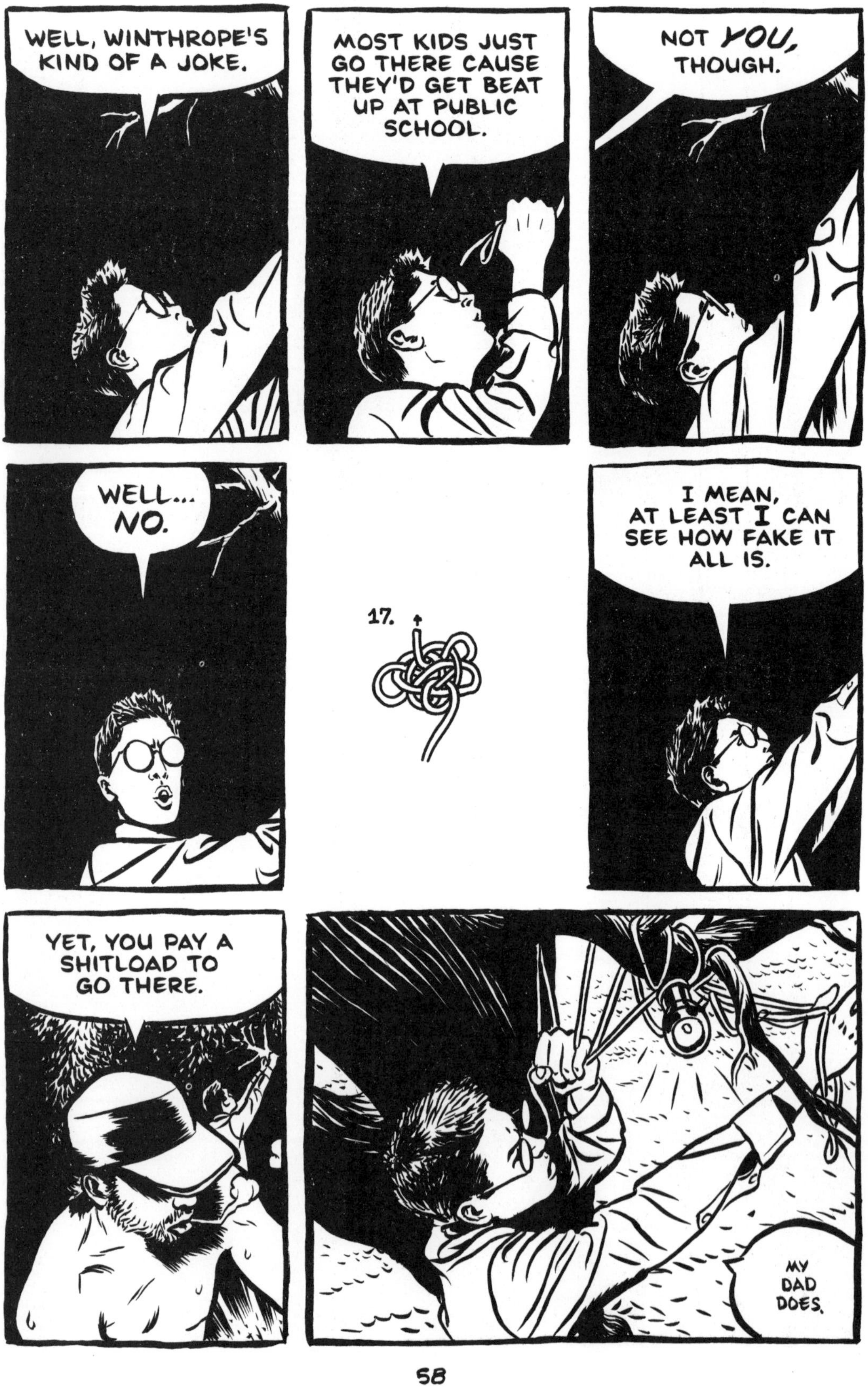
WELL, WINTHROPE'S KIND OF A JOKE.
MOST KIDS JUST GO THERE CAUSE THEY'D GET BEAT UP AT PUBLIC SCHOOL.
NOT YOU, THOUGH.
WELL... NO.
17.
I MEAN, AT LEAST I CAN SEE HOW FAKE IT ALL IS.
YET, YOU PAY A SHITLOAD TO GO THERE.
MY DAD DOES.

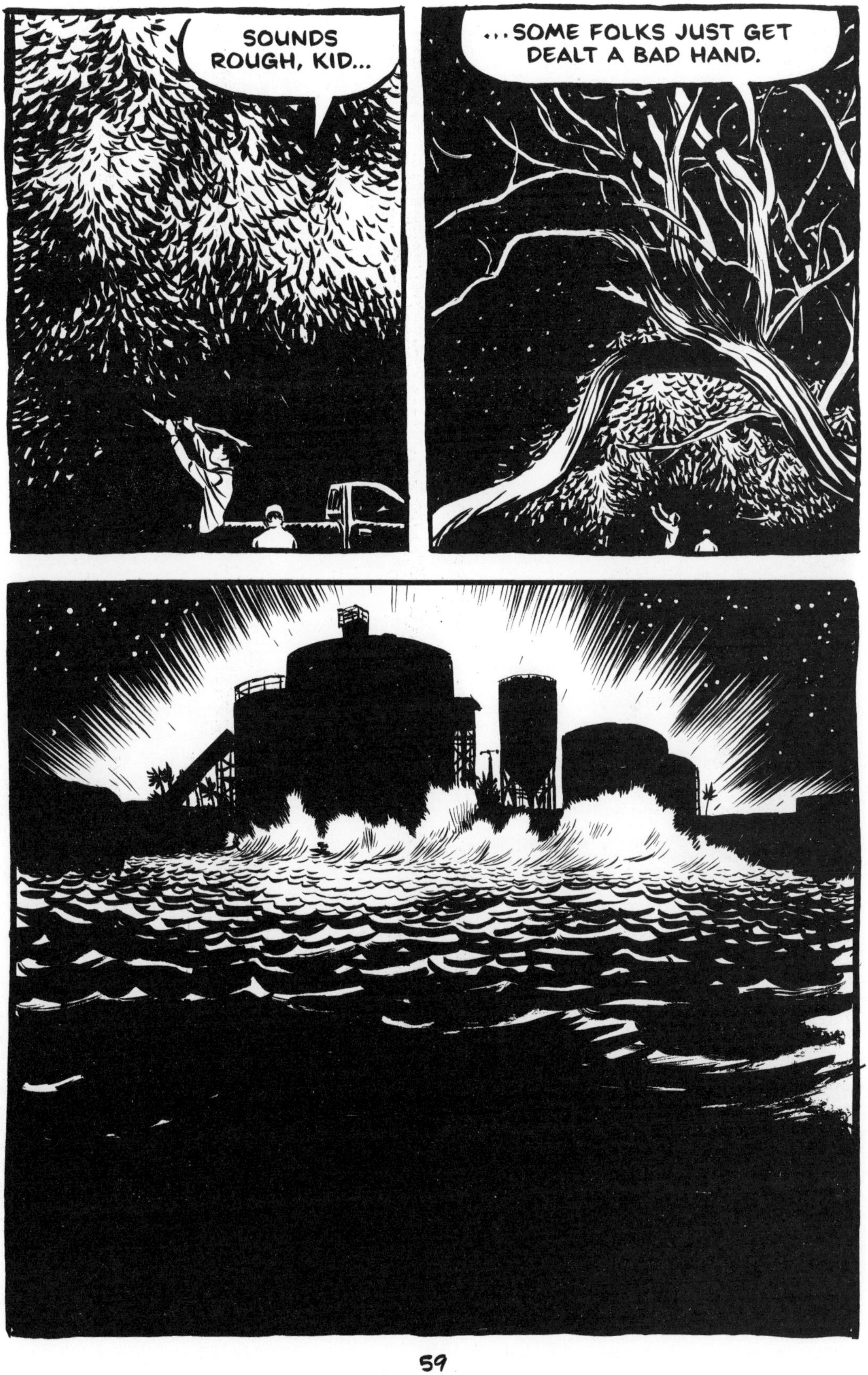
SOUNDS ROUGH, KID...
...SOME FOLKS JUST GET DEALT A BAD HAND.

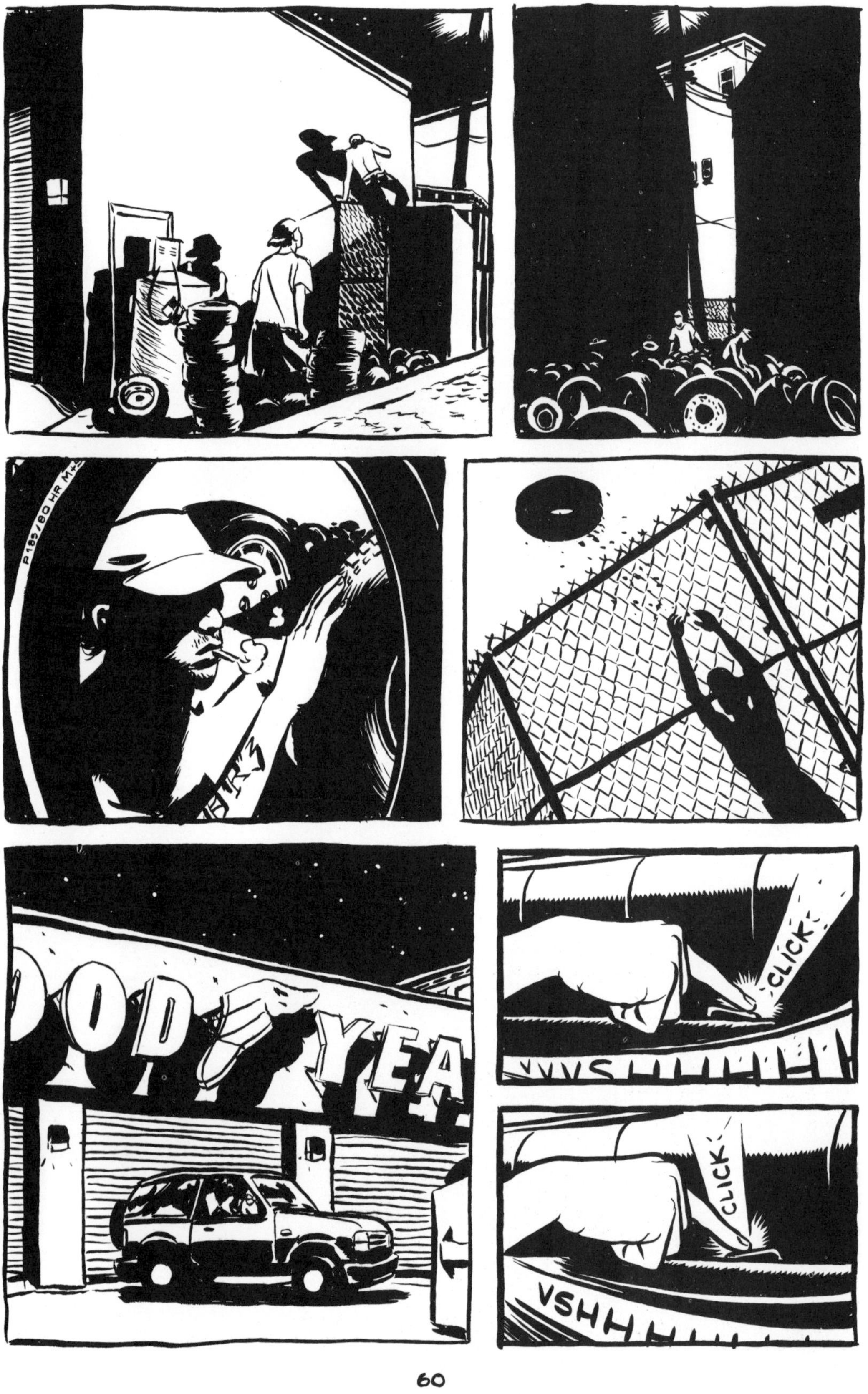
OOD YEA
CLICK
VSHHHHH
CLICK
VSHHHHH

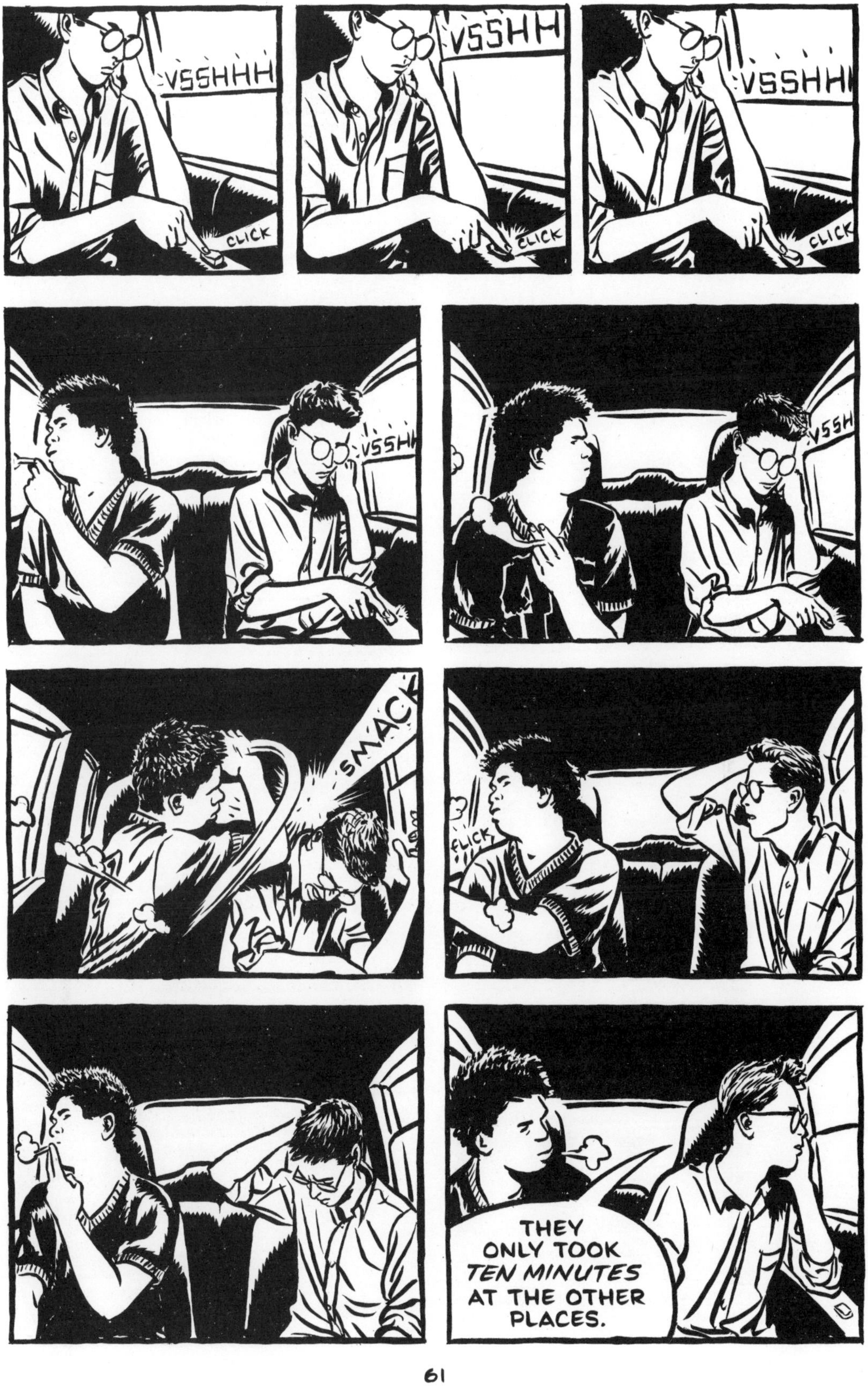
VSSHHH
CLICK
VSSHH
CLICK
VSSHH
CLICK
VSSH
VSSH
SMACK
FLICK
THEY ONLY TOOK *TEN MINUTES* AT THE OTHER PLACES.

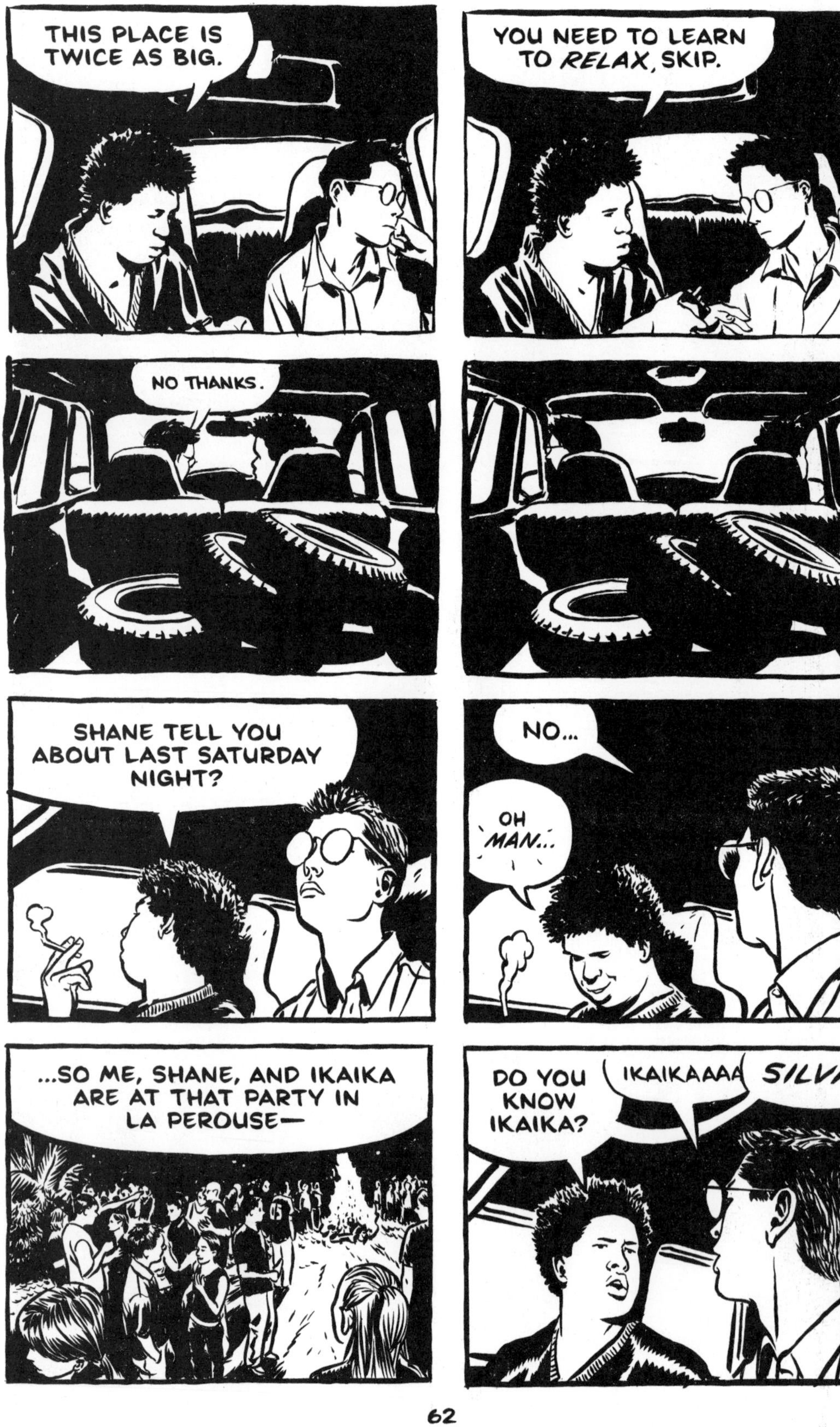
THIS PLACE IS TWICE AS BIG.
YOU NEED TO LEARN TO RELAX, SKIP.
NO THANKS.
SHANE TELL YOU ABOUT LAST SATURDAY NIGHT?
NO...
OH MAN...
...SO ME, SHANE, AND IKAIKA ARE AT THAT PARTY IN LA PEROUSE—
DO YOU KNOW IKAIKA?
IKAIKAAAA
SILVA.

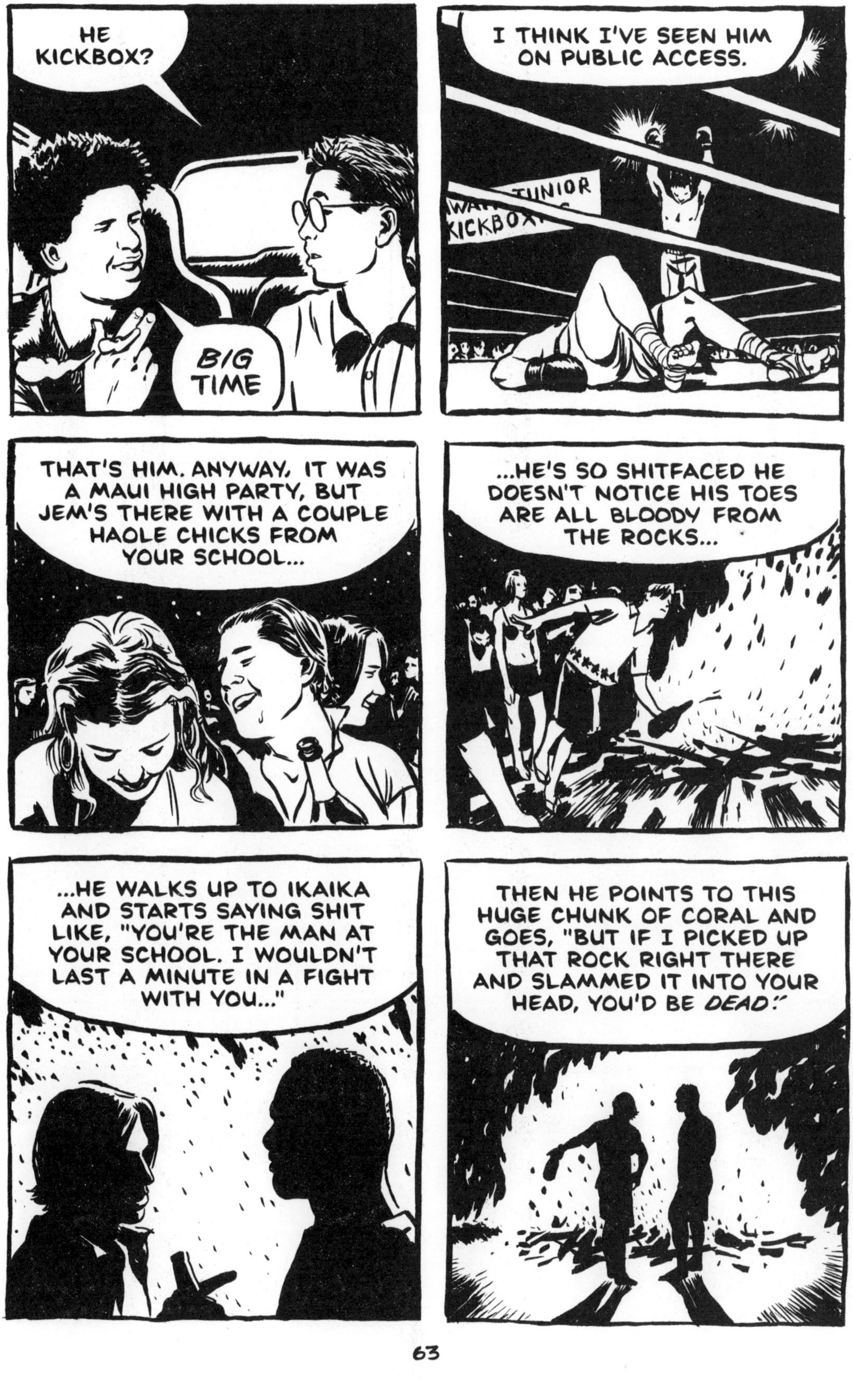
HE KICKBOX?
BIG TIME
I THINK I'VE SEEN HIM ON PUBLIC ACCESS.
JUNIOR
KICKBOX
THAT'S HIM. ANYWAY, IT WAS A MAUI HIGH PARTY, BUT JEM'S THERE WITH A COUPLE HAOLE CHICKS FROM YOUR SCHOOL...
...HE'S SO SHITFACED HE DOESN'T NOTICE HIS TOES ARE ALL BLOODY FROM THE ROCKS...
...HE WALKS UP TO IKAIKA AND STARTS SAYING SHIT LIKE, "YOU'RE THE MAN AT YOUR SCHOOL. I WOULDN'T LAST A MINUTE IN A FIGHT WITH YOU..."
THEN HE POINTS TO THIS HUGE CHUNK OF CORAL AND GOES, "BUT IF I PICKED UP THAT ROCK RIGHT THERE AND SLAMMED IT INTO YOUR HEAD, YOU'D BE *DEAD*."

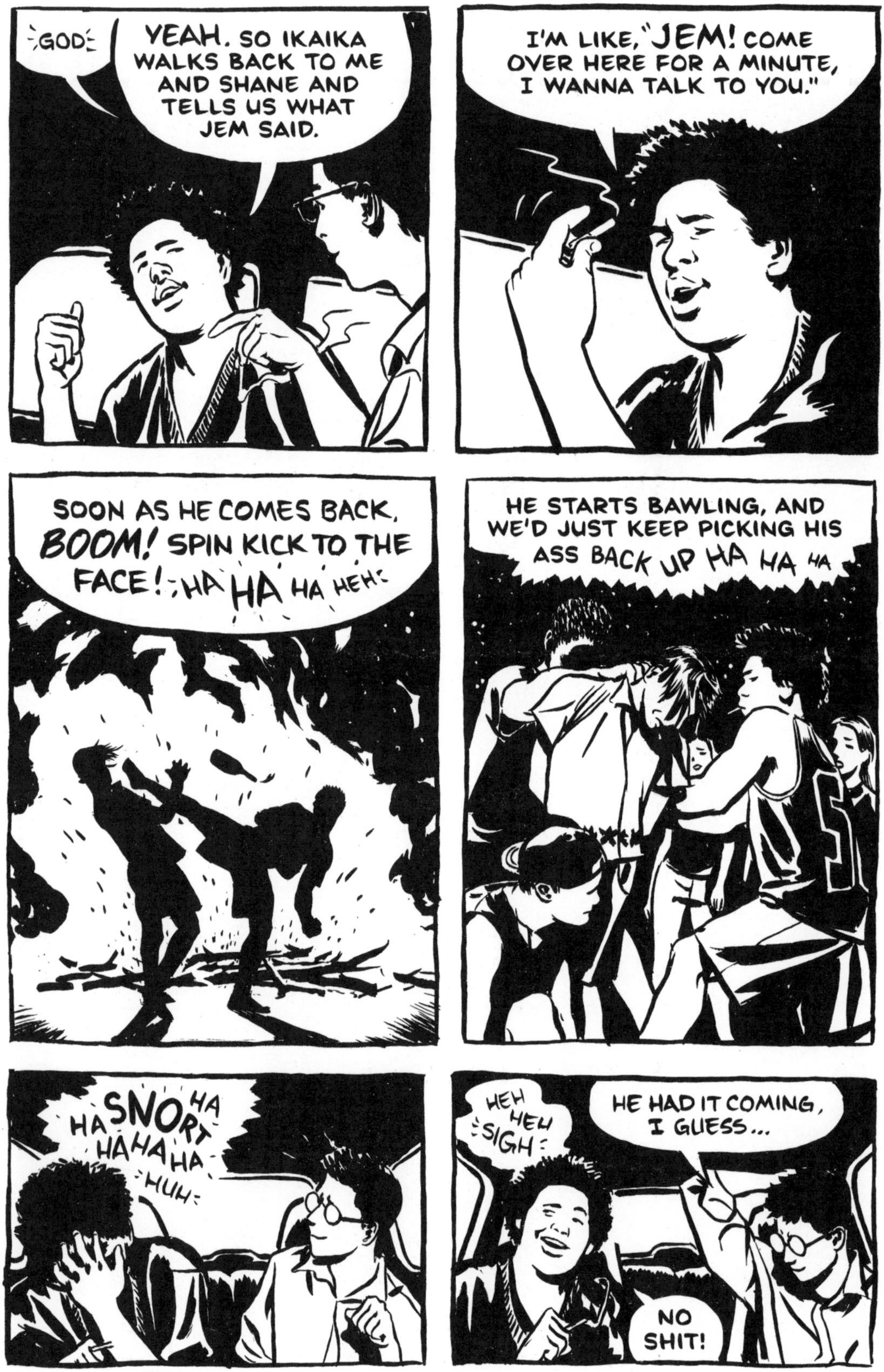
GOD
YEAH. SO IKAIKA WALKS BACK TO ME AND SHANE AND TELLS US WHAT JEM SAID.
I'M LIKE, "JEM! COME OVER HERE FOR A MINUTE, I WANNA TALK TO YOU."
SOON AS HE COMES BACK, BOOM! SPIN KICK TO THE FACE! HA HA HA HEH
HE STARTS BAWLING, AND WE'D JUST KEEP PICKING HIS ASS BACK UP HA HA HA
HA SNORT HA HA HA HA HA
HUH
HEH HEH SIGH
HE HAD IT COMING, I GUESS...
NO SHIT!

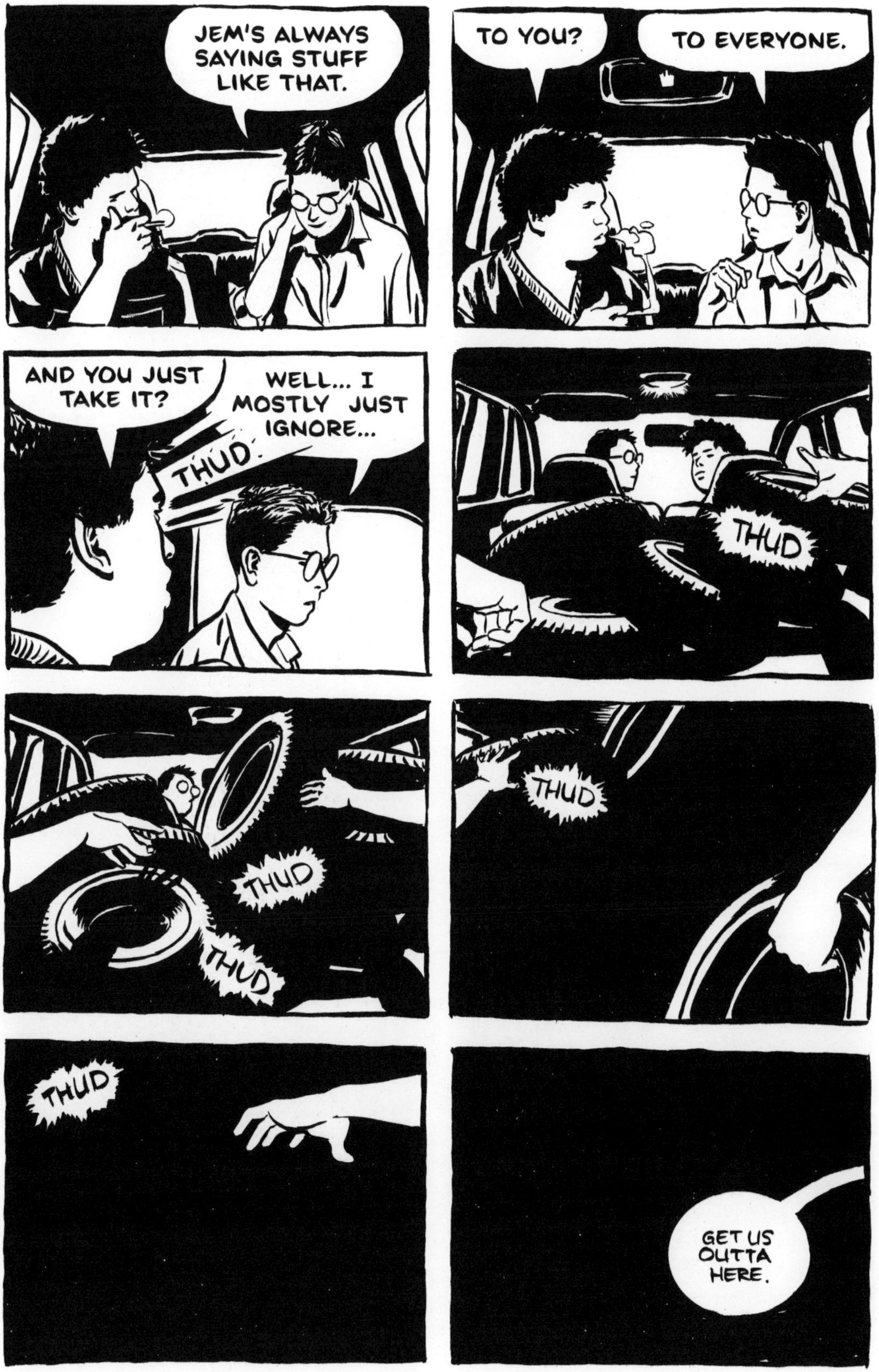
JEM'S ALWAYS SAYING STUFF LIKE THAT.
TO YOU?
TO EVERYONE.
AND YOU JUST TAKE IT?
WELL... I MOSTLY JUST IGNORE...
THUD
THUD
THUD
THUD
THUD
THUD
GET US OUTTA HERE.

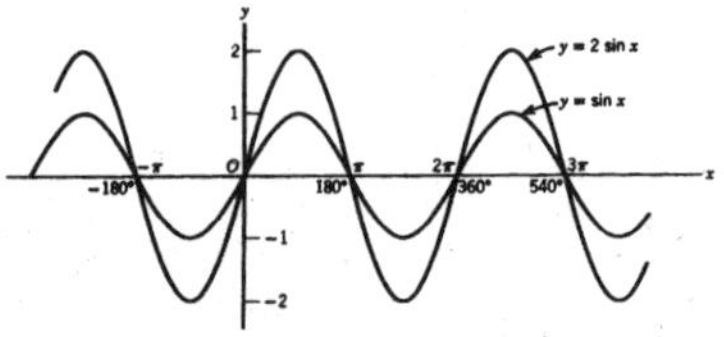
y = 2 sin x
y = sin x

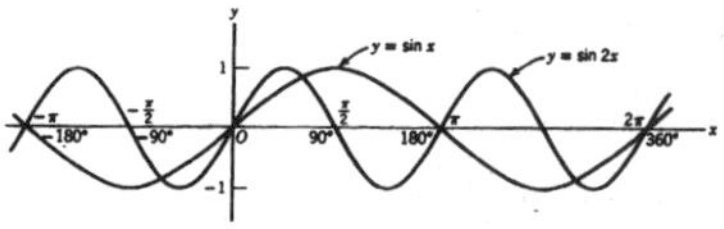
y = sin x
y = sin 2x

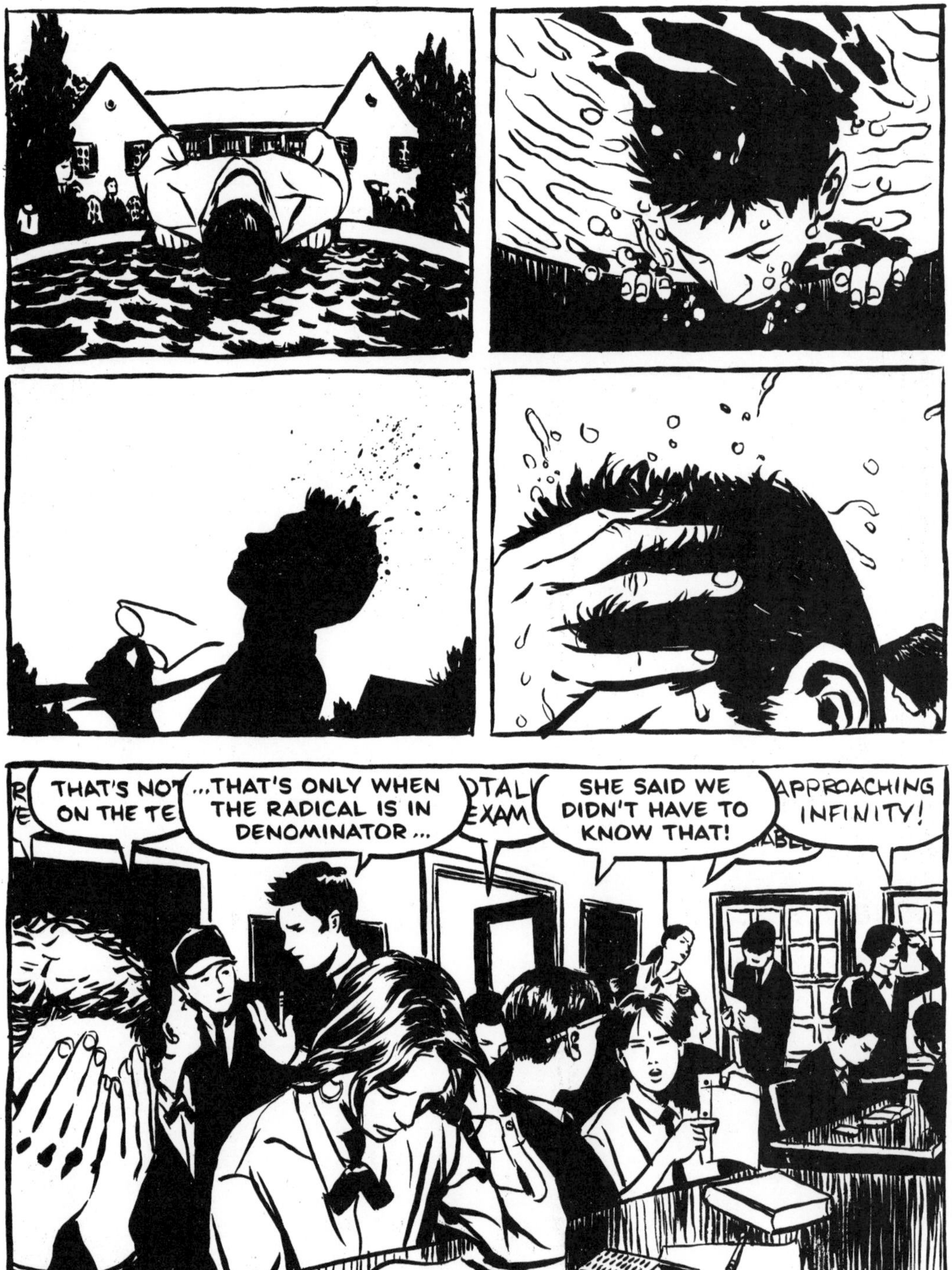
THAT'S NOT ON THE TE
...THAT'S ONLY WHEN THE RADICAL IS IN DENOMINATOR...
TAL EXAM
SHE SAID WE DIDN'T HAVE TO KNOW THAT!
APPROACHING INFINITY!

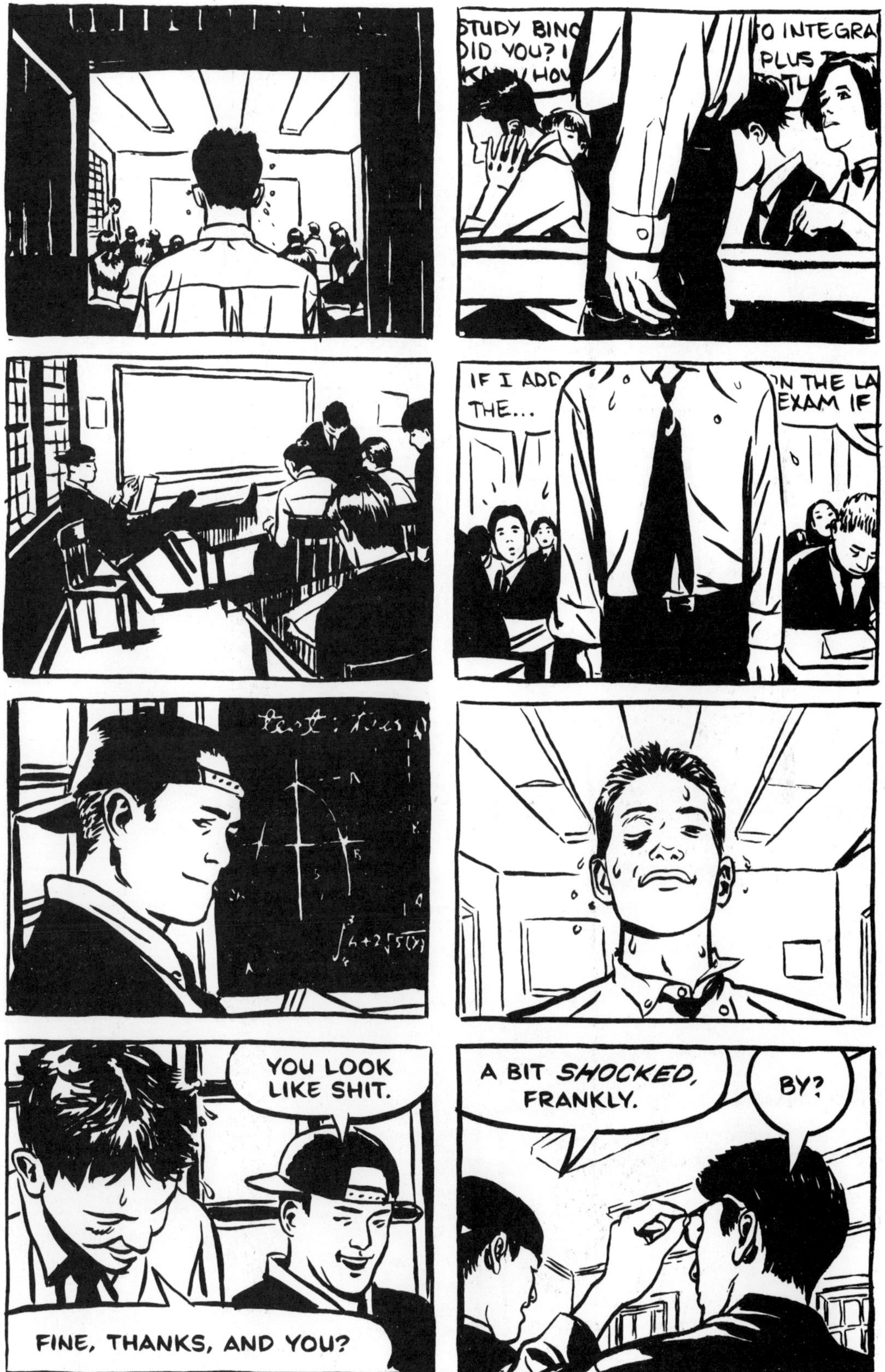

YOU LOOK LIKE SHIT.
FINE, THANKS, AND YOU?
A BIT *SHOCKED,* FRANKLY.
BY?

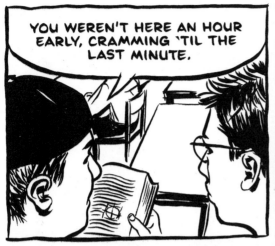

YOU WEREN'T HERE AN HOUR EARLY, CRAMMING 'TIL THE LAST MINUTE.
PUT YOUR BOOKS UNDER YOUR DESKS AND SPREAD OUT...
I'LL IMPROVISE.
...THERE ARE FIFTY QUESTIONS.
...YOU HAVE ONE HOUR...
Calculus
trigonometric,
Formula 12,2,2
y=sinx

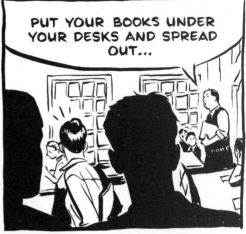

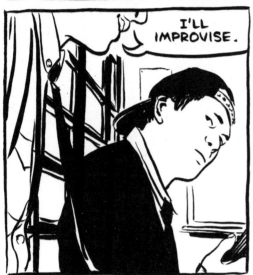

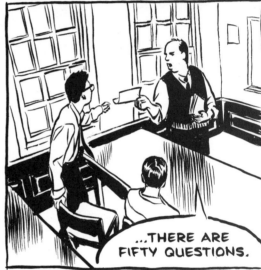

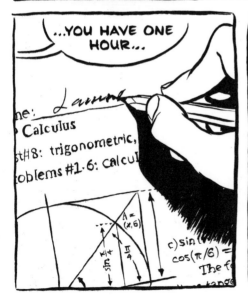

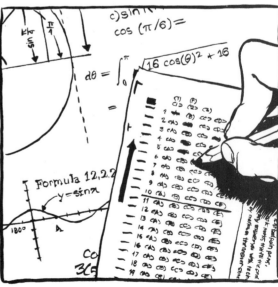

Formula 12.2.2
y=sin x
d)
180°
B
cos(π/6)
3(5x
3(x
THE NEXT FEW DAYS AT WINTHROPE ARE A BREEZE.

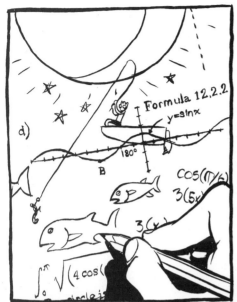

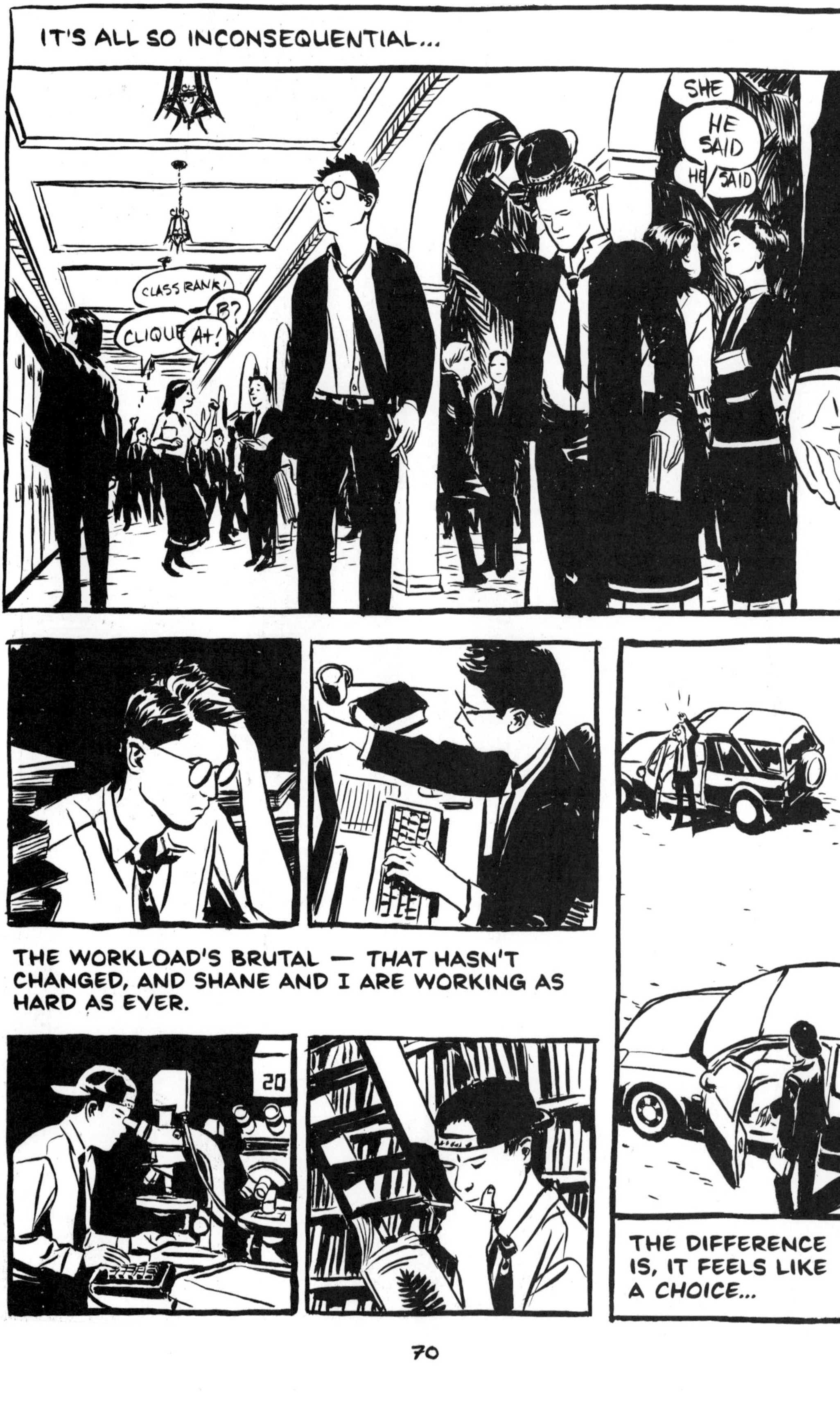
IT'S ALL SO INCONSEQUENTIAL...
CLASS RANK!
CLIQUE
A+!
B?
SHE
HE SAID
HE SAID
THE WORKLOAD'S BRUTAL — THAT HASN'T CHANGED, AND SHANE AND I ARE WORKING AS HARD AS EVER.
20
THE DIFFERENCE IS, IT FEELS LIKE A CHOICE...

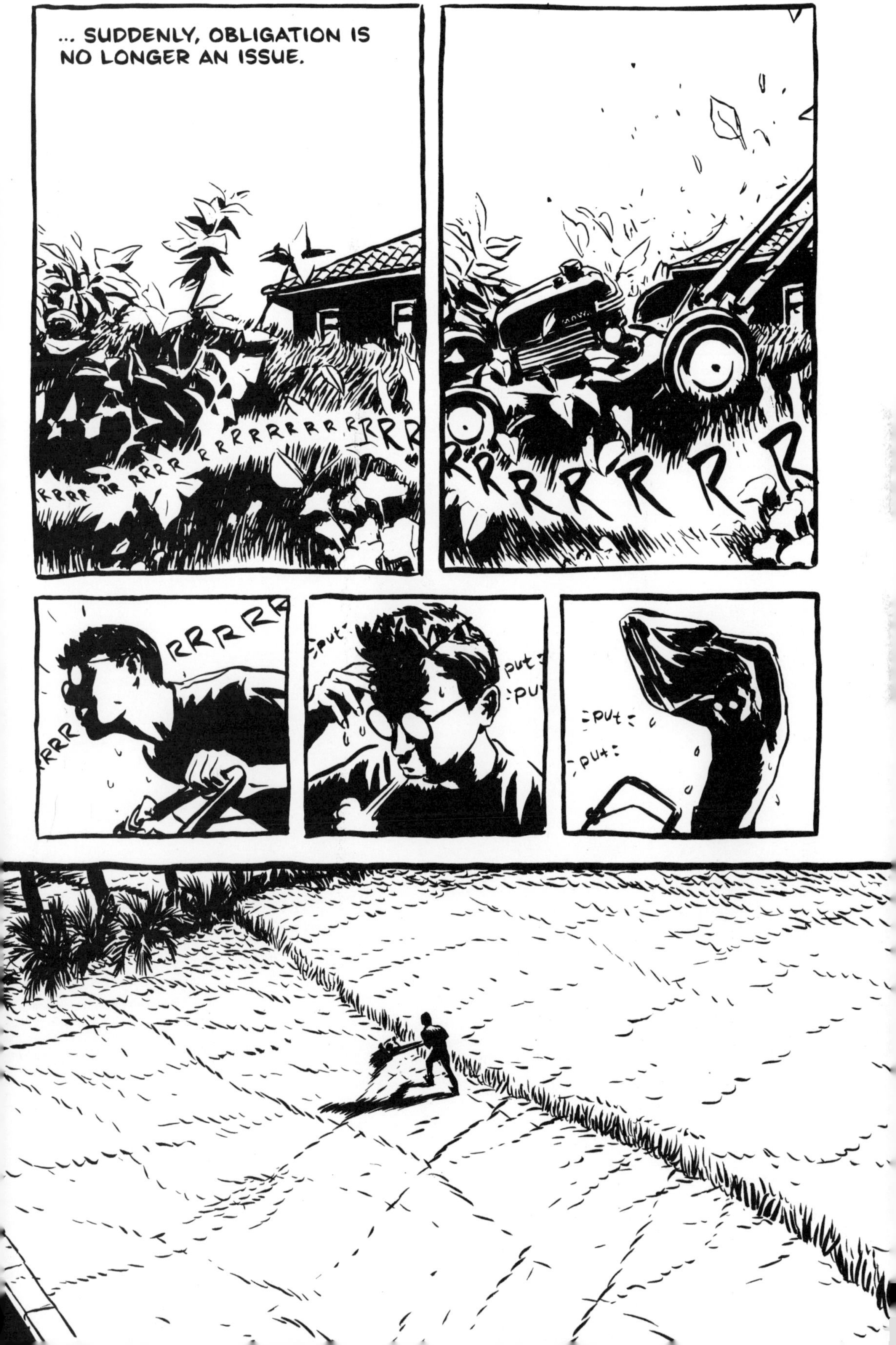

... SUDDENLY, OBLIGATION IS NO LONGER AN ISSUE.
RRRR RR RRRR RRRRRRRRRRRRRRR
RRRRRRR
RRRRR
RRR
put
put
PU
put
put

I WENT TO JON'S HOUSE JUST ONCE MORE THAT WEEK.

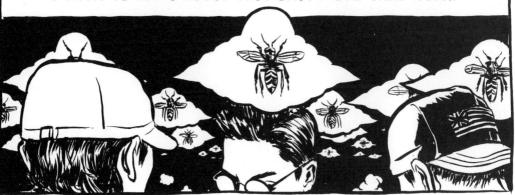

THE NIGHT BEGAN PRETTY MUCH THE WAY IT HAD LAST TIME...

...BUT WAS CUT SHORT WHEN WE RETURNED HOME TO FIND JON HAD A VISITOR.

...TWO, ACTUALLY.

JON STEPPED OUT OF THE CAR WITHOUT A WORD. I WATCHED HIM SHRINK IN THE REAR-VIEW AS SHANE PULLED BACK ONTO THE ROAD.

73

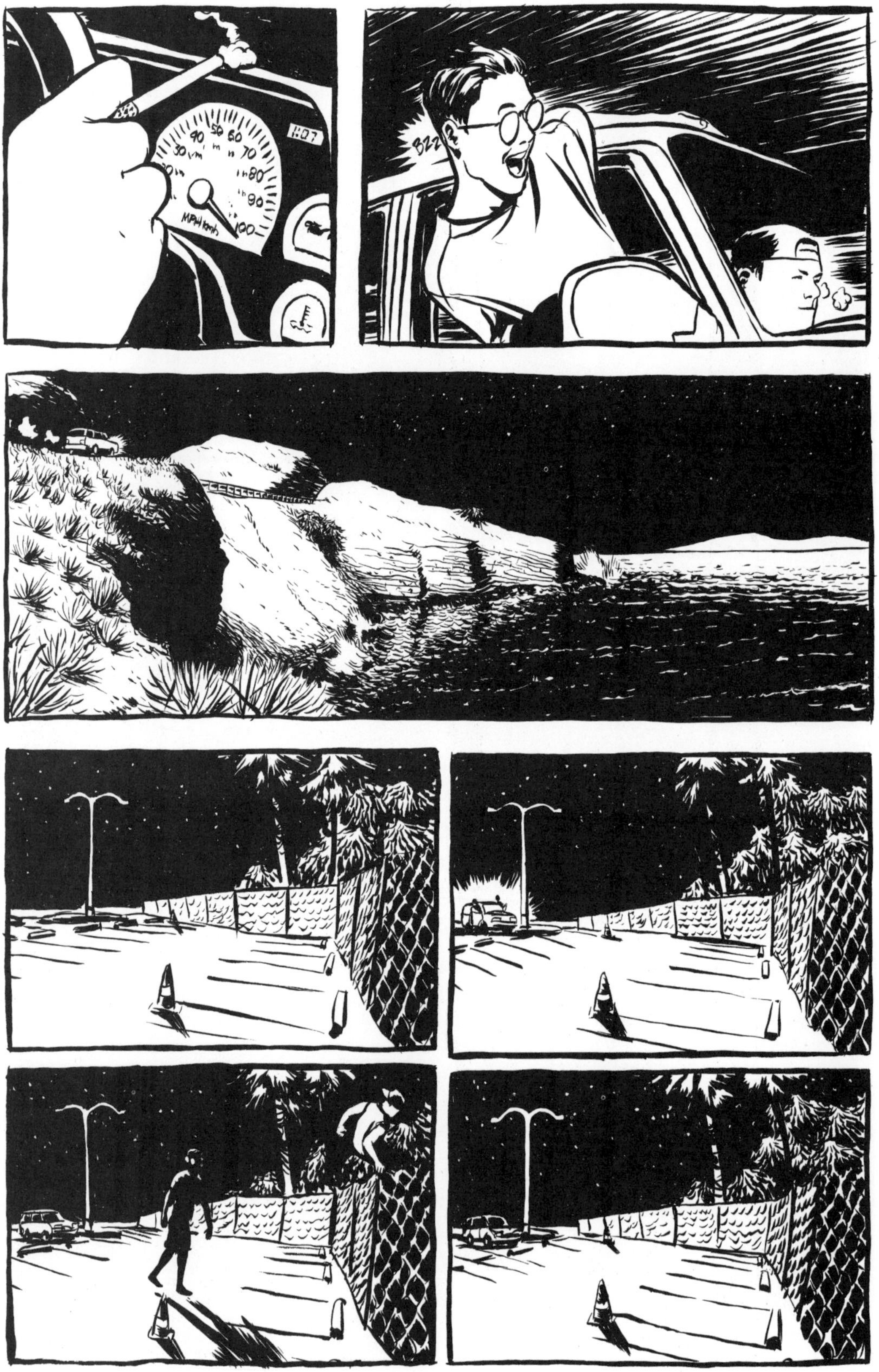
BZZ

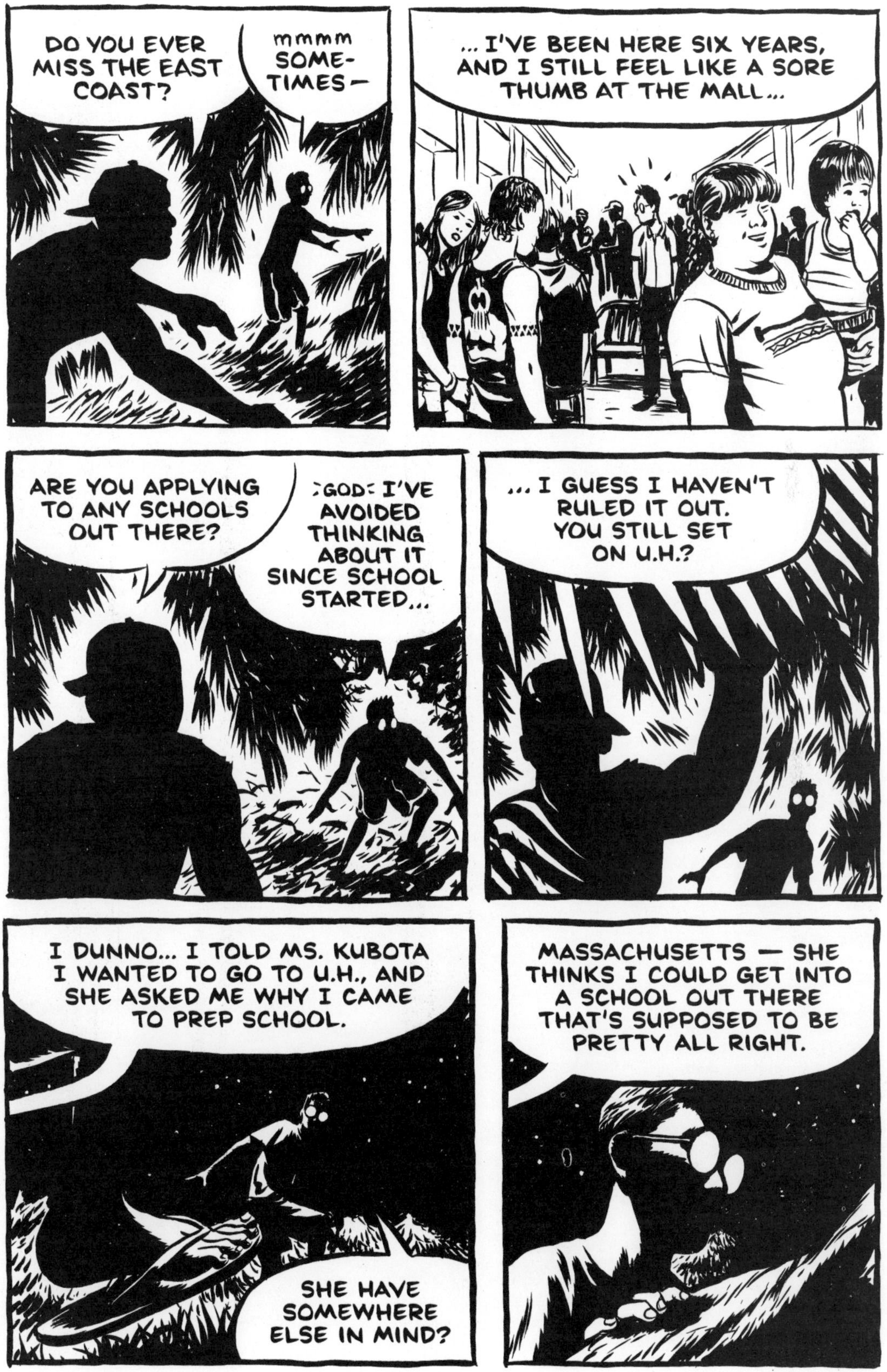
DO YOU EVER MISS THE EAST COAST?
mmmm SOME-TIMES—
... I'VE BEEN HERE SIX YEARS, AND I STILL FEEL LIKE A SORE THUMB AT THE MALL...
ARE YOU APPLYING TO ANY SCHOOLS OUT THERE?
:GOD: I'VE AVOIDED THINKING ABOUT IT SINCE SCHOOL STARTED...
... I GUESS I HAVEN'T RULED IT OUT. YOU STILL SET ON U.H.?
I DUNNO... I TOLD MS. KUBOTA I WANTED TO GO TO U.H., AND SHE ASKED ME WHY I CAME TO PREP SCHOOL.
SHE HAVE SOMEWHERE ELSE IN MIND?
MASSACHUSETTS — SHE THINKS I COULD GET INTO A SCHOOL OUT THERE THAT'S SUPPOSED TO BE PRETTY ALL RIGHT.

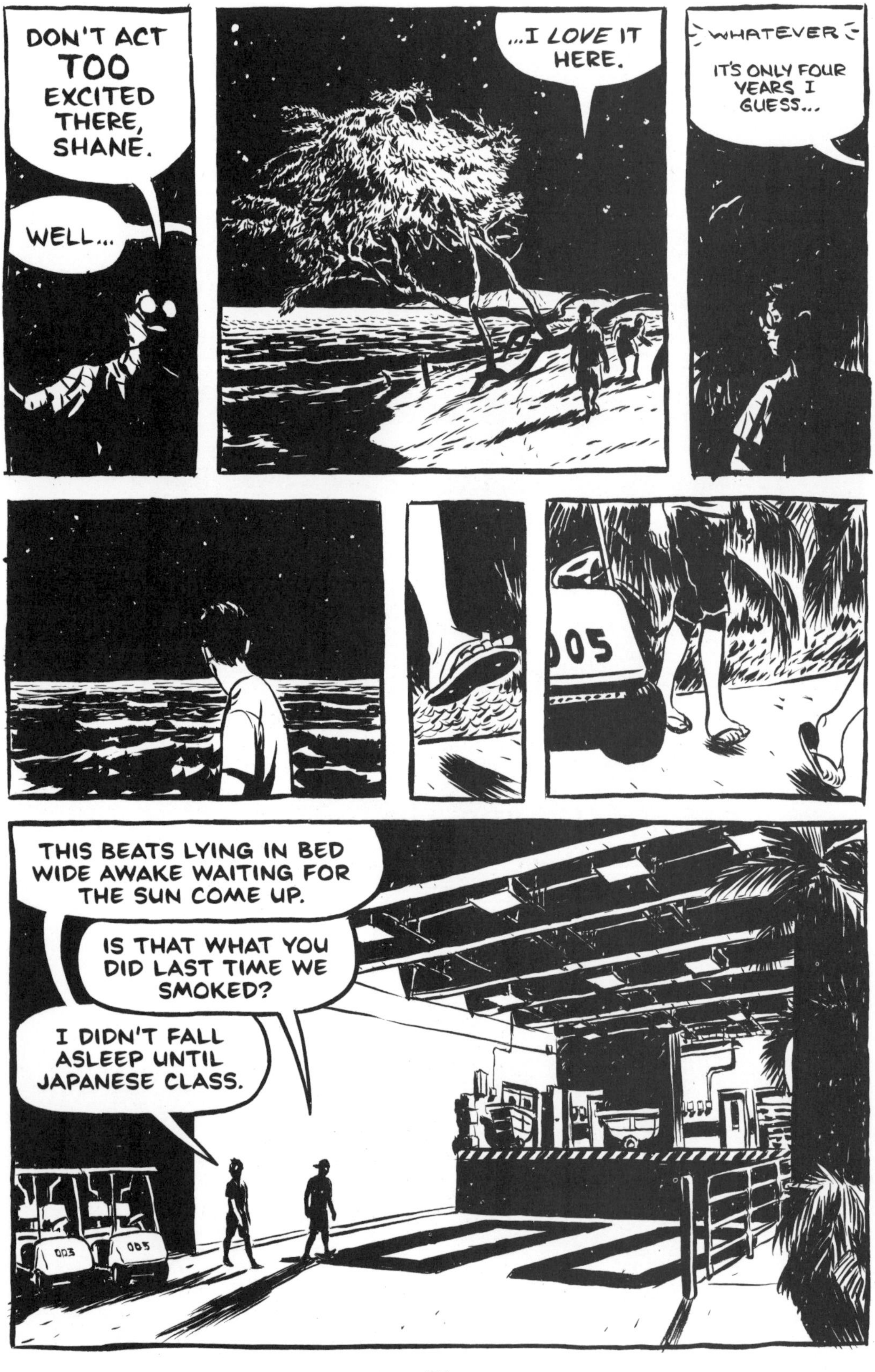
DON'T ACT TOO EXCITED THERE, SHANE.
WELL...
...I LOVE IT HERE.
WHATEVER
IT'S ONLY FOUR YEARS I GUESS...
005
THIS BEATS LYING IN BED WIDE AWAKE WAITING FOR THE SUN COME UP.
IS THAT WHAT YOU DID LAST TIME WE SMOKED?
I DIDN'T FALL ASLEEP UNTIL JAPANESE CLASS.
003
005

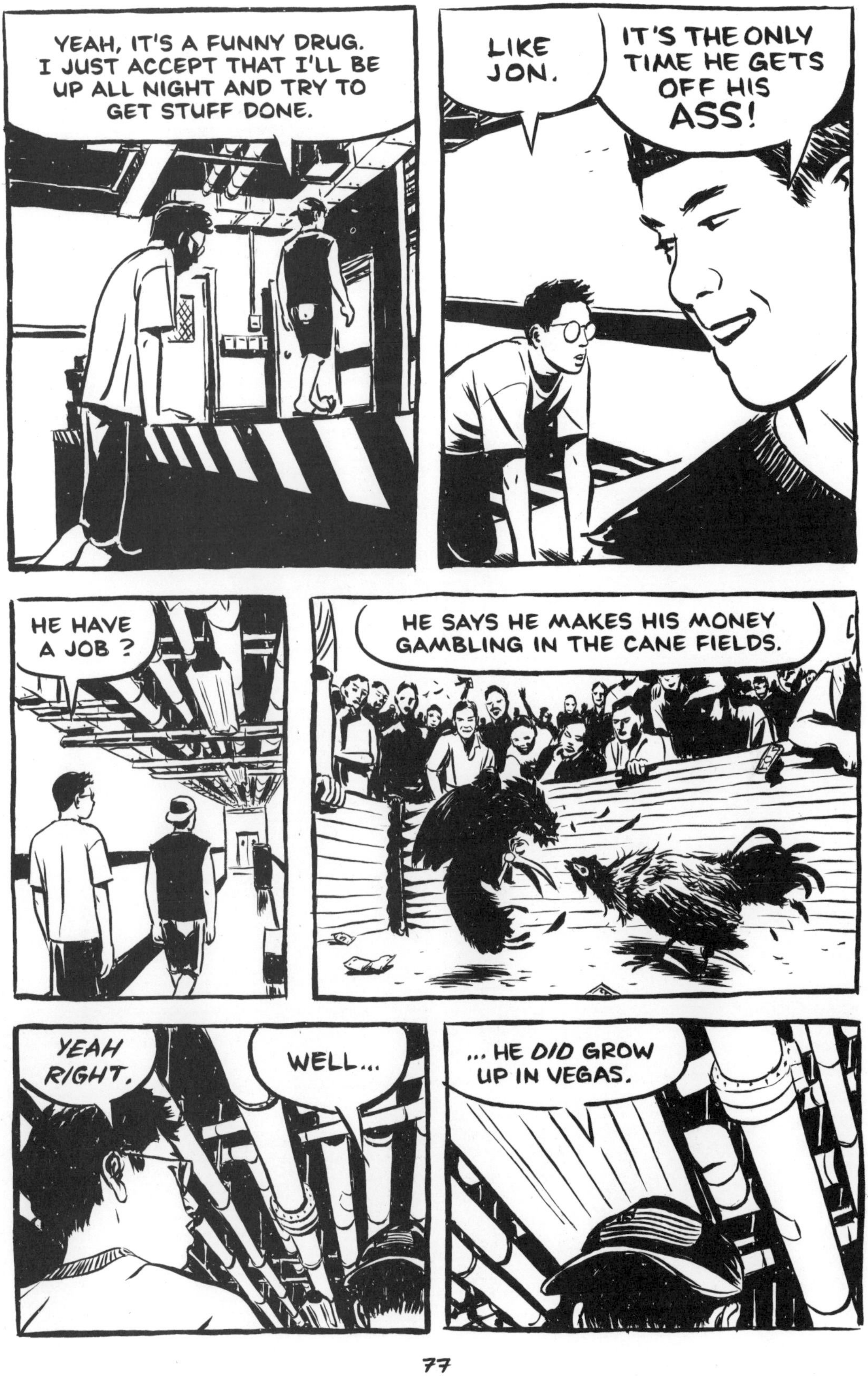
YEAH, IT'S A FUNNY DRUG. I JUST ACCEPT THAT I'LL BE UP ALL NIGHT AND TRY TO GET STUFF DONE.
LIKE JON.
IT'S THE ONLY TIME HE GETS OFF HIS ASS!
HE HAVE A JOB ?
HE SAYS HE MAKES HIS MONEY GAMBLING IN THE CANE FIELDS.
YEAH RIGHT.
WELL...
... HE DID GROW UP IN VEGAS.

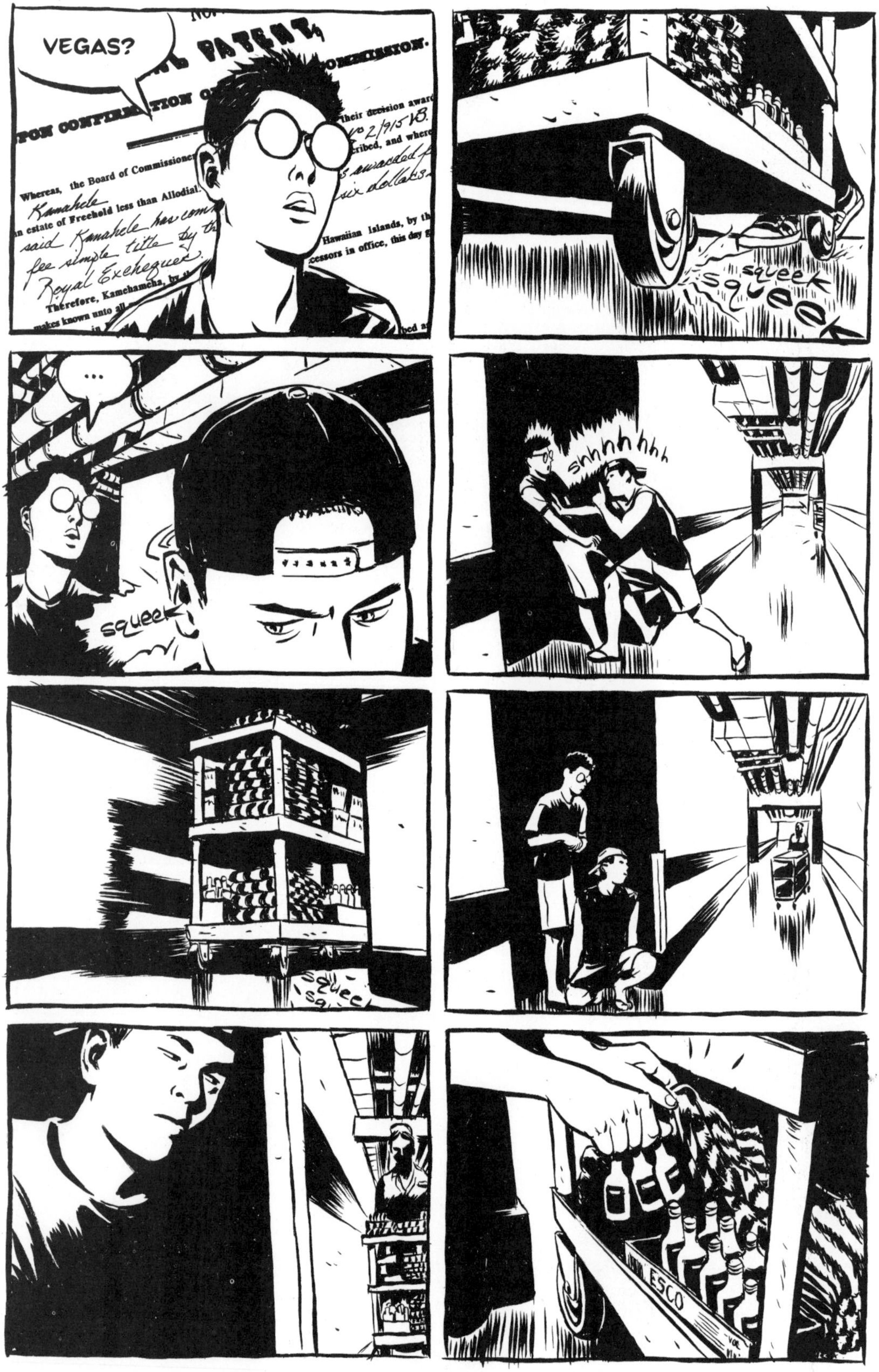
VEGAS?
UPON CONFIRMA
Whereas, the Board of Commissioner
Kamahele
an estate of Freehold less than Allodial.
said Kamahele has comm
fee simple title by th
Royal Exchequer
Therefore, Kamehameha, by th
Hawaiian Islands, by the
cessors in office, this day g
squeek
squeek
...
squeek
shhhhhhh
ESCO

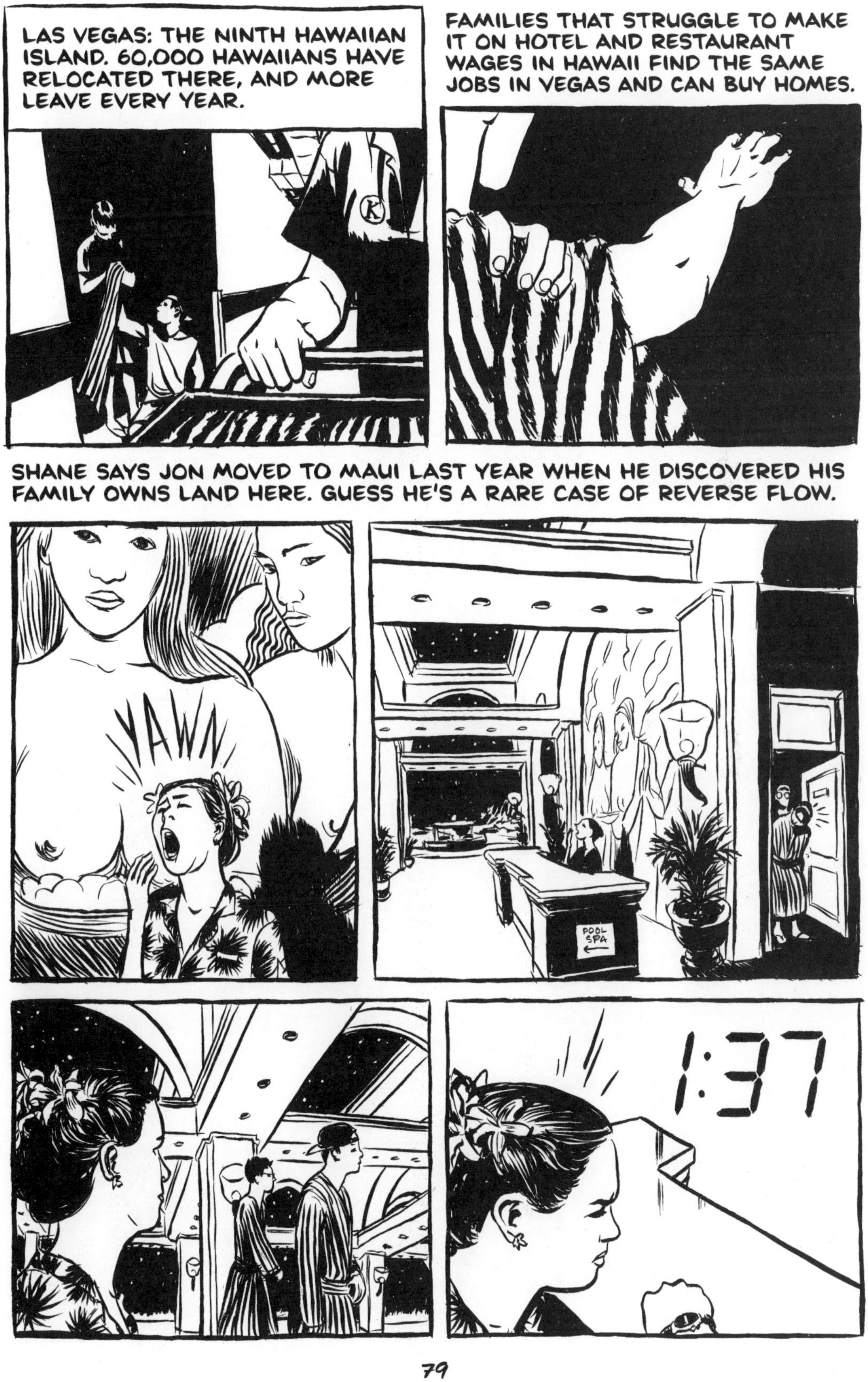
LAS VEGAS: THE NINTH HAWAIIAN ISLAND. 60,000 HAWAIIANS HAVE RELOCATED THERE, AND MORE LEAVE EVERY YEAR.
FAMILIES THAT STRUGGLE TO MAKE IT ON HOTEL AND RESTAURANT WAGES IN HAWAII FIND THE SAME JOBS IN VEGAS AND CAN BUY HOMES.
SHANE SAYS JON MOVED TO MAUI LAST YEAR WHEN HE DISCOVERED HIS FAMILY OWNS LAND HERE. GUESS HE'S A RARE CASE OF REVERSE FLOW.
YAWN
POOL SPA
1:37

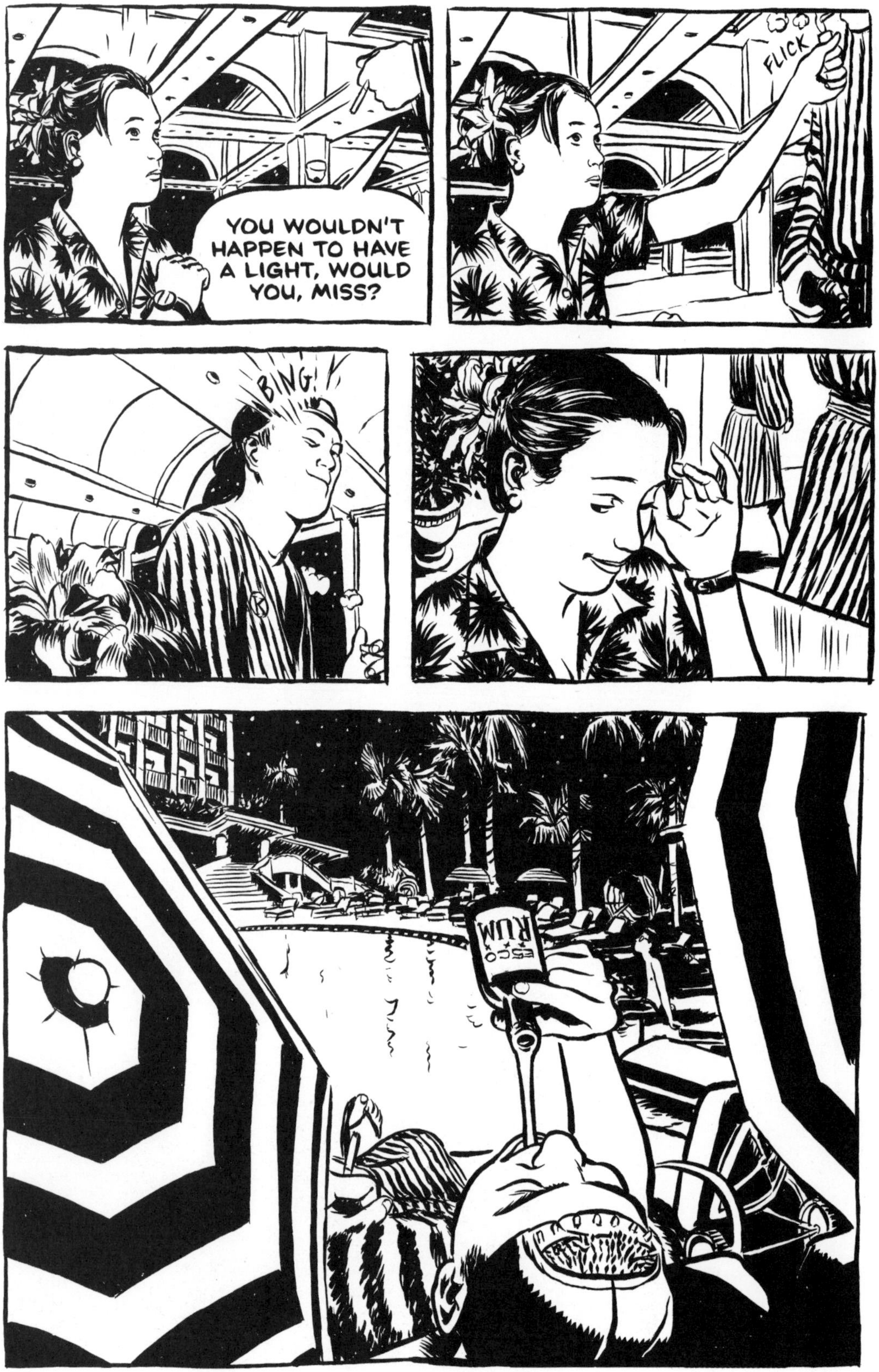
YOU WOULDN'T HAPPEN TO HAVE A LIGHT, WOULD YOU, MISS?
FLICK
BING!

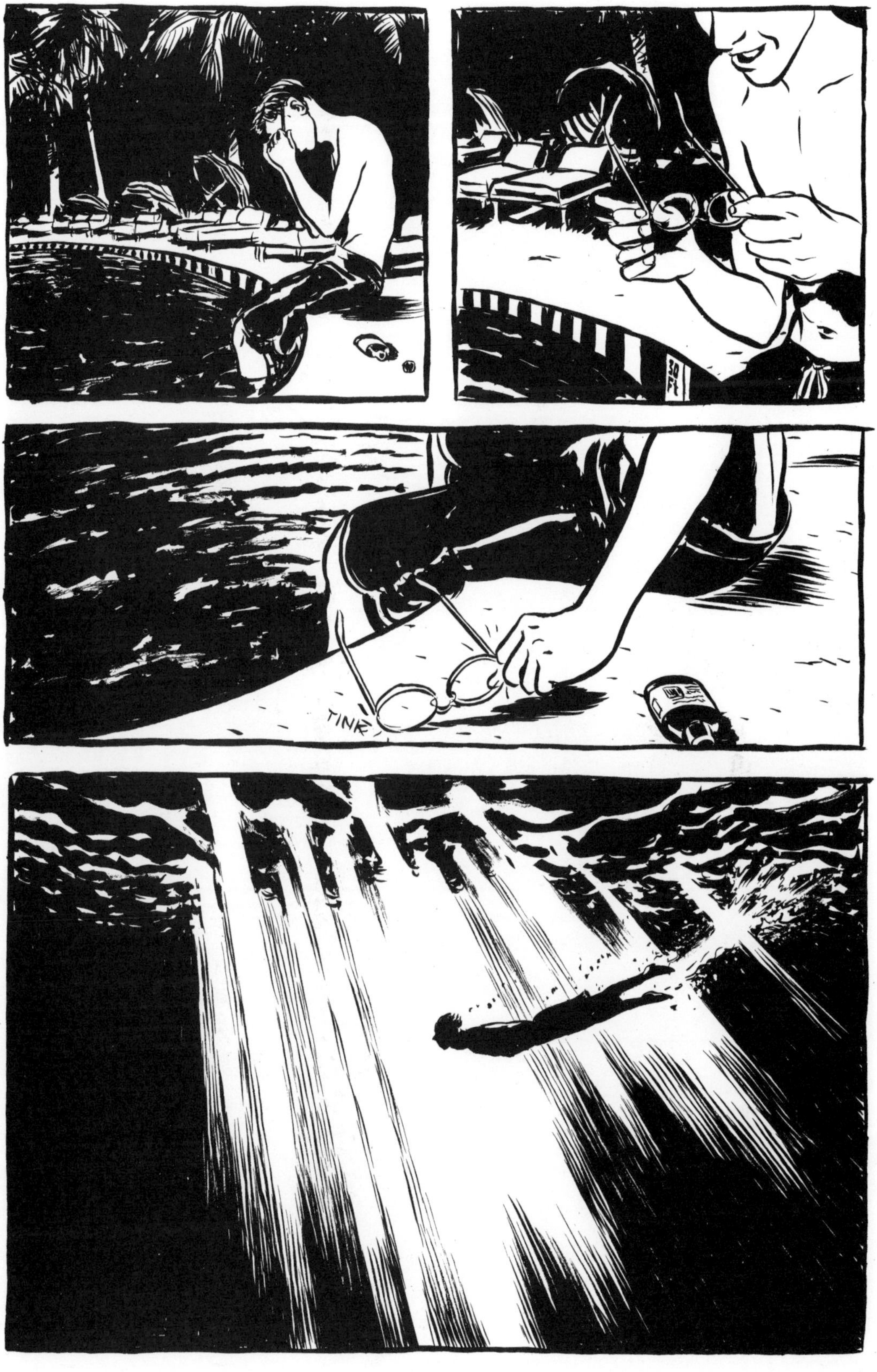
30 Ft
TINK

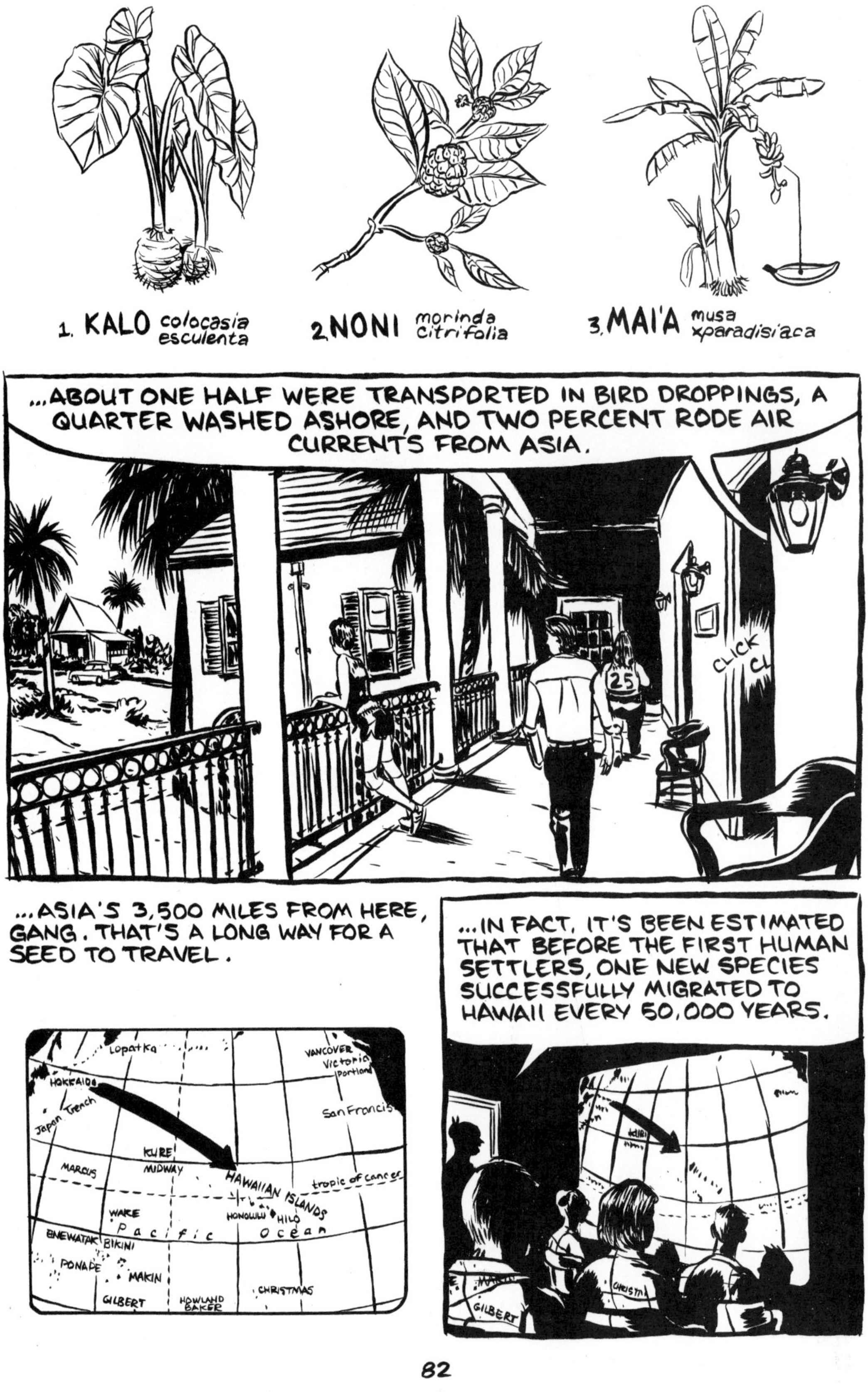

1. KALO colocasia esculenta
2. NONI morinda citrifolia
3. MAI'A musa xparadisiaca
...ABOUT ONE HALF WERE TRANSPORTED IN BIRD DROPPINGS, A QUARTER WASHED ASHORE, AND TWO PERCENT RODE AIR CURRENTS FROM ASIA.
25
CLICK
...ASIA'S 3,500 MILES FROM HERE, GANG. THAT'S A LONG WAY FOR A SEED TO TRAVEL.
Lopatka
VANCOUVER
Victoria
Portland
HOKKAIDO
Japan Trench
San Francis
KURE
MARCUS
MIDWAY
HAWAIIAN ISLANDS
tropic of cancer
WAKE
HONOLULU
HILO
Pacific Ocean
ENEWATAK
BIKINI
PONAPE
MAKIN
GILBERT
HOWLAND BAKER
CHRISTMAS
...IN FACT, IT'S BEEN ESTIMATED THAT BEFORE THE FIRST HUMAN SETTLERS, ONE NEW SPECIES SUCCESSFULLY MIGRATED TO HAWAII EVERY 50,000 YEARS.
GILBERT

THAT'S HOW ISOLATED WE ARE OUT HERE, FOLKS...

CLICK

...IN ANY CASE, HUMANS MANAGED TO FIND THEIR WAY HERE ABOUT 1,200 YEARS AGO. THEIR CARGO INCLUDED ALMOST THIRTY NEW SPECIES OF FLORA...

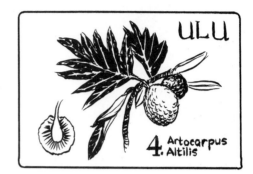

ULU

4. Artocarpus Altilis

...AND FOUR NEW ANIMALS: THE FERAL PIG, LAND FOWL, DOG, AND RAT. THE LATTER WAS AN ACCIDENT.

5. Sus Scrofa

THE IMPACT THIS HAD ON HAWAII'S ECOSYSTEM WAS *HUGE*...

CLICK

THE DRYLAND FORESTS THAT COVERED THE LEEWARD SIDE OF THE ISLANDS WERE ELIMINATED, MOSTLY BY THE INTRODUCED PIG POPULATION.

CLICK CLICK

YAWN

37

WE NOW KNOW FROM FOSSIL DISCOVERIES OF ALMOST FIFTY EXTINCT SPECIES OF BIRDS, MANY ENDEMIC TO THESE DEFORESTED REGIONS.

A.
B.
C.
D.
E.
F.
G.
H.
I.
J.

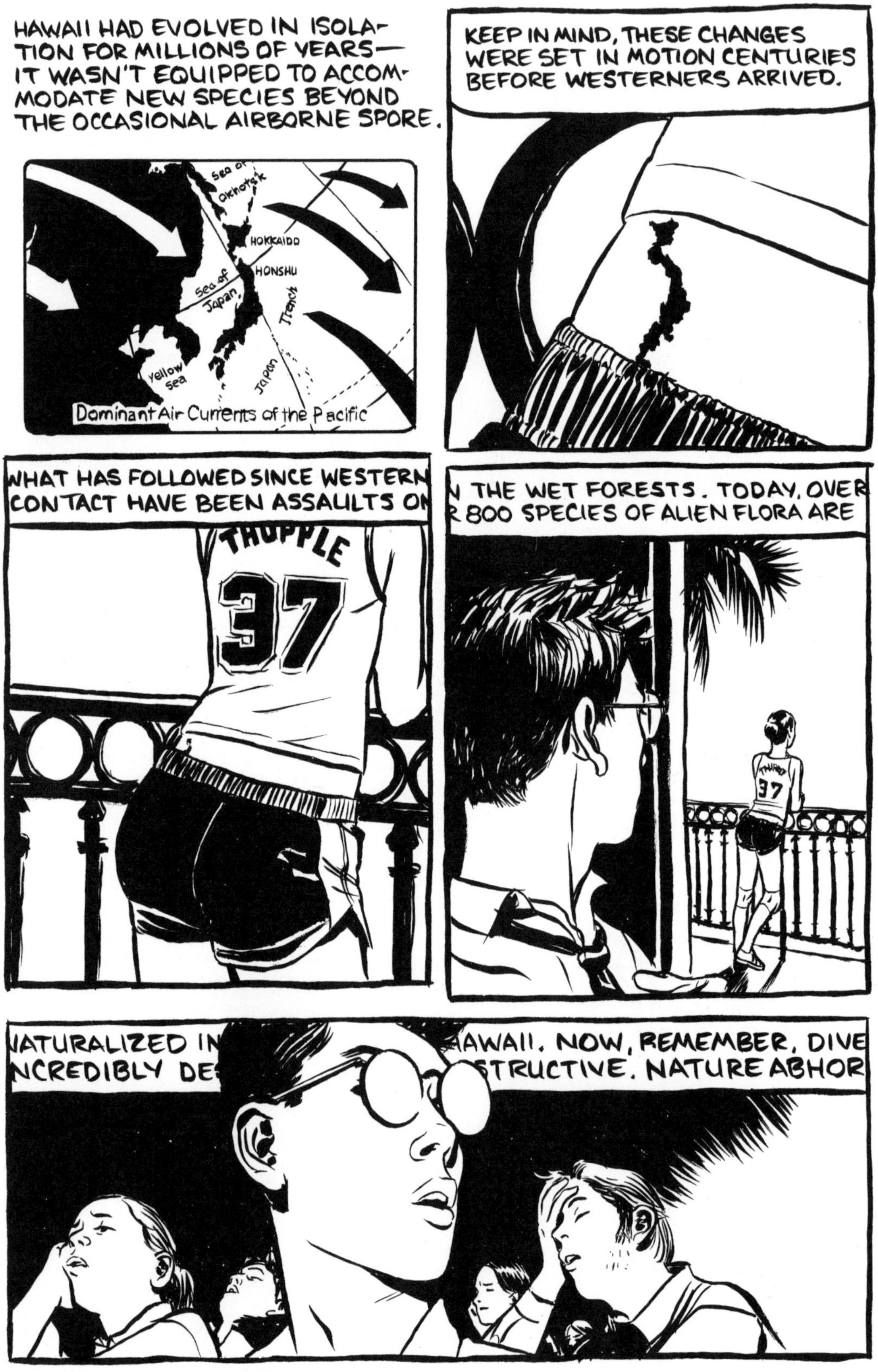
HAWAII HAD EVOLVED IN ISOLATION FOR MILLIONS OF YEARS— IT WASN'T EQUIPPED TO ACCOMMODATE NEW SPECIES BEYOND THE OCCASIONAL AIRBORNE SPORE.
KEEP IN MIND, THESE CHANGES WERE SET IN MOTION CENTURIES BEFORE WESTERNERS ARRIVED.
Sea of Okhotsk
HOKKAIDO
HONSHU
Sea of Japan
Japan Trench
Yellow sea
Dominant Air Currents of the Pacific
WHAT HAS FOLLOWED SINCE WESTERN CONTACT HAVE BEEN ASSAULTS ON
THUPPLE
37
N THE WET FORESTS. TODAY, OVER 800 SPECIES OF ALIEN FLORA ARE
NATURALIZED IN
NCREDIBLY DE
HAWAII. NOW, REMEMBER, DIVE
STRUCTIVE. NATURE ABHOR

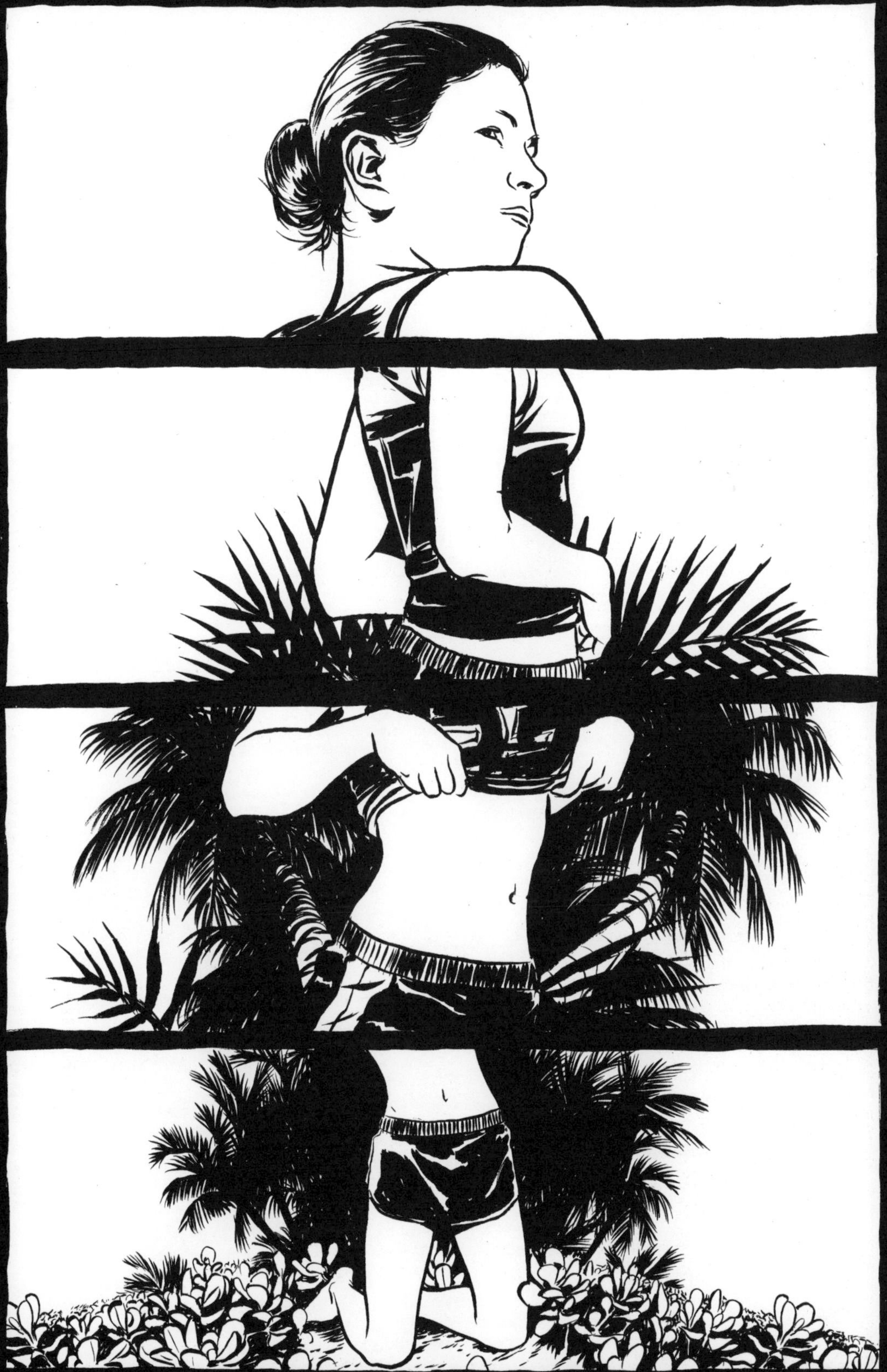

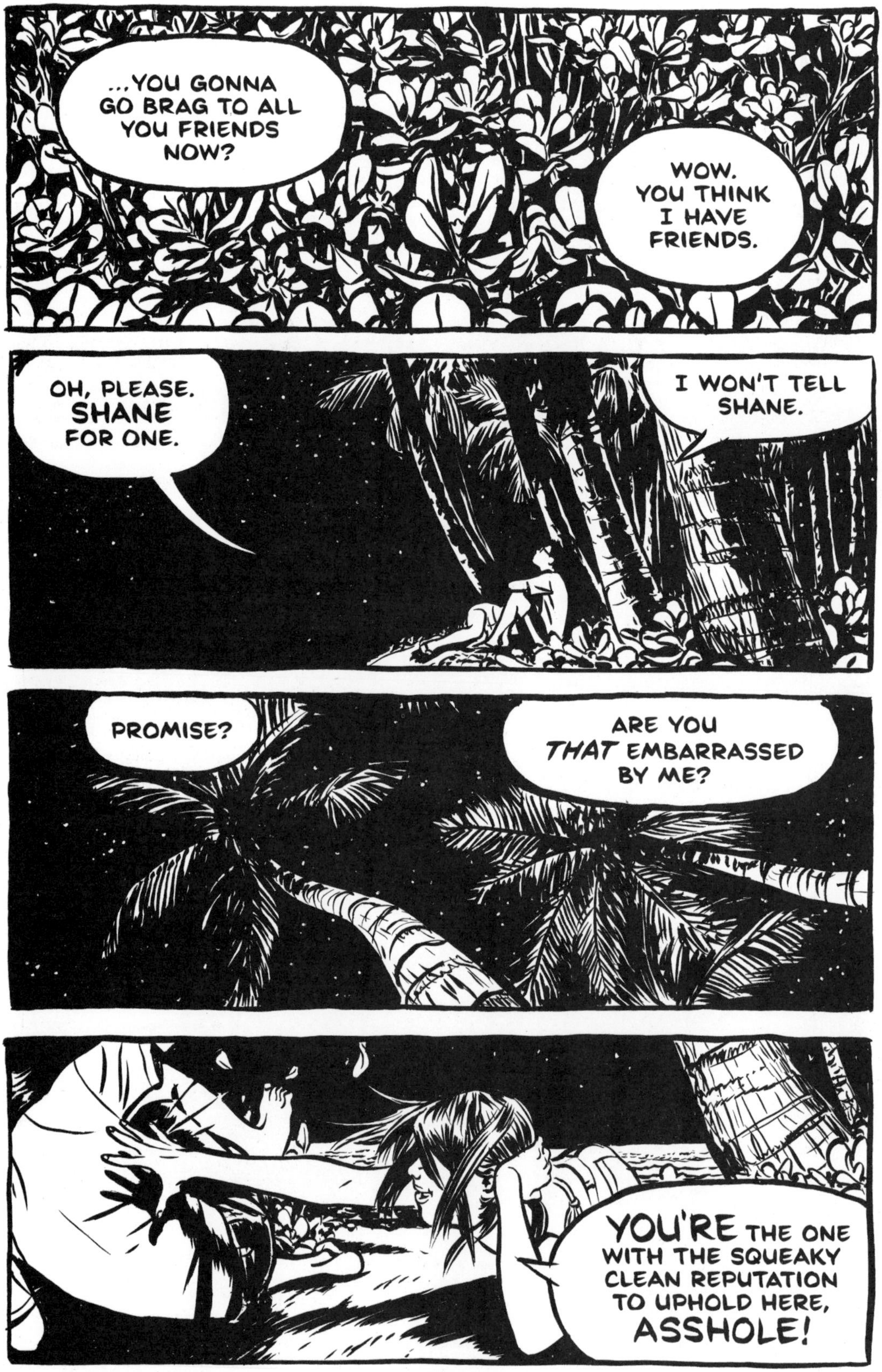
...YOU GONNA GO BRAG TO ALL YOU FRIENDS NOW?
WOW. YOU THINK I HAVE FRIENDS.
OH, PLEASE. SHANE FOR ONE.
I WON'T TELL SHANE.
PROMISE?
ARE YOU *THAT* EMBARRASSED BY ME?
YOU'RE THE ONE WITH THE SQUEAKY CLEAN REPUTATION TO UPHOLD HERE, ASSHOLE!

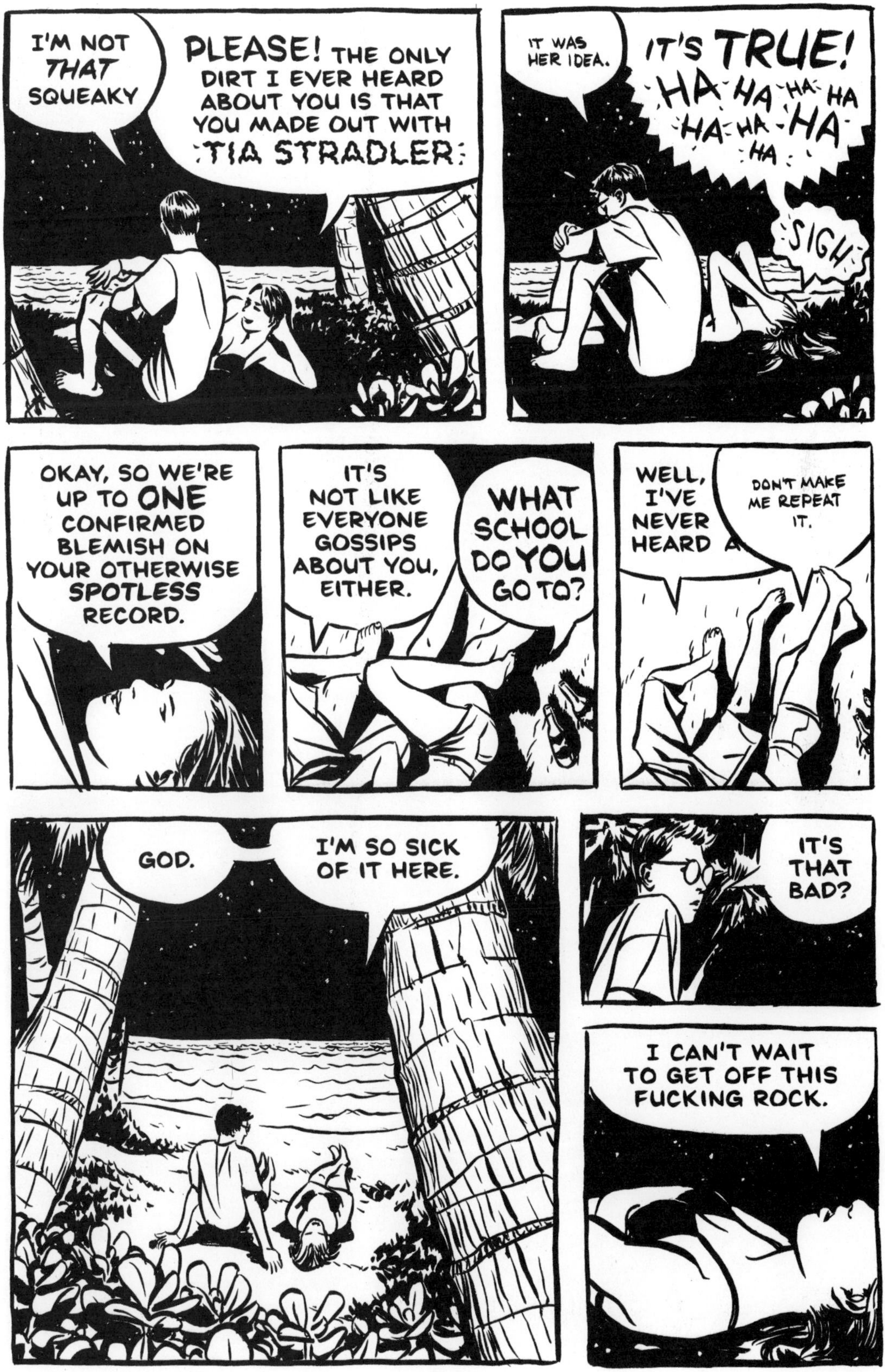
I'M NOT THAT SQUEAKY
PLEASE! THE ONLY DIRT I EVER HEARD ABOUT YOU IS THAT YOU MADE OUT WITH TIA STRADLER
IT WAS HER IDEA.
IT'S TRUE! HA HA HA HA HA HA HA HA
SIGH
OKAY, SO WE'RE UP TO ONE CONFIRMED BLEMISH ON YOUR OTHERWISE SPOTLESS RECORD.
IT'S NOT LIKE EVERYONE GOSSIPS ABOUT YOU, EITHER.
WHAT SCHOOL DO YOU GO TO?
WELL, I'VE NEVER HEARD A
DON'T MAKE ME REPEAT IT.
GOD.
I'M SO SICK OF IT HERE.
IT'S THAT BAD?
I CAN'T WAIT TO GET OFF THIS FUCKING ROCK.

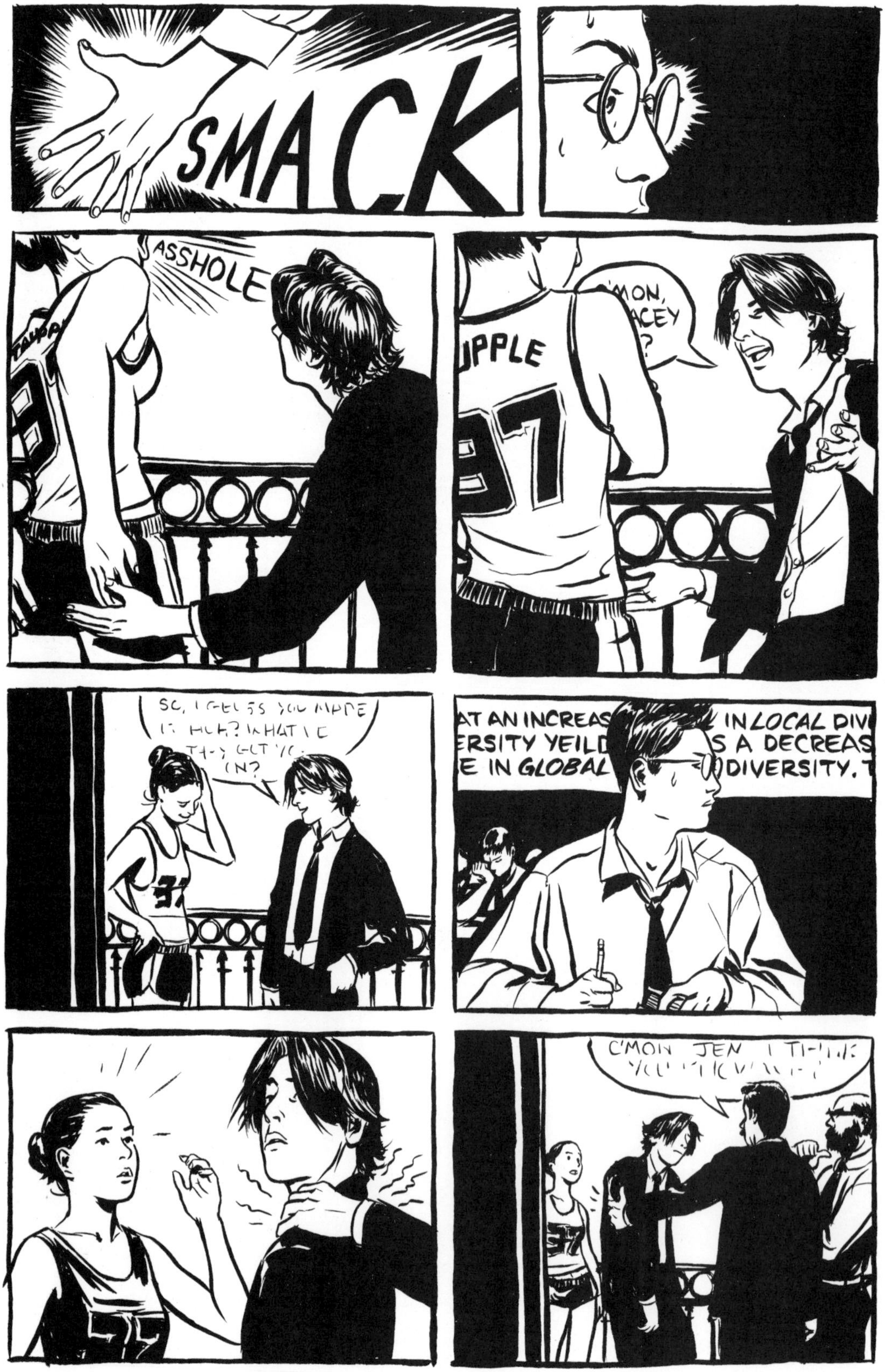
SMACK
ASSHOLE
'MON,
ACEY
?
UPPLE
AT AN INCREAS
IN LOCAL DIV
ERSITY YEILD
S A DECREAS
E IN GLOBAL
DIVERSITY. T
C'MON JEN

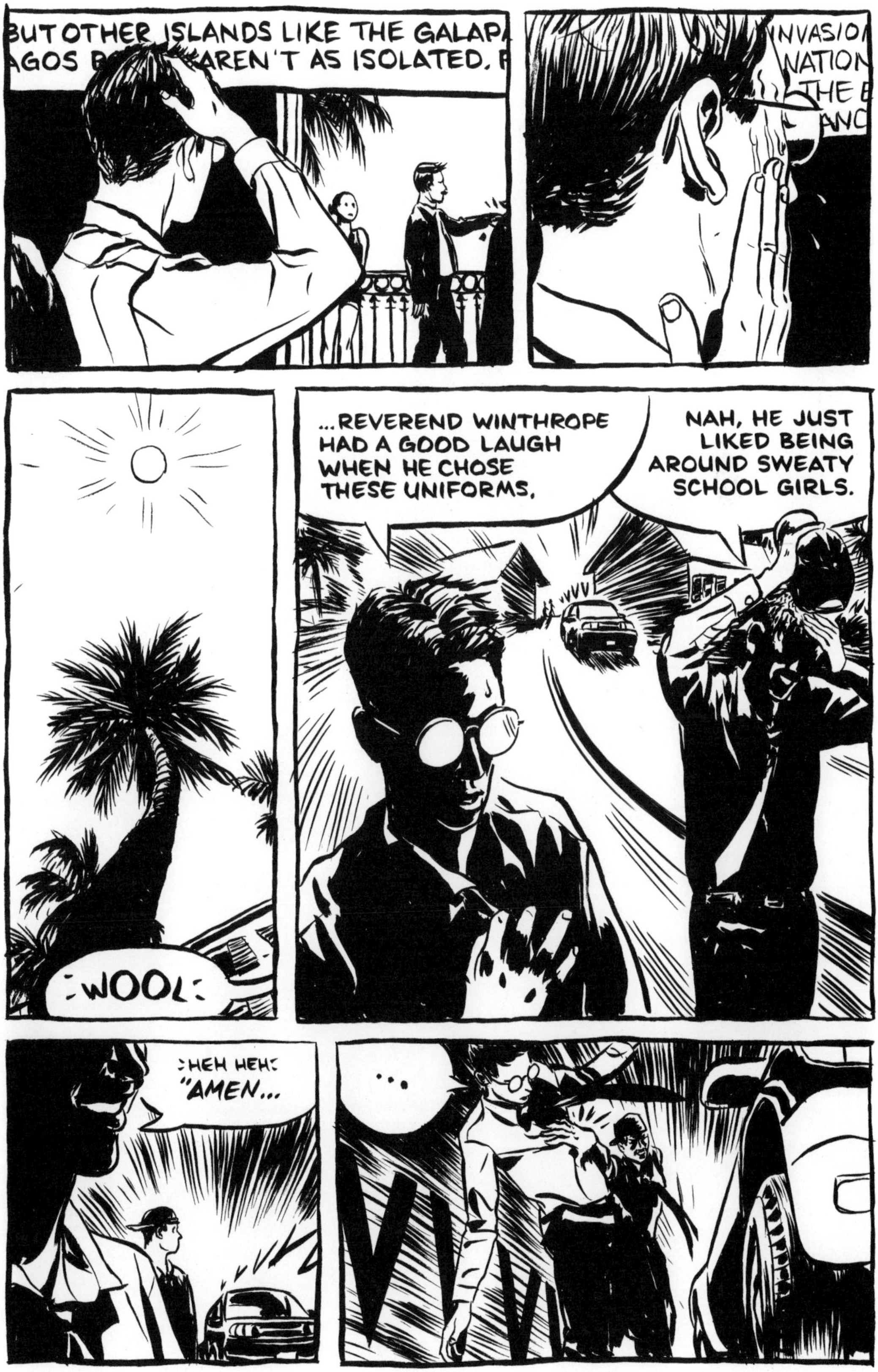
BUT OTHER ISLANDS LIKE THE GALAPA
AGOS B AREN'T AS ISOLATED.
INVASION
NATION
THE
ANC
...REVEREND WINTHROPE HAD A GOOD LAUGH WHEN HE CHOSE THESE UNIFORMS.
NAH, HE JUST LIKED BEING AROUND SWEATY SCHOOL GIRLS.
WOOL
HEH HEH
"AMEN...
...

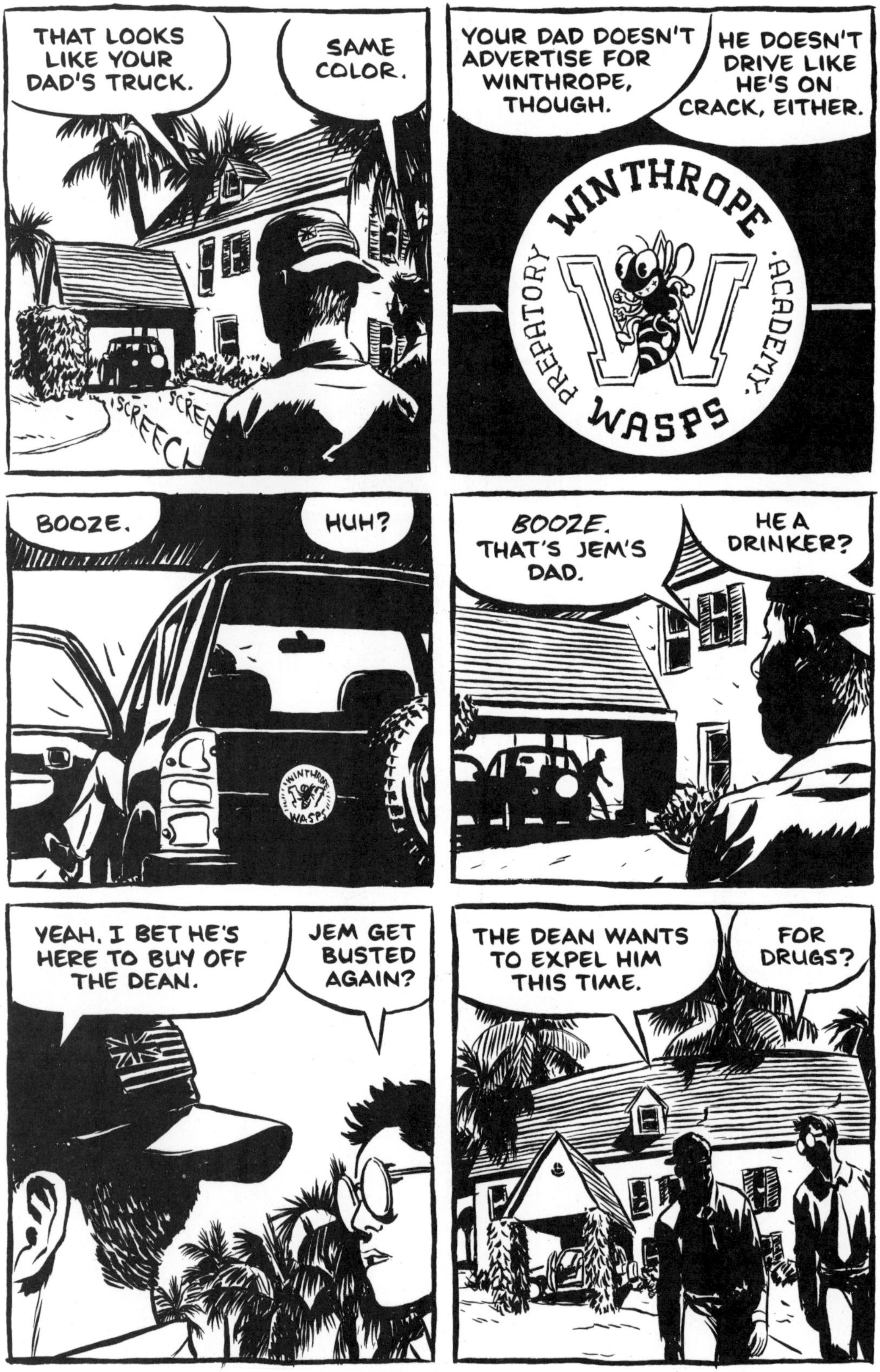
THAT LOOKS LIKE YOUR DAD'S TRUCK.
SAME COLOR.
SCREECH
SCREE
YOUR DAD DOESN'T ADVERTISE FOR WINTHROPE, THOUGH.
HE DOESN'T DRIVE LIKE HE'S ON CRACK, EITHER.
WINTHROPE
PREPATORY ACADEMY
WASPS
BOOZE.
HUH?
WINTHROPE WASPS
BOOZE. THAT'S JEM'S DAD.
HE A DRINKER?
YEAH. I BET HE'S HERE TO BUY OFF THE DEAN.
JEM GET BUSTED AGAIN?
THE DEAN WANTS TO EXPEL HIM THIS TIME.
FOR DRUGS?

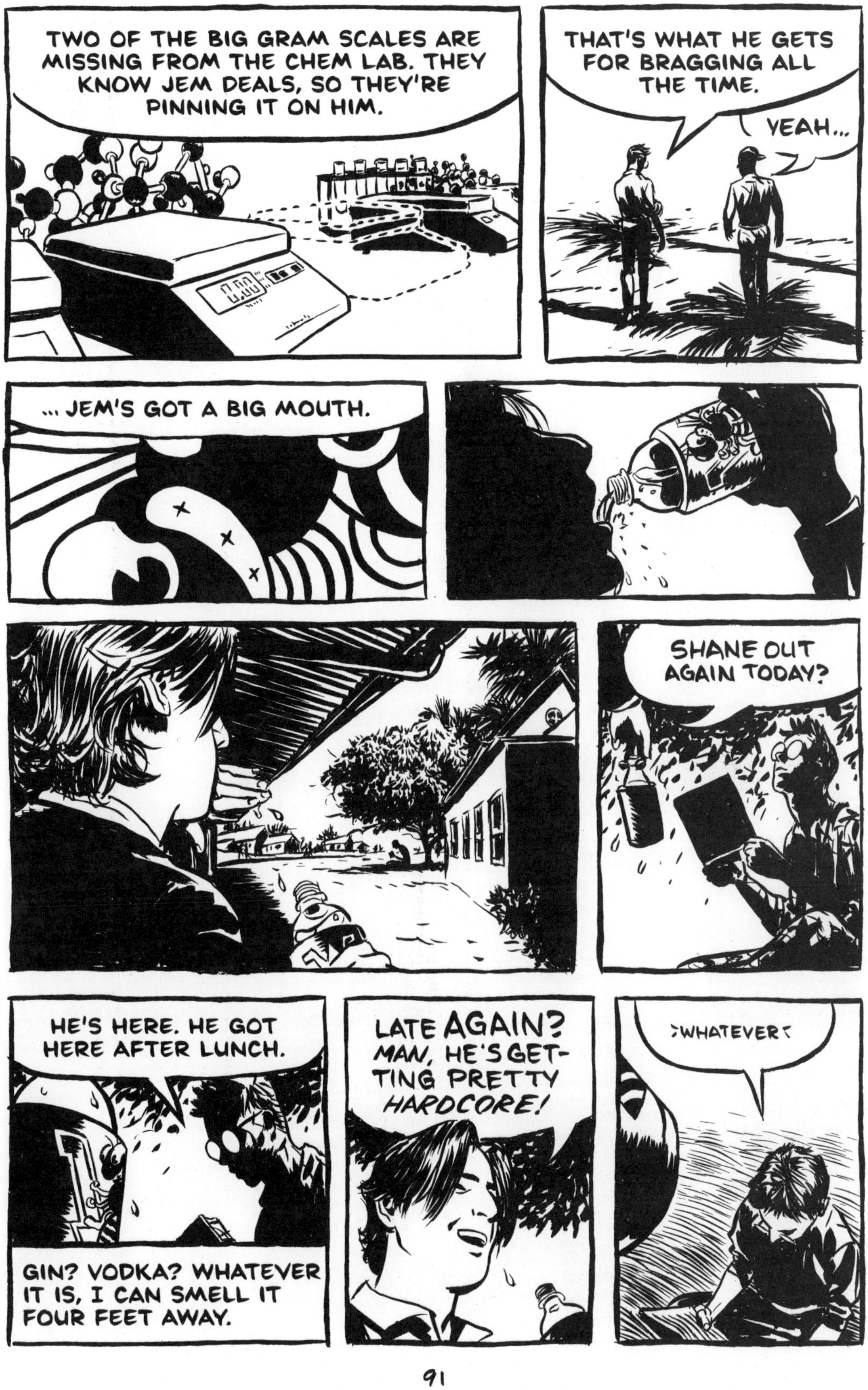
TWO OF THE BIG GRAM SCALES ARE MISSING FROM THE CHEM LAB. THEY KNOW JEM DEALS, SO THEY'RE PINNING IT ON HIM.
THAT'S WHAT HE GETS FOR BRAGGING ALL THE TIME.
YEAH...
... JEM'S GOT A BIG MOUTH.
SHANE OUT AGAIN TODAY?
HE'S HERE. HE GOT HERE AFTER LUNCH.
GIN? VODKA? WHATEVER IT IS, I CAN SMELL IT FOUR FEET AWAY.
LATE AGAIN? MAN, HE'S GETTING PRETTY HARDCORE!
WHATEVER

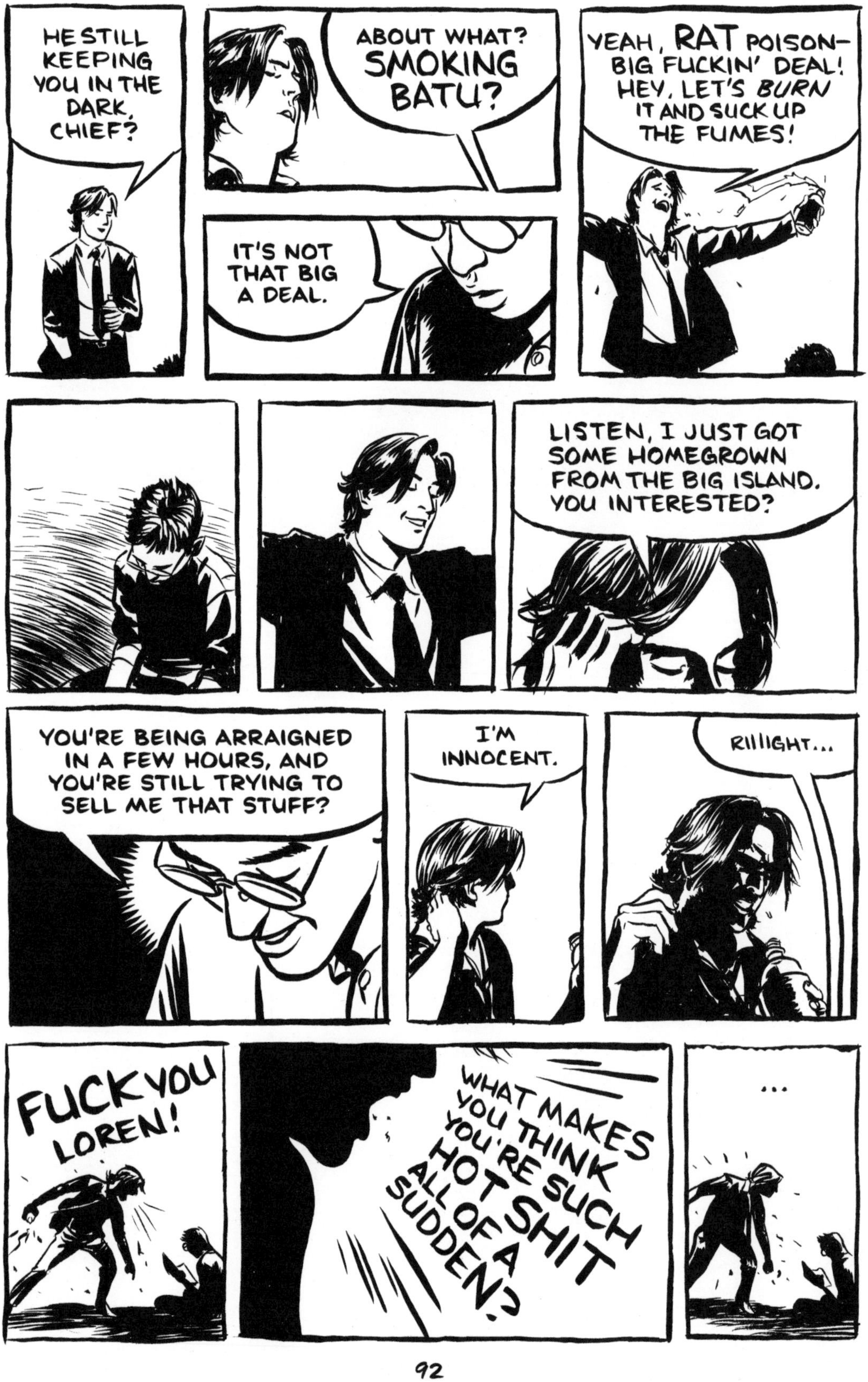
HE STILL KEEPING YOU IN THE DARK, CHIEF?
ABOUT WHAT? SMOKING BATU?
IT'S NOT THAT BIG A DEAL.
YEAH, RAT POISON- BIG FUCKIN' DEAL! HEY, LET'S *BURN* IT AND SUCK UP THE FUMES!
LISTEN, I JUST GOT SOME HOMEGROWN FROM THE BIG ISLAND. YOU INTERESTED?
YOU'RE BEING ARRAIGNED IN A FEW HOURS, AND YOU'RE STILL TRYING TO SELL ME THAT STUFF?
I'M INNOCENT.
RIIIIGHT...
FUCK YOU LOREN!
WHAT MAKES YOU THINK YOU'RE SUCH HOT SHIT ALL OF A SUDDEN?
...

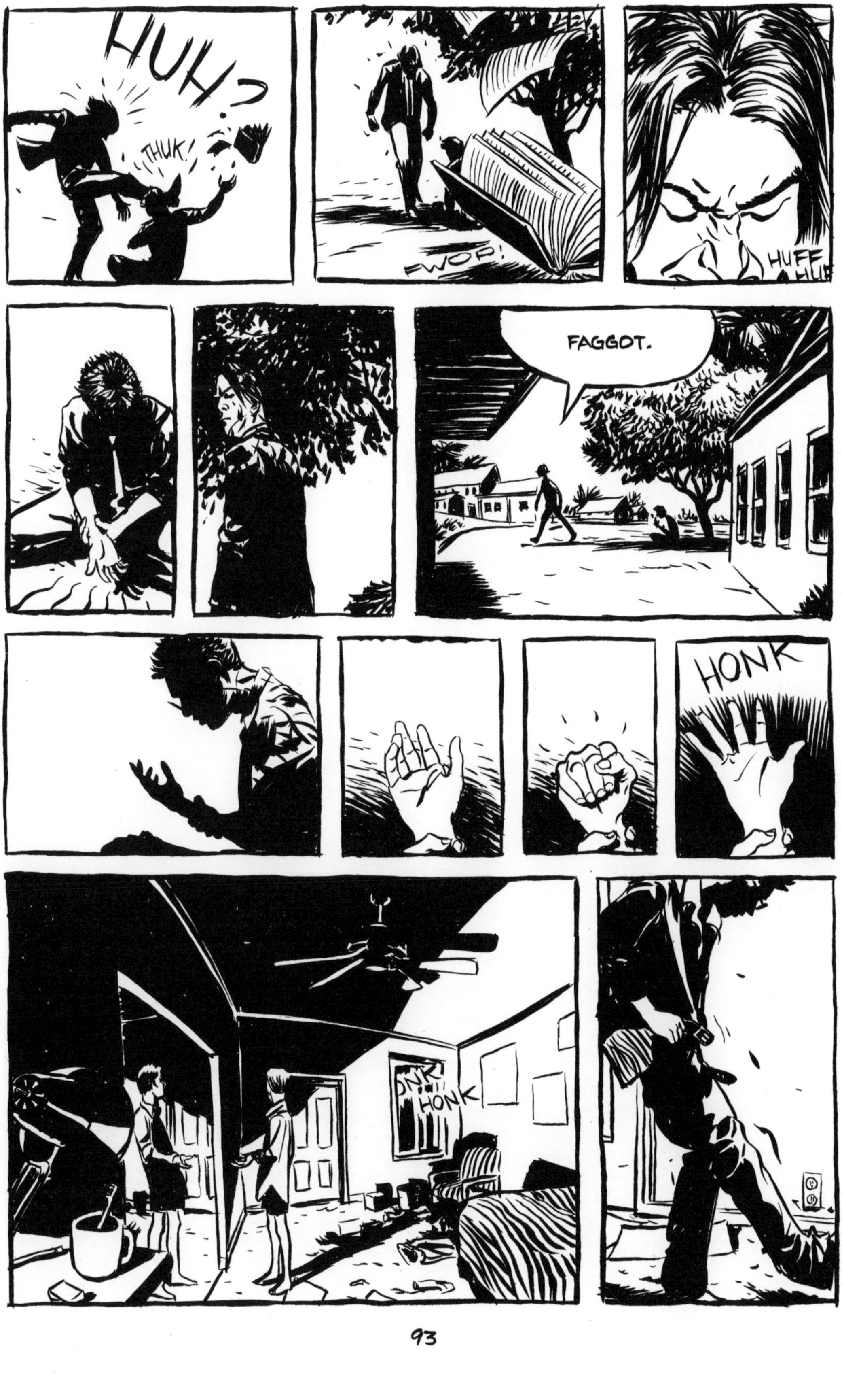
HUH!?
THUK!
FWOP!
HUFF
FAGGOT.
HONK
HONK

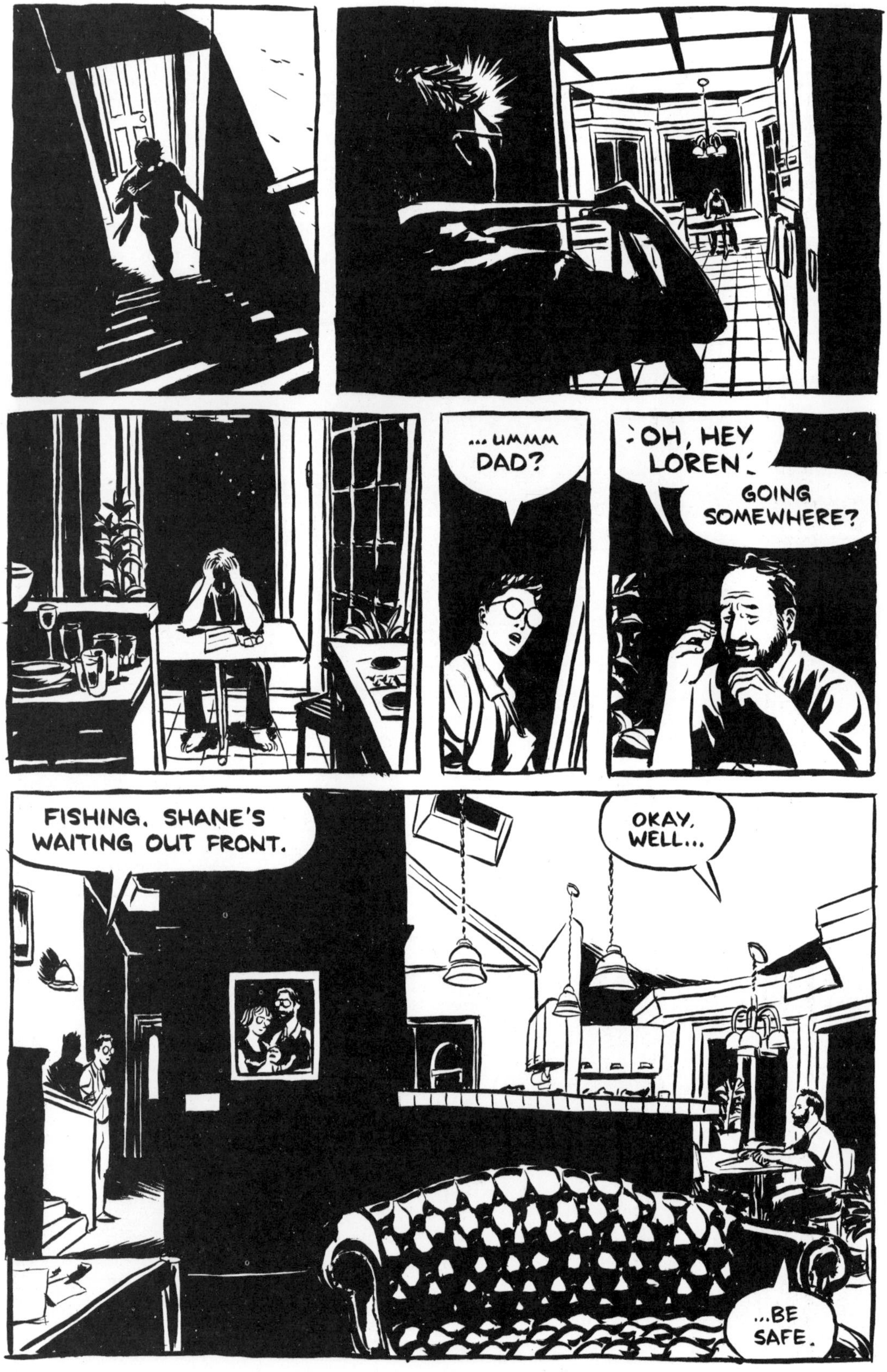
...UMMM
DAD?
OH, HEY
LOREN.
GOING
SOMEWHERE?
FISHING. SHANE'S
WAITING OUT FRONT.
OKAY,
WELL...
...BE
SAFE.

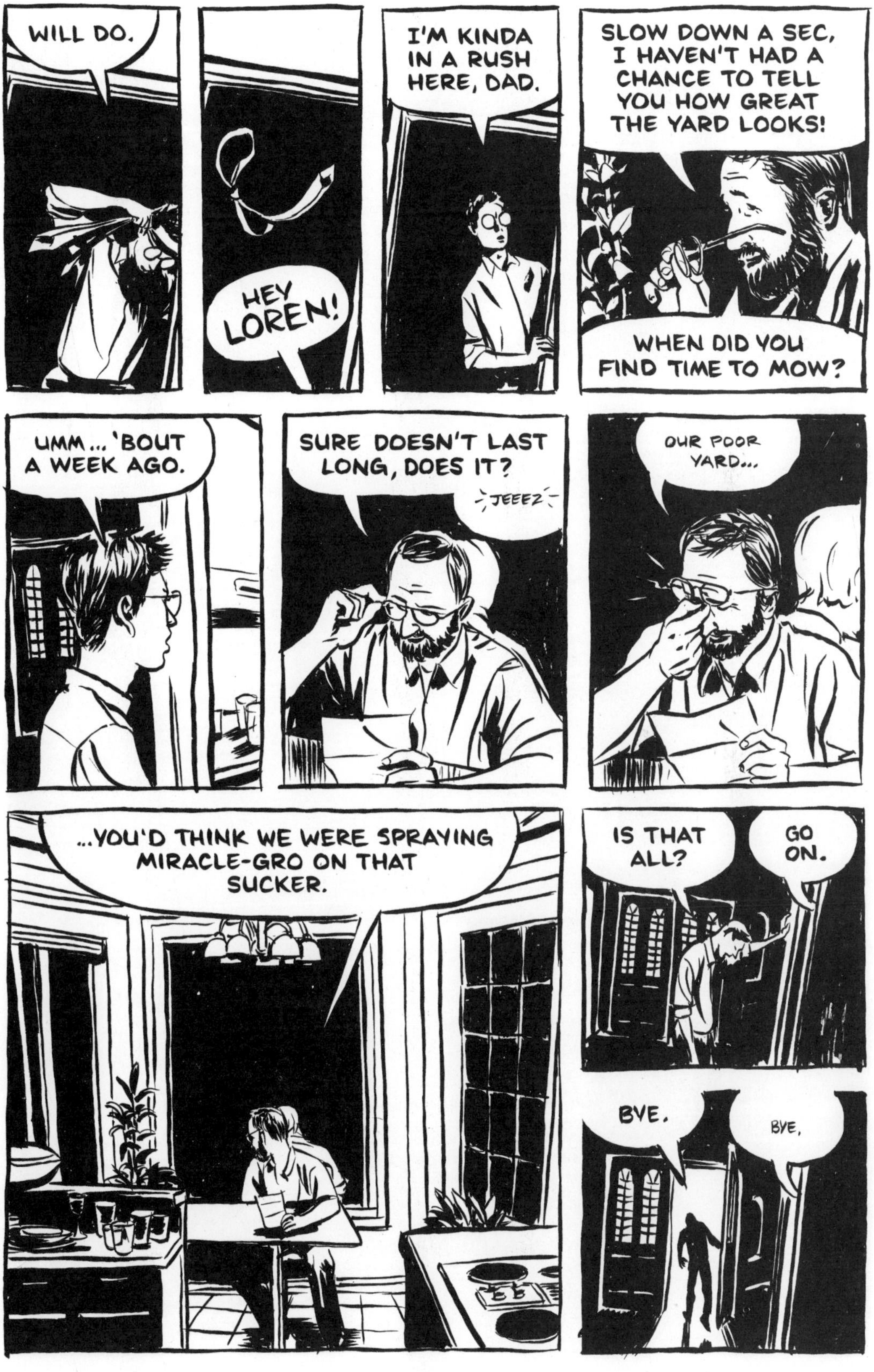
WILL DO.
HEY LOREN!
I'M KINDA IN A RUSH HERE, DAD.
SLOW DOWN A SEC, I HAVEN'T HAD A CHANCE TO TELL YOU HOW GREAT THE YARD LOOKS!
WHEN DID YOU FIND TIME TO MOW?
UMM... 'BOUT A WEEK AGO.
SURE DOESN'T LAST LONG, DOES IT?
JEEEZ
OUR POOR YARD...
...YOU'D THINK WE WERE SPRAYING MIRACLE-GRO ON THAT SUCKER.
IS THAT ALL?
GO ON.
BYE.
BYE,

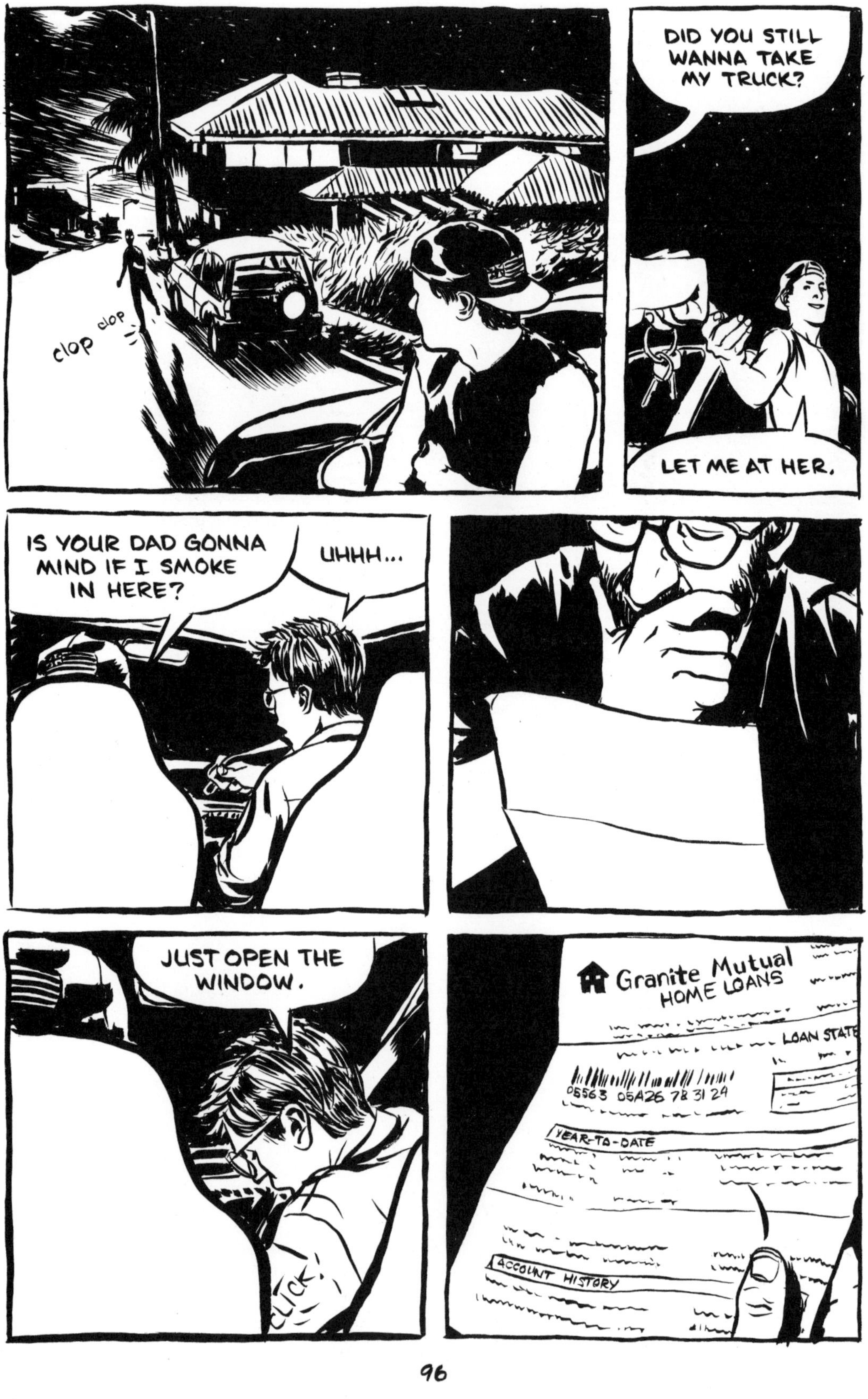
clop clop
DID YOU STILL WANNA TAKE MY TRUCK?
LET ME AT HER.
IS YOUR DAD GONNA MIND IF I SMOKE IN HERE?
UHHH...
JUST OPEN THE WINDOW.
CLICK
Granite Mutual HOME LOANS
LOAN STATE
05563 05A26 78 31 24
YEAR-TO-DATE
ACCOUNT HISTORY

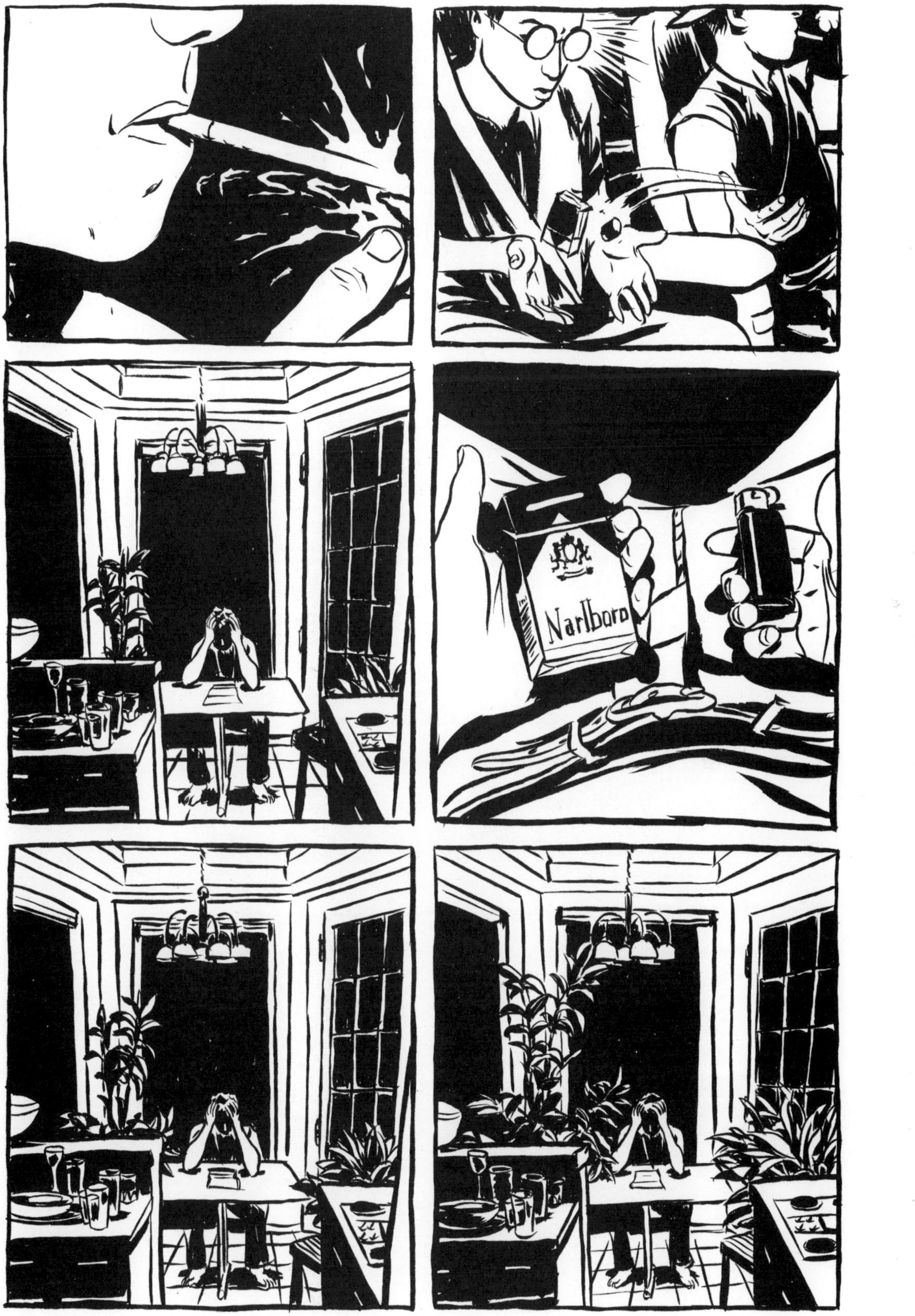
FFSS
Narlboro

WHAT DO YOU THINK YOUR PARENTS WOULD DO IF THEY FOUND OUT YOU SMOKE BATU?

WELL, MY DAD'S BEEN HAVING TROUBLE STAYING AWAKE AT WORK LATELY—HE'D PROBABLY ASK FOR A HOOK UP.

REALLY?

THEY'D **FREAK.**

C'MON!

YOU HAVING REGRETS?

NO...

...IT JUST SEEMS ... *EASY* FOR YOU—

MEANWHILE, I FREEZE UP THINKING ABOUT WHAT MY *DAD* WOULD SAY.

THAT'S THE *LAST* THING THAT SHOULD STOP YOU.

HE'S YOUR *DAD*— HE'LL FORGIVE YOU.

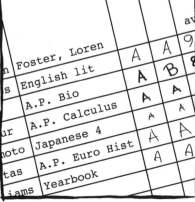

		av
n Foster, Loren	A A	9
s English lit	A B	8
A.P. Bio	A A	
ur A.P. Calculus	A A	
hoto Japanese 4	A A	
tas A.P. Euro Hist	A A	
iams Yearbook		

FLICK

MY DAD'S A WORKAHOLIC. HE DOESN'T EVEN TAKE WEEKENDS OFF ANYMORE.

HE NEEDS TO HIT THE LINKS!

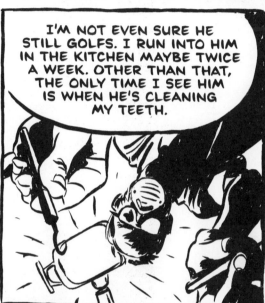

I'M NOT EVEN SURE HE STILL GOLFS. I RUN INTO HIM IN THE KITCHEN MAYBE TWICE A WEEK. OTHER THAN THAT, THE ONLY TIME I SEE HIM IS WHEN HE'S CLEANING MY TEETH.

HE MUST LOVE HIS JOB.

I THINK HE HATES IT. HE'S ALWAYS SO *TIRED*...

I GUESS IT PAYS, THOUGH — PAYS MY TUITION... PAYS FOR OUR HOUSE...

YARD SOLD SEPERATELY.

EXACTLY—THERE'S NEVER *ENOUGH*.

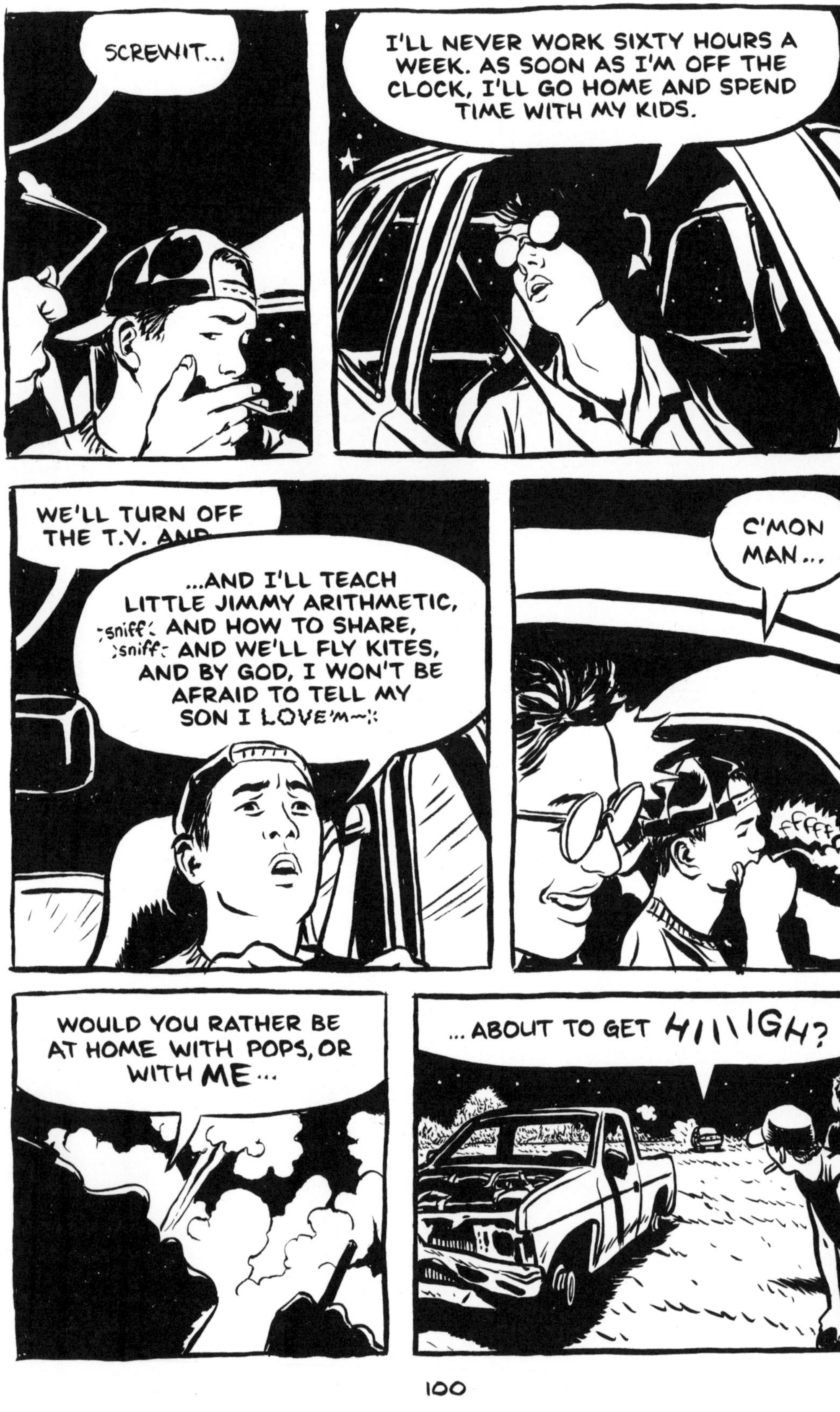
SCREWIT...
I'LL NEVER WORK SIXTY HOURS A WEEK. AS SOON AS I'M OFF THE CLOCK, I'LL GO HOME AND SPEND TIME WITH MY KIDS.
WE'LL TURN OFF THE T.V. AND
...AND I'LL TEACH LITTLE JIMMY ARITHMETIC, sniff AND HOW TO SHARE, sniff AND WE'LL FLY KITES, AND BY GOD, I WON'T BE AFRAID TO TELL MY SON I LOVE'M~
C'MON MAN...
WOULD YOU RATHER BE AT HOME WITH POPS, OR WITH ME...
...ABOUT TO GET HIIIIGH?

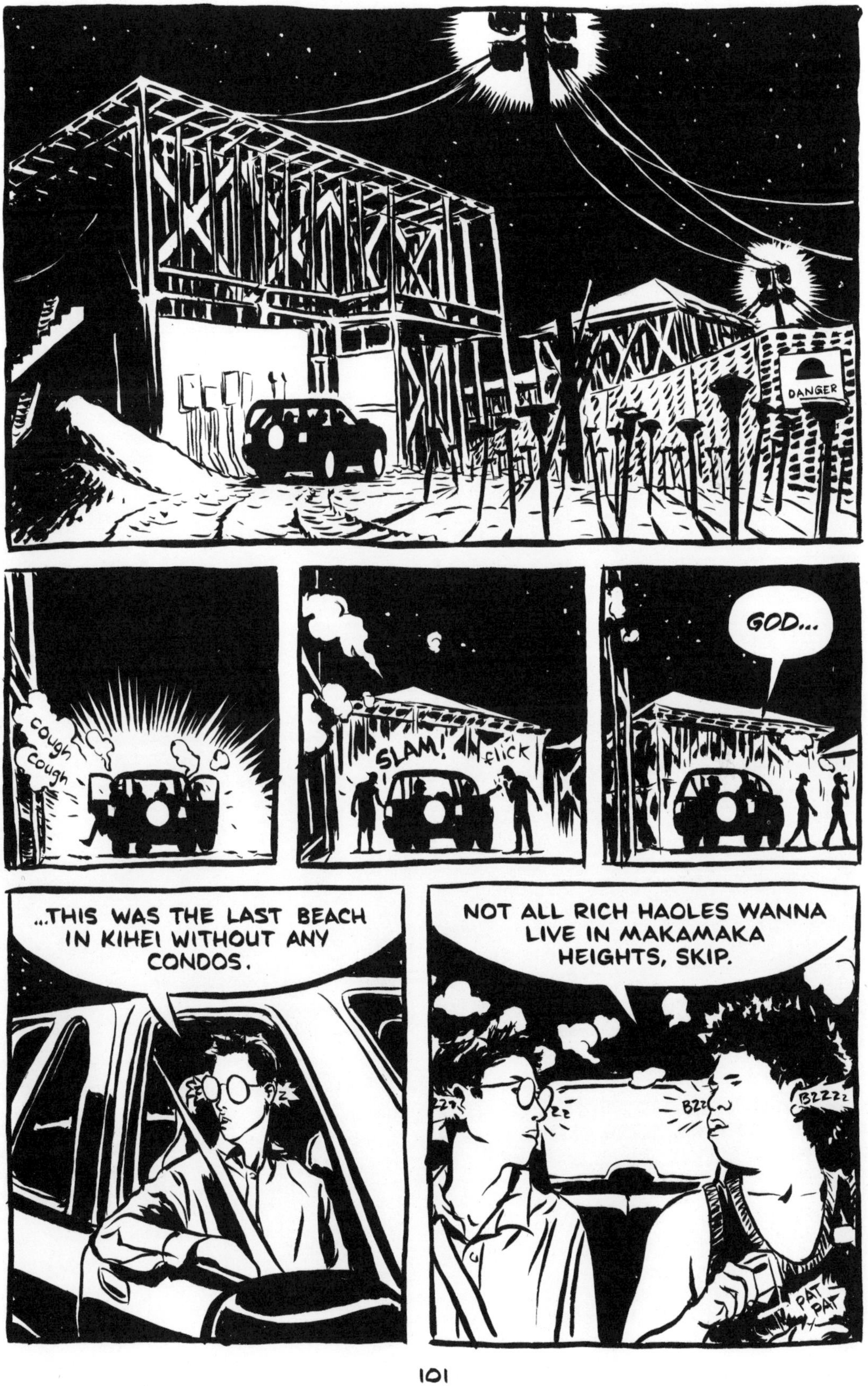
DANGER
cough cough
SLAM!
flick
GOD...
...THIS WAS THE LAST BEACH IN KIHEI WITHOUT ANY CONDOS.
NOT ALL RICH HAOLES WANNA LIVE IN MAKAMAKA HEIGHTS, SKIP.
BZZ
BZZZZ
PAT PAT

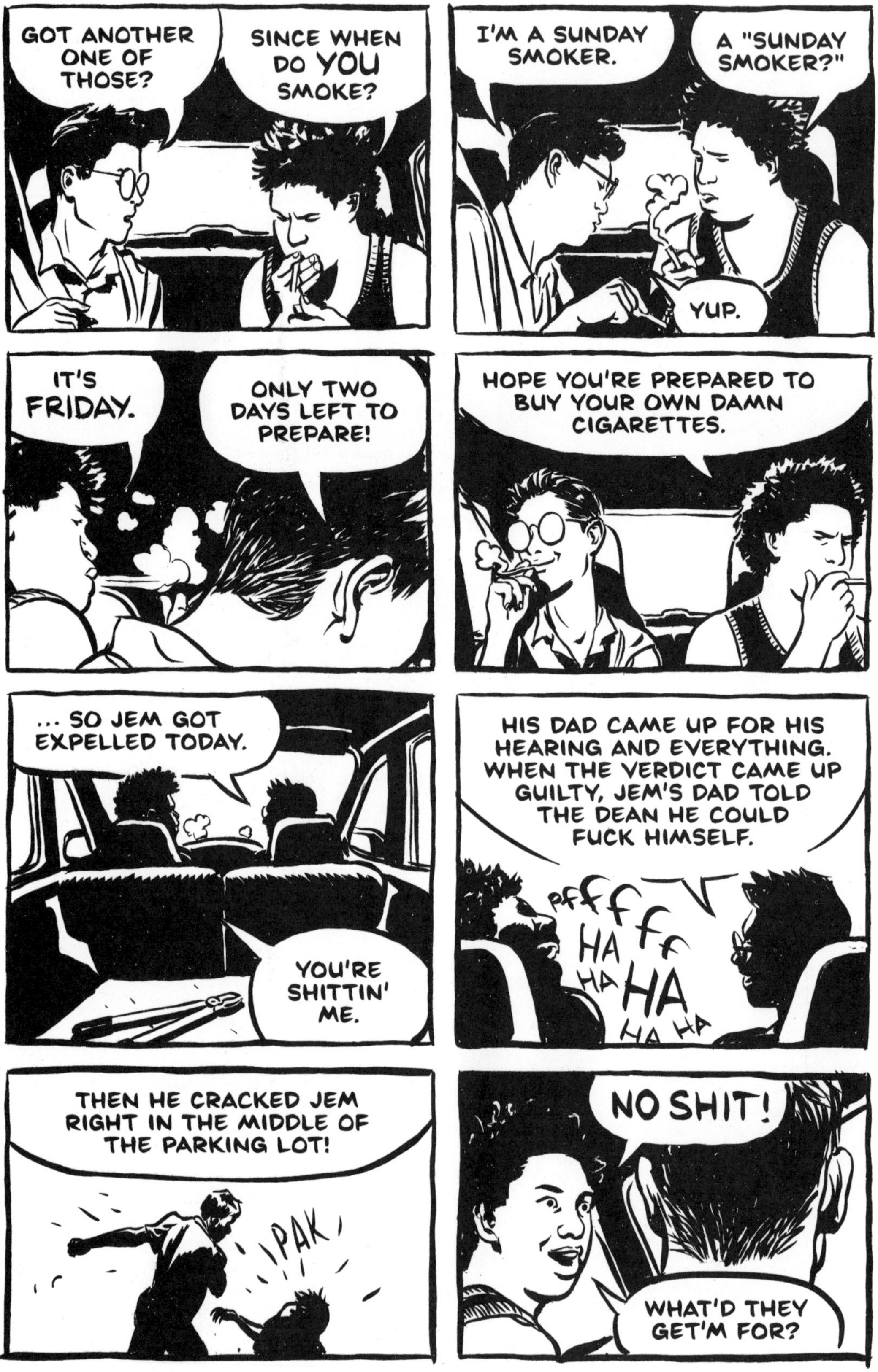
GOT ANOTHER ONE OF THOSE?
SINCE WHEN DO YOU SMOKE?
I'M A SUNDAY SMOKER.
A "SUNDAY SMOKER?"
YUP.
IT'S FRIDAY.
ONLY TWO DAYS LEFT TO PREPARE!
HOPE YOU'RE PREPARED TO BUY YOUR OWN DAMN CIGARETTES.
... SO JEM GOT EXPELLED TODAY.
YOU'RE SHITTIN' ME.
HIS DAD CAME UP FOR HIS HEARING AND EVERYTHING. WHEN THE VERDICT CAME UP GUILTY, JEM'S DAD TOLD THE DEAN HE COULD FUCK HIMSELF.
PFFFFF
HA HA HA HA HA HA
THEN HE CRACKED JEM RIGHT IN THE MIDDLE OF THE PARKING LOT!
PAK
NO SHIT!
WHAT'D THEY GET'M FOR?

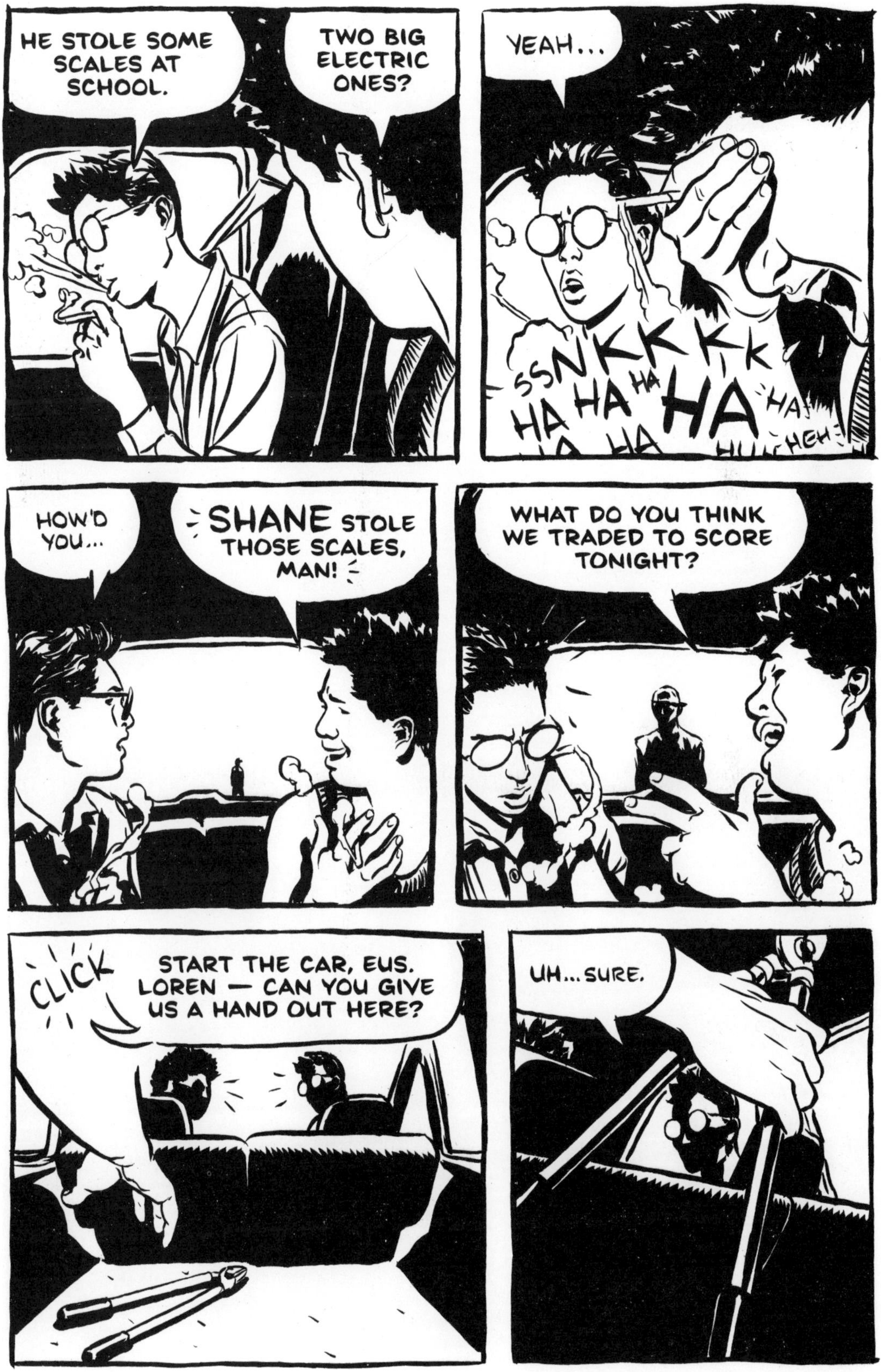
HE STOLE SOME SCALES AT SCHOOL.
TWO BIG ELECTRIC ONES?
YEAH...
SSNKKKK
HA HA HA HA HA
HOW'D YOU...
SHANE STOLE THOSE SCALES, MAN!
WHAT DO YOU THINK WE TRADED TO SCORE TONIGHT?
CLICK
START THE CAR, EUS. LOREN — CAN YOU GIVE US A HAND OUT HERE?
UH... SURE.

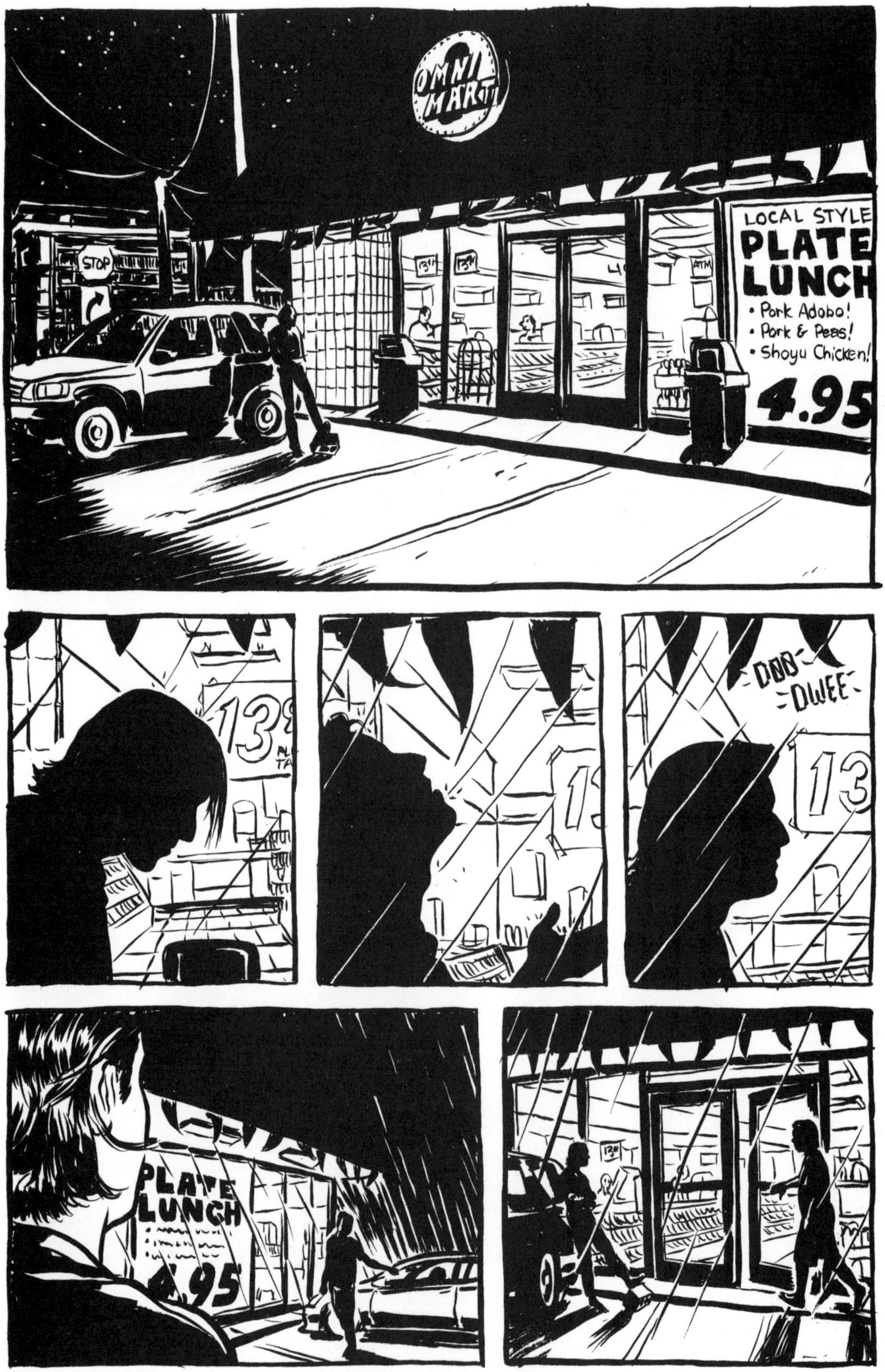
OMNI MART
STOP
ATM
LOCAL STYLE
PLATE LUNCH
• Pork Adobo!
• Pork & Peas!
• Shoyu Chicken!
4.95
DOO DWEE
PLATE LUNCH
4.95

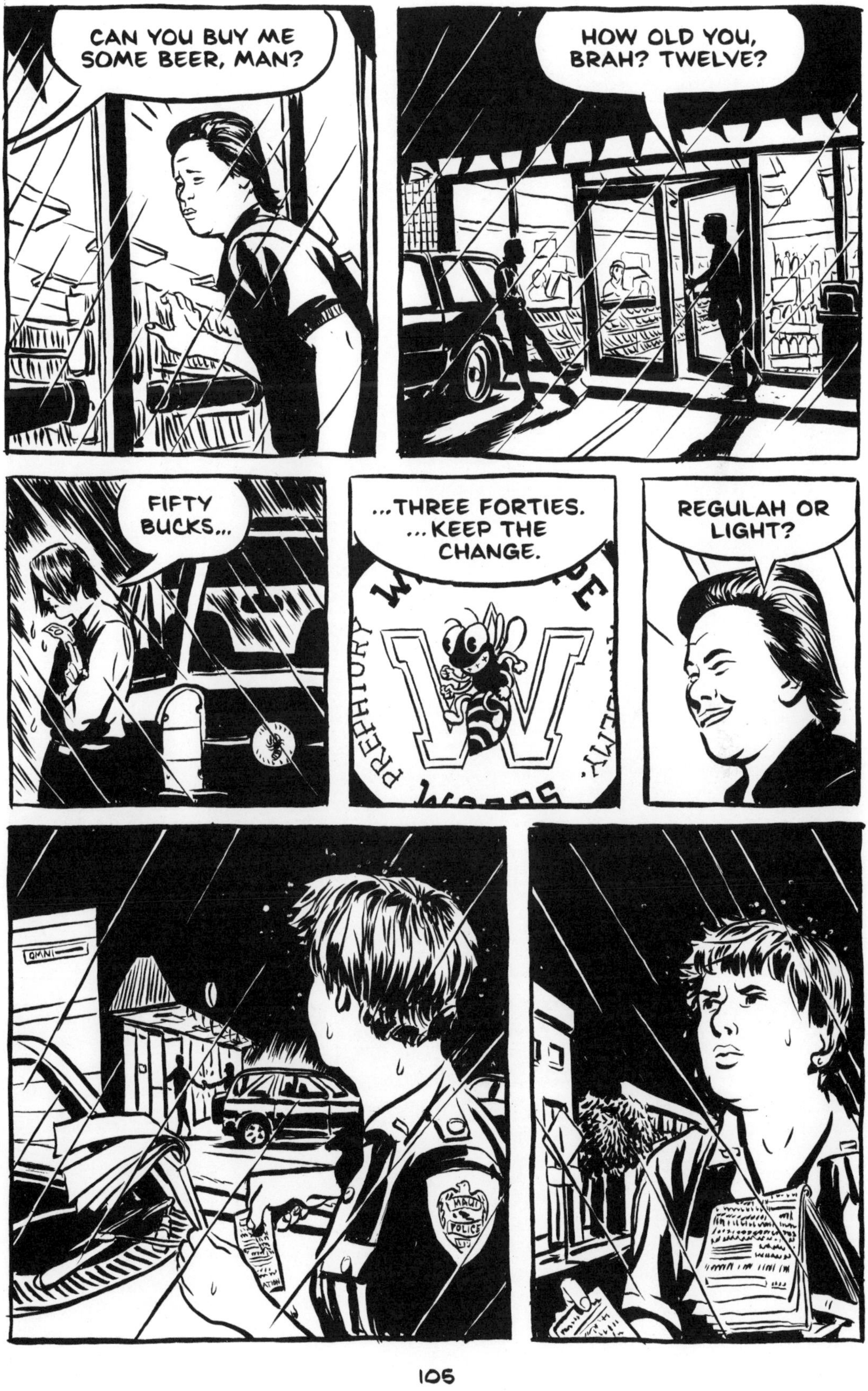
CAN YOU BUY ME SOME BEER, MAN?
HOW OLD YOU, BRAH? TWELVE?
FIFTY BUCKS...
...THREE FORTIES. ...KEEP THE CHANGE.
REGULAH OR LIGHT?

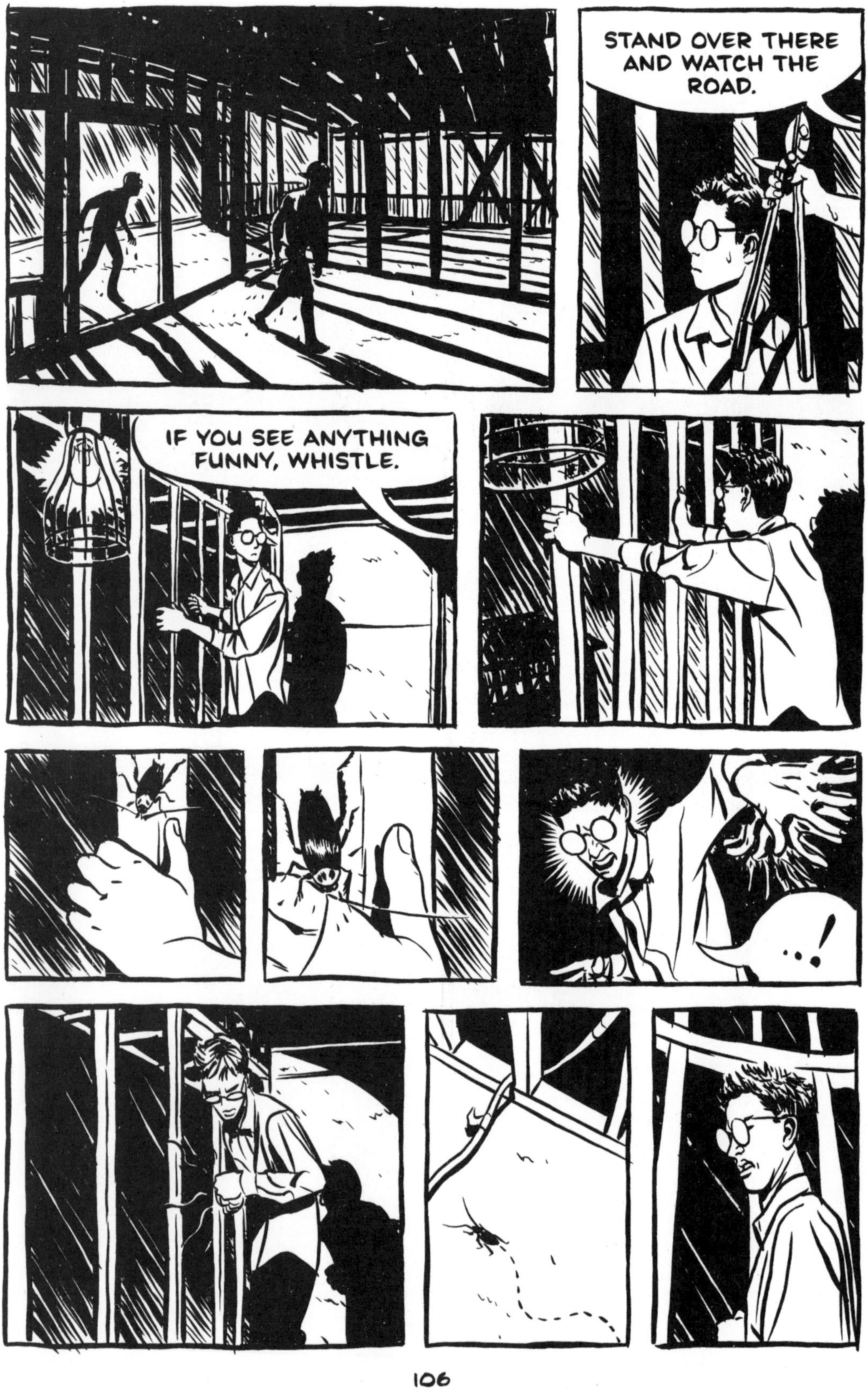
STAND OVER THERE AND WATCH THE ROAD.
IF YOU SEE ANYTHING FUNNY, WHISTLE.
..!

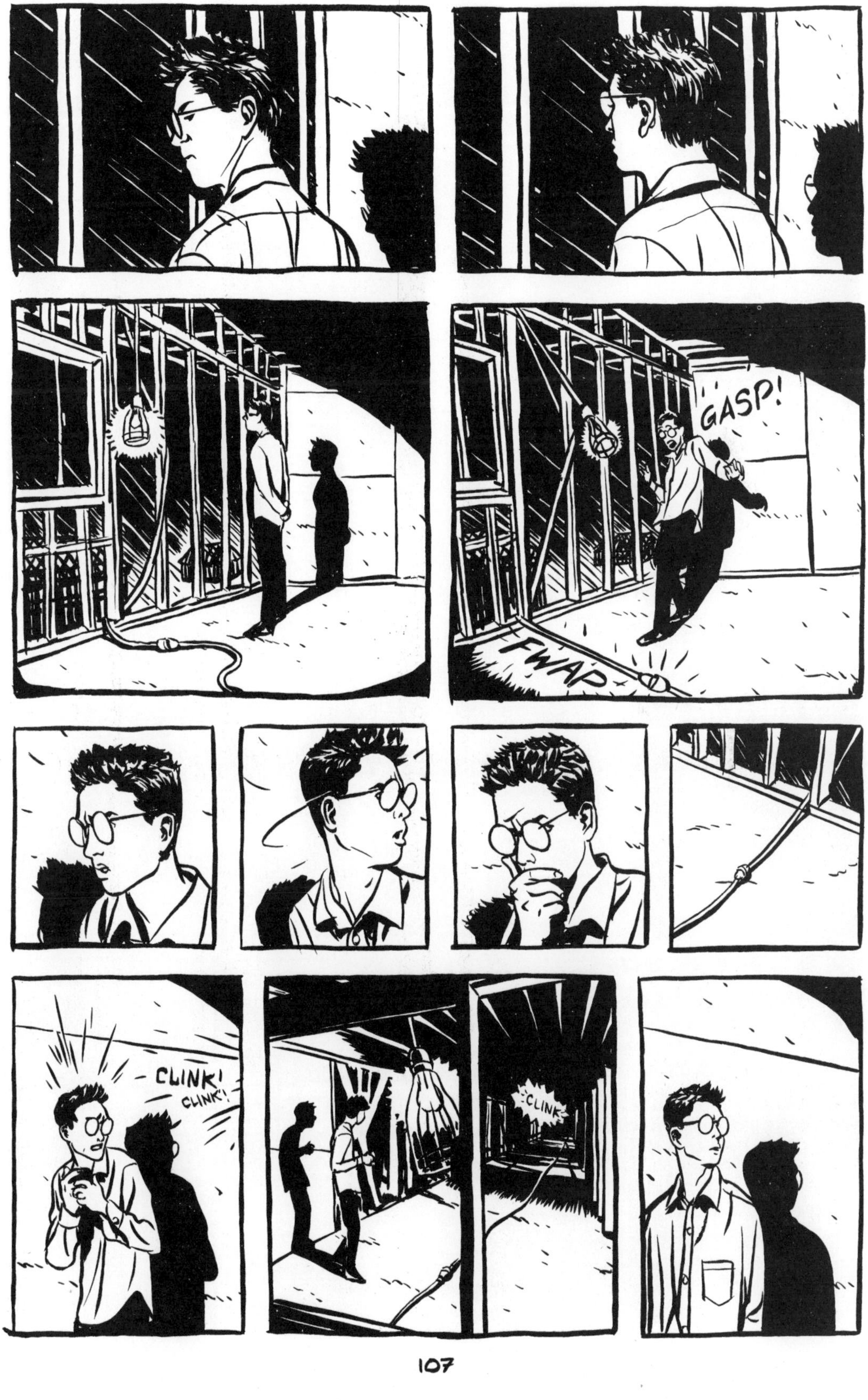
GASP!
FWAP
CLINK!
CLINK!
CLINK

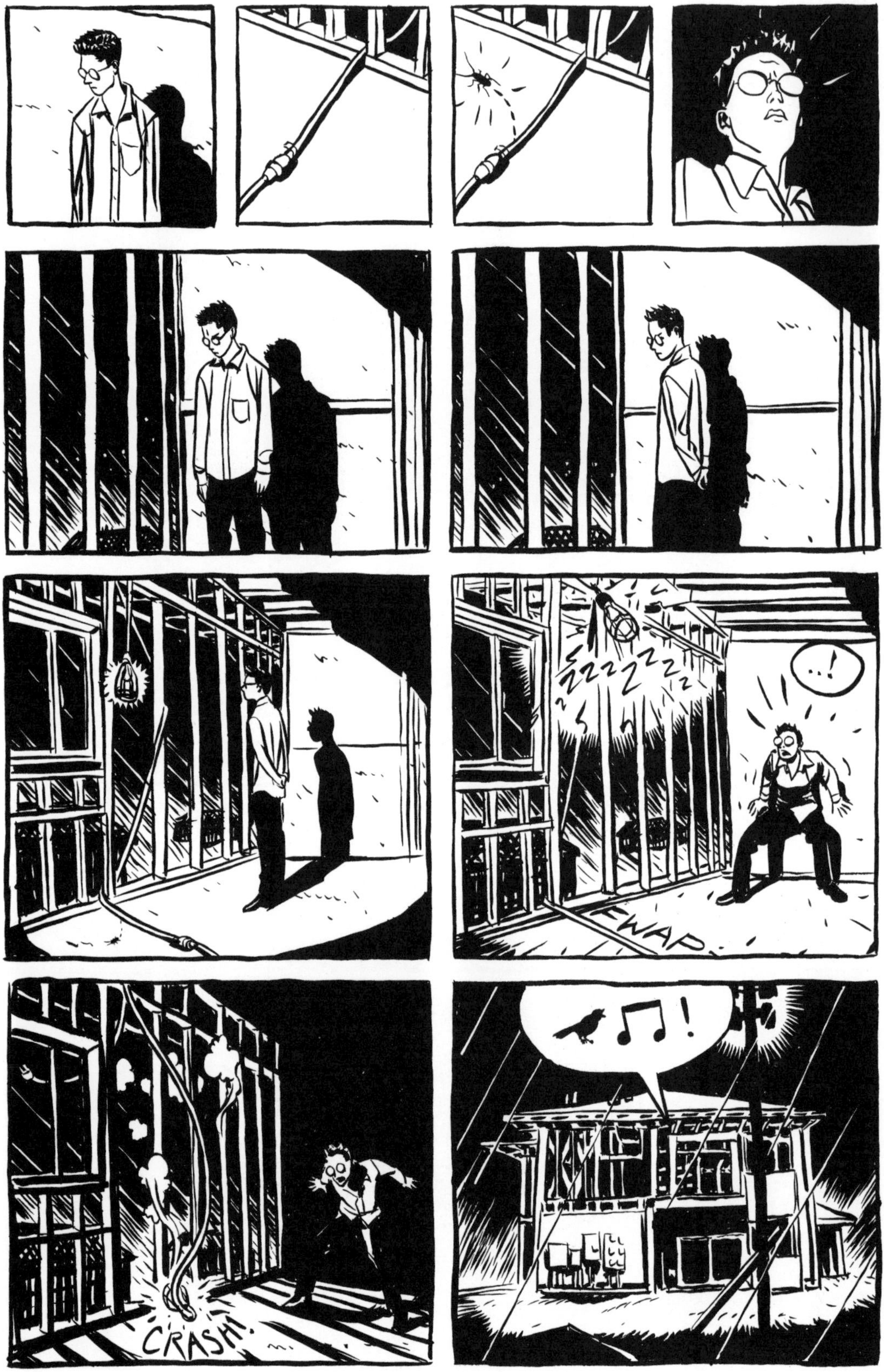
..!
FWAP
CRASH!
♫ !

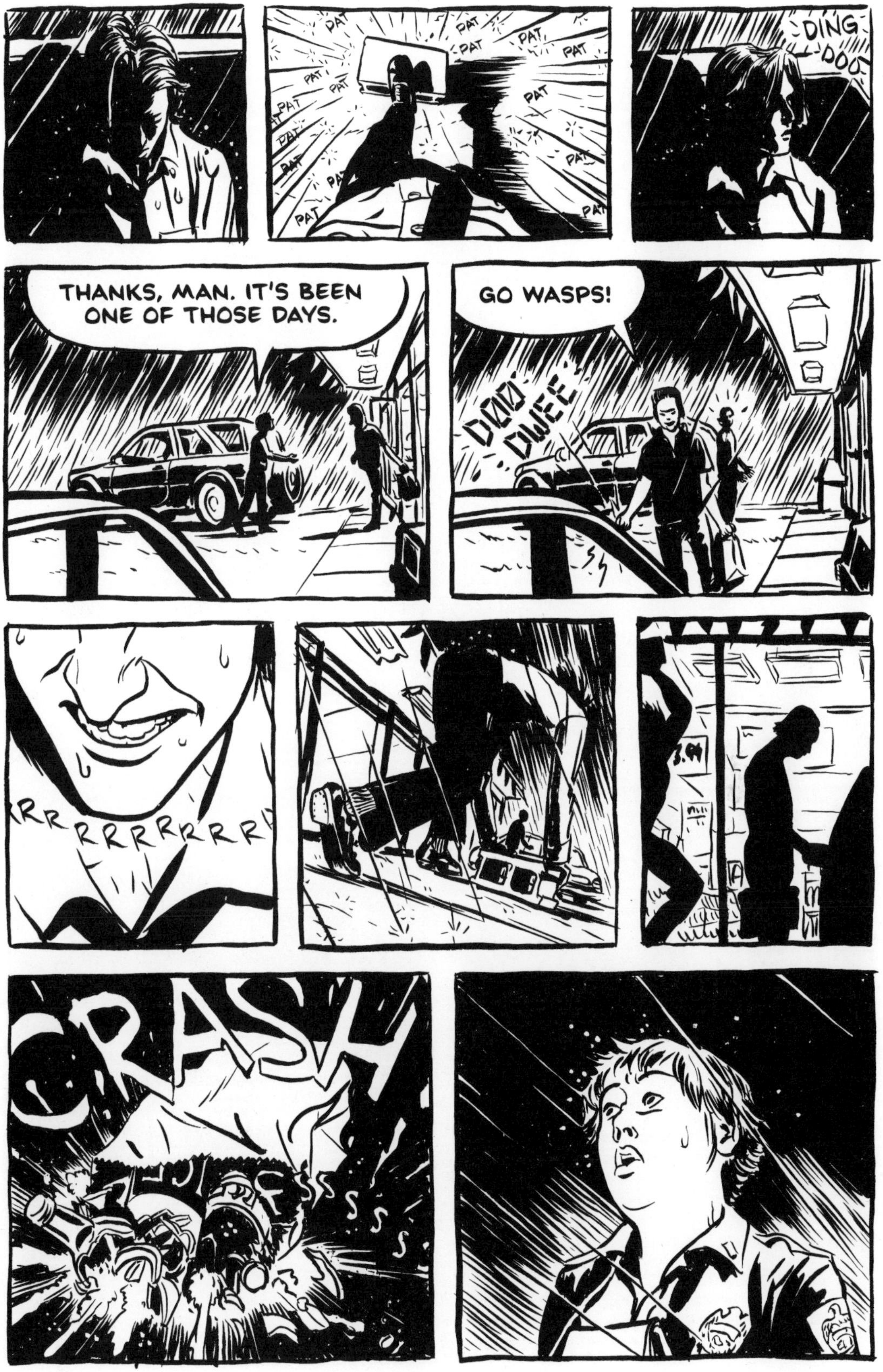
PAT PAT PAT PAT PAT PAT PAT PAT PAT PAT PAT PAT PAT PAT PAT
DING DOO
THANKS, MAN. IT'S BEEN ONE OF THOSE DAYS.
GO WASPS!
DOO DWEE
RRRRRRRRRR
CRASH
SSSSS

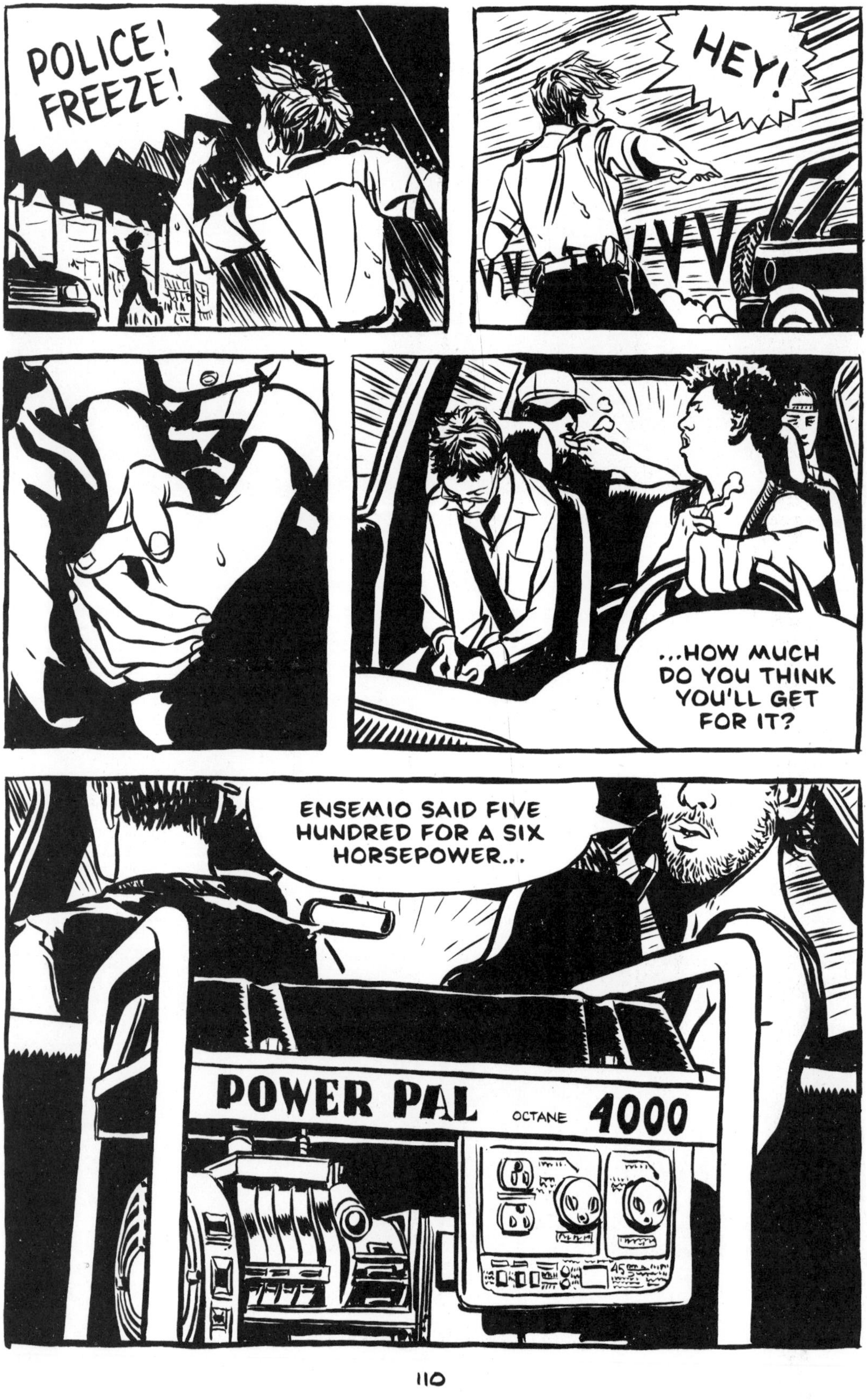
POLICE! FREEZE!
HEY!
...HOW MUCH DO YOU THINK YOU'LL GET FOR IT?
ENSEMIO SAID FIVE HUNDRED FOR A SIX HORSEPOWER...
POWER PAL
OCTANE
4000

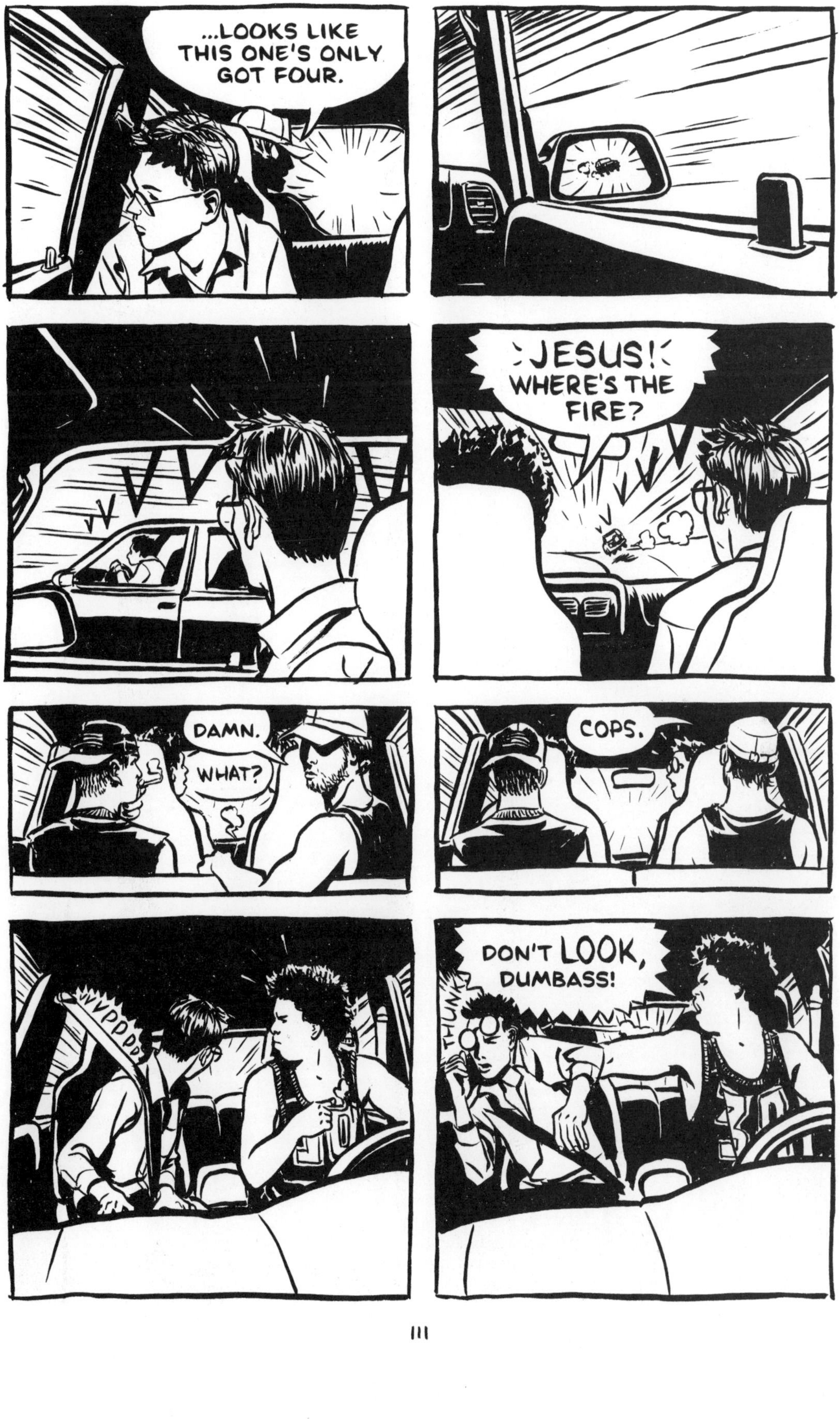
...LOOKS LIKE THIS ONE'S ONLY GOT FOUR.
JESUS! WHERE'S THE FIRE?
DAMN.
WHAT?
COPS.
WVPPPP
THUNK
DON'T LOOK, DUMBASS!

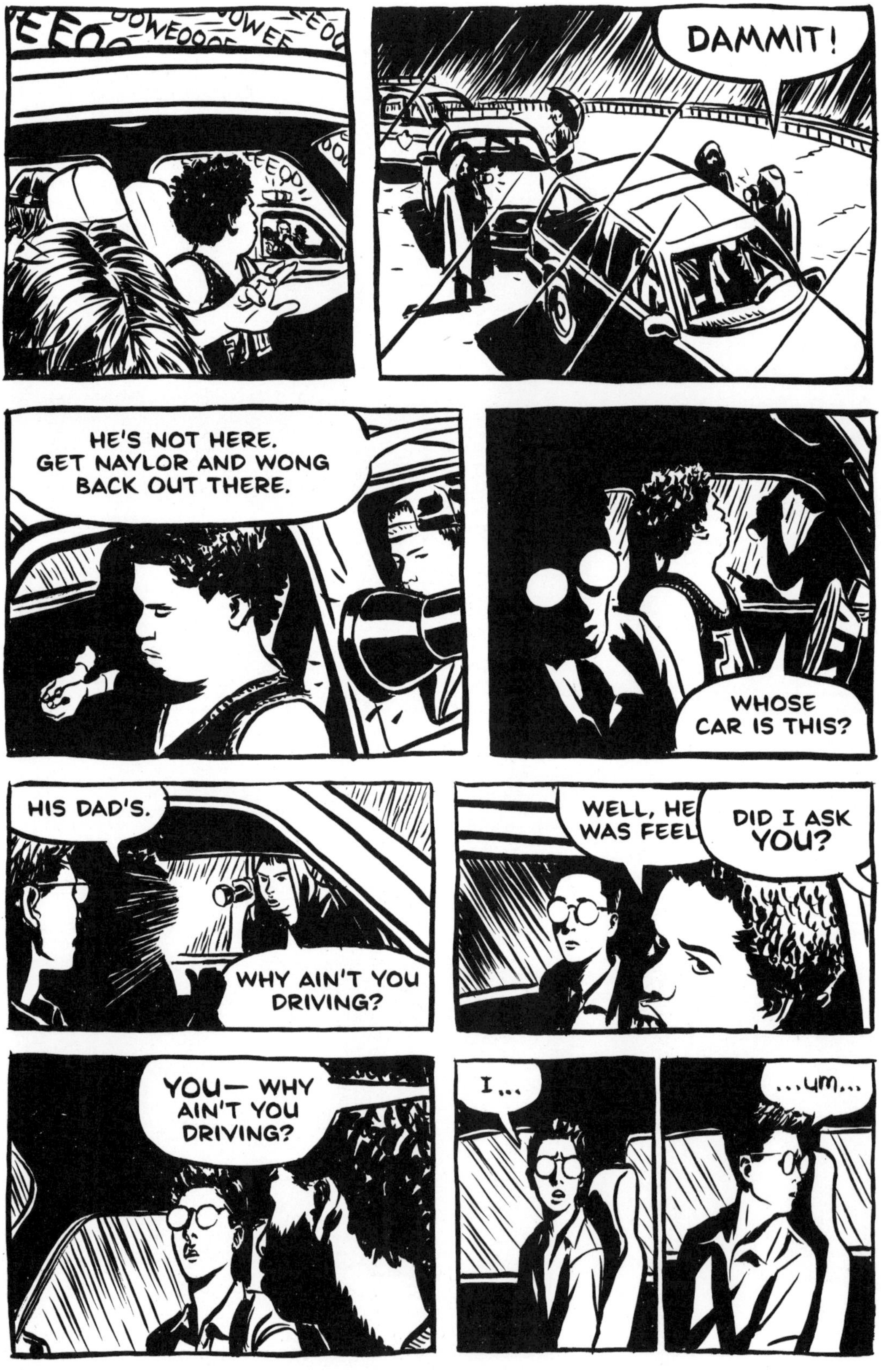
DAMMIT!
HE'S NOT HERE. GET NAYLOR AND WONG BACK OUT THERE.
WHOSE CAR IS THIS?
HIS DAD'S.
WHY AIN'T YOU DRIVING?
WELL, HE WAS FEEL
DID I ASK YOU?
YOU— WHY AIN'T YOU DRIVING?
I...
...um...

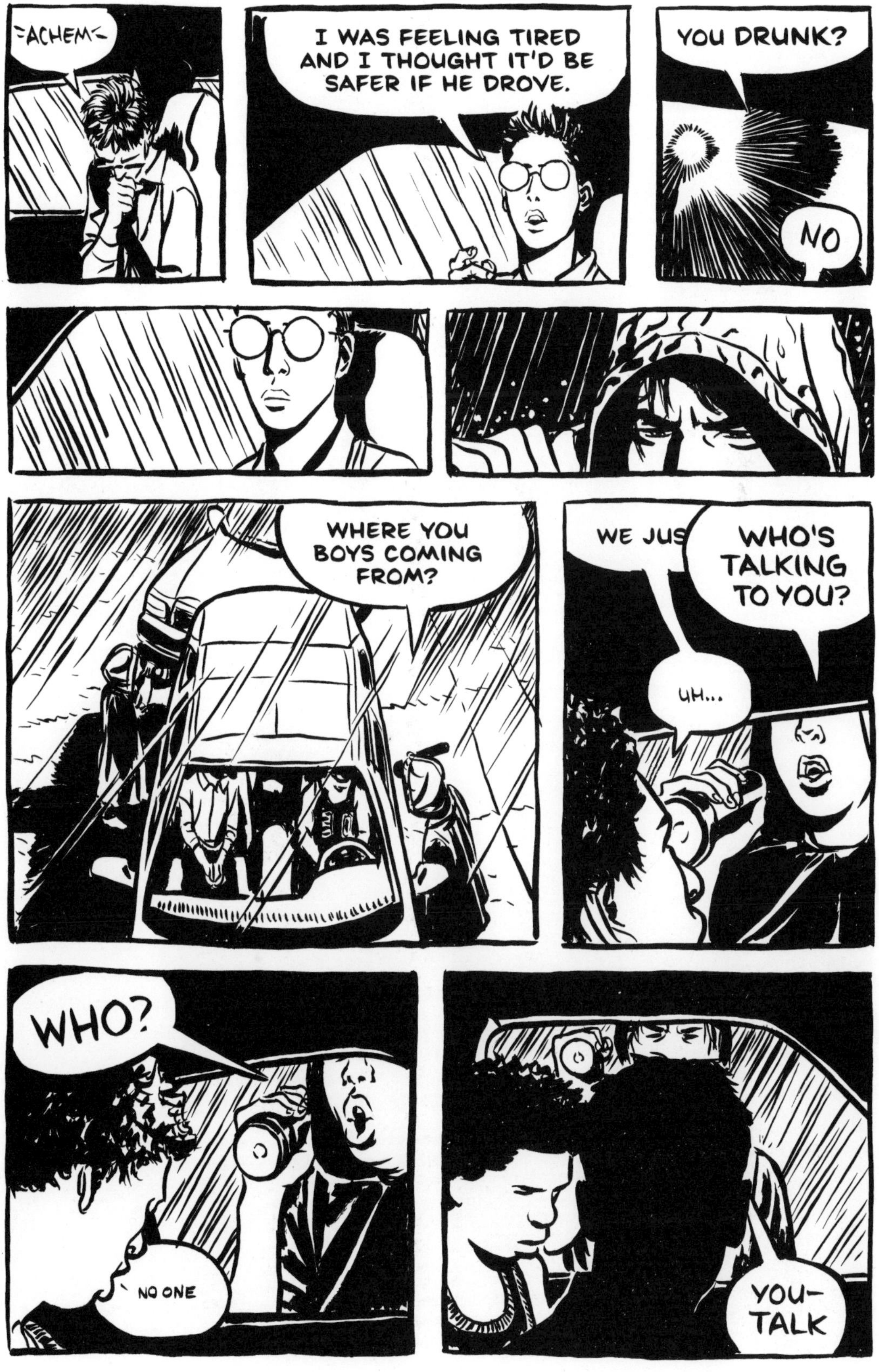
=ACHEM=
I WAS FEELING TIRED AND I THOUGHT IT'D BE SAFER IF HE DROVE.
YOU DRUNK?
NO
WHERE YOU BOYS COMING FROM?
WE JUS
WHO'S TALKING TO YOU?
UH...
WHO?
NO ONE
YOU-TALK

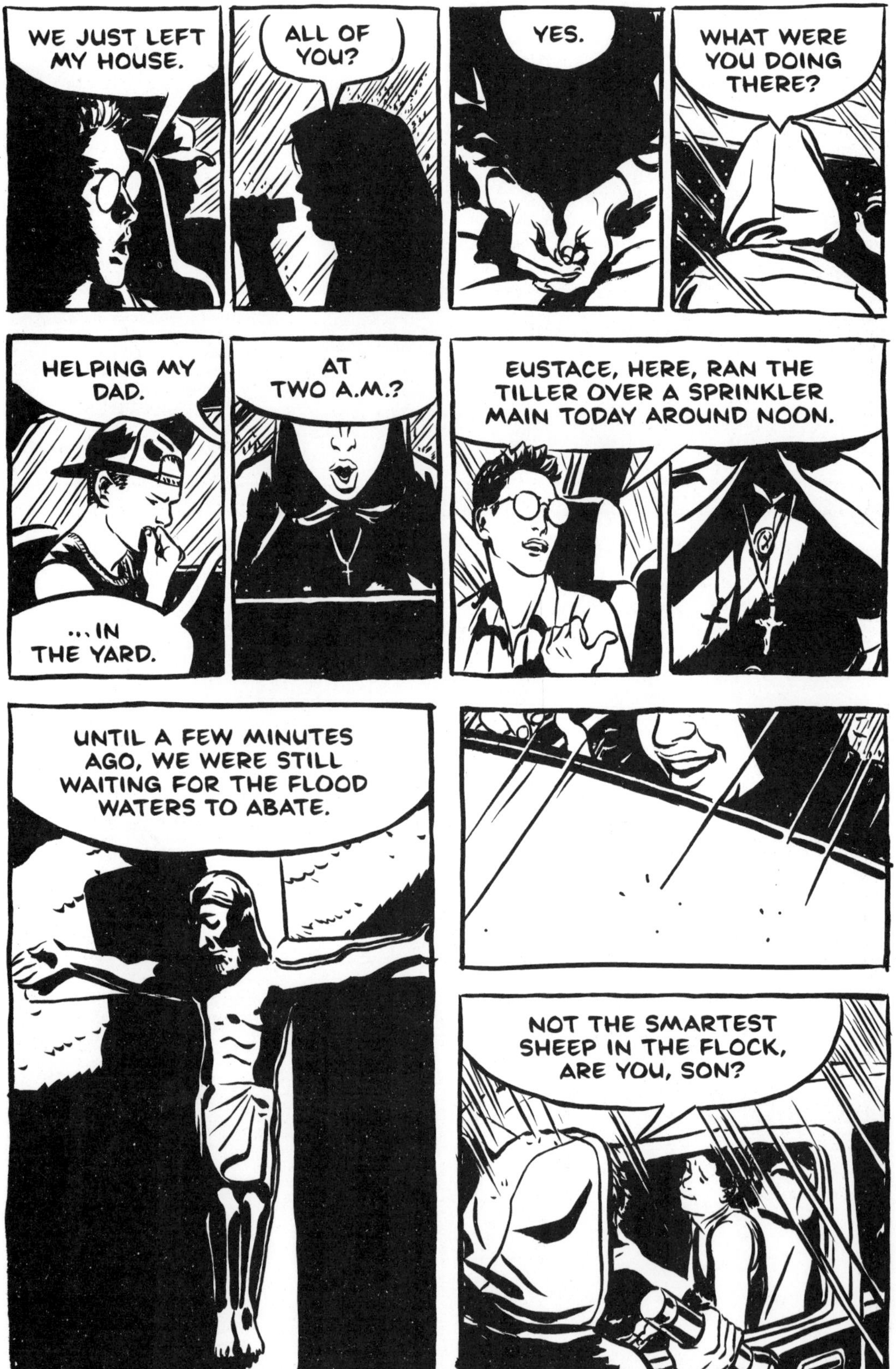
WE JUST LEFT MY HOUSE.
ALL OF YOU?
YES.
WHAT WERE YOU DOING THERE?
HELPING MY DAD.
...IN THE YARD.
AT TWO A.M.?
EUSTACE, HERE, RAN THE TILLER OVER A SPRINKLER MAIN TODAY AROUND NOON.
UNTIL A FEW MINUTES AGO, WE WERE STILL WAITING FOR THE FLOOD WATERS TO ABATE.
NOT THE SMARTEST SHEEP IN THE FLOCK, ARE YOU, SON?

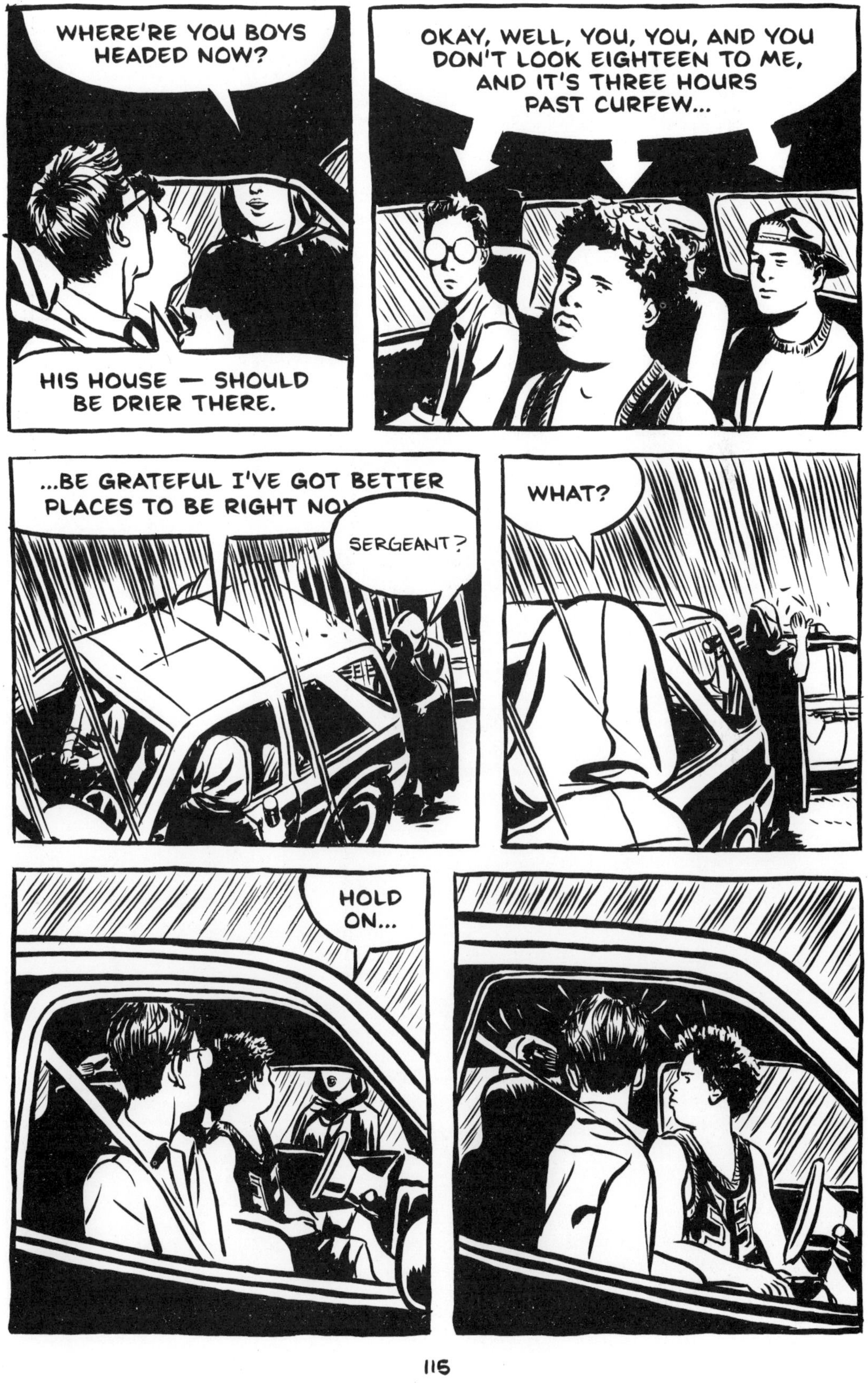
WHERE'RE YOU BOYS HEADED NOW?
HIS HOUSE — SHOULD BE DRIER THERE.
OKAY, WELL, YOU, YOU, AND YOU DON'T LOOK EIGHTEEN TO ME, AND IT'S THREE HOURS PAST CURFEW...
...BE GRATEFUL I'VE GOT BETTER PLACES TO BE RIGHT NO
SERGEANT?
WHAT?
HOLD ON...

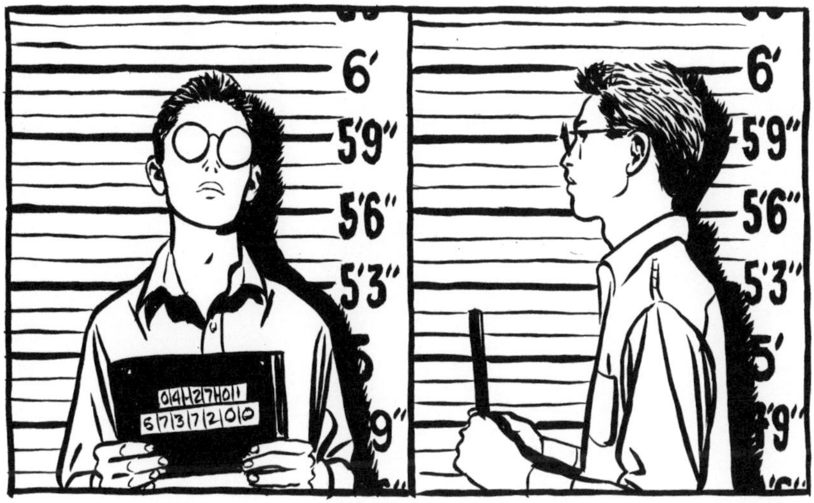

6'
5'9"
5'6"
5'3"
5'
04-27-01
67372000
6'
5'9"
5'6"
5'3"
5'

LEAVE BLANK	CRIMINAL	(STAPLE HERE)	LEAVE BLANK
		STATE USAGE NFF SECOND SUBMISSION ☐ APPROXAMATE CLASS ☐ AMPUTATION ☐ SCAR	

STATE USAGE	LAST NAME, FIRST NAME, MIDDLE NAME, SUFFIX Foster, Loren
SIGNATURE OF PERSON FINGER PRINTED Loren Foster	SOCIAL SECURITY NO. 575-26-0572
ALIASES/MAIDEN LAST NAME, FIRST NAME, MIDDLE NAME, SUFFIX	LEAVE BLANK

FBI NO.	STATE IDENTIFICATION NO.	DATE OF BIRTH MM DD YY	SEX	RACE	HIEGHT	WEIGHT	EYES	HAIR
8634-29	78-378	03 17 83	M	W	6'0"	140	Br	Bl

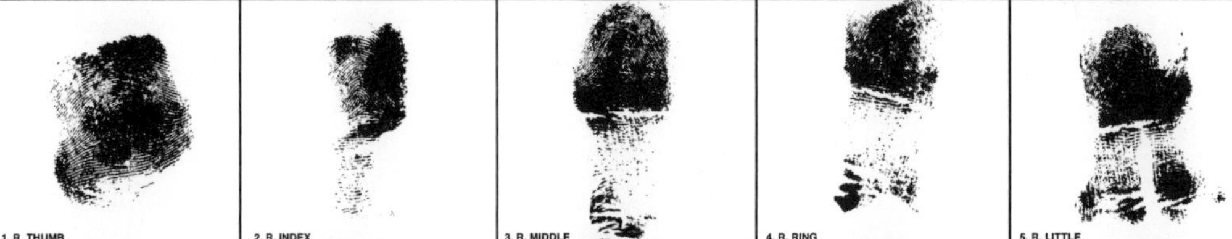

1. R. THUMB | 2. R. INDEX | 3. R. MIDDLE | 4. R. RING | 5. R. LITTLE

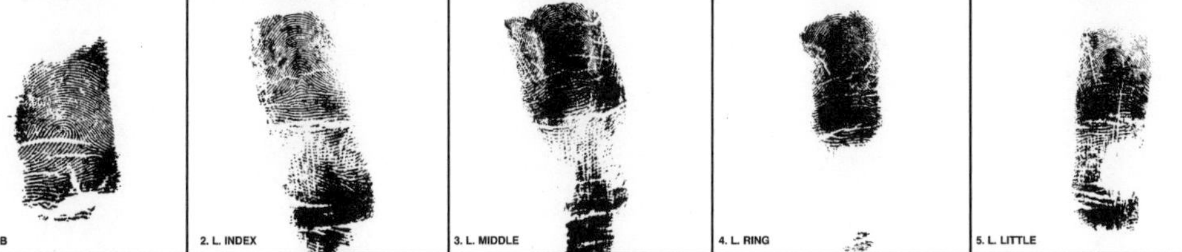

1. L. THUMB | 2. L. INDEX | 3. L. MIDDLE | 4. L. RING | 5. L. LITTLE

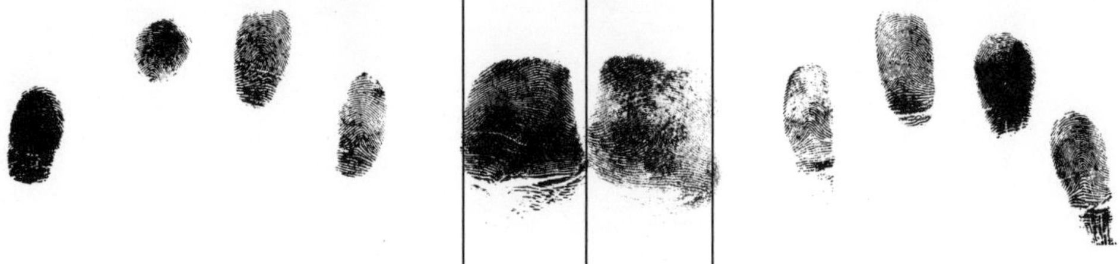

LEFT FOUR FINGERS TAKE SIMULTANEOUSLY | L. THUMB | R. THUMB | RIGHT FOUR FINGERS TAKEN SIMULTANEOUSLY

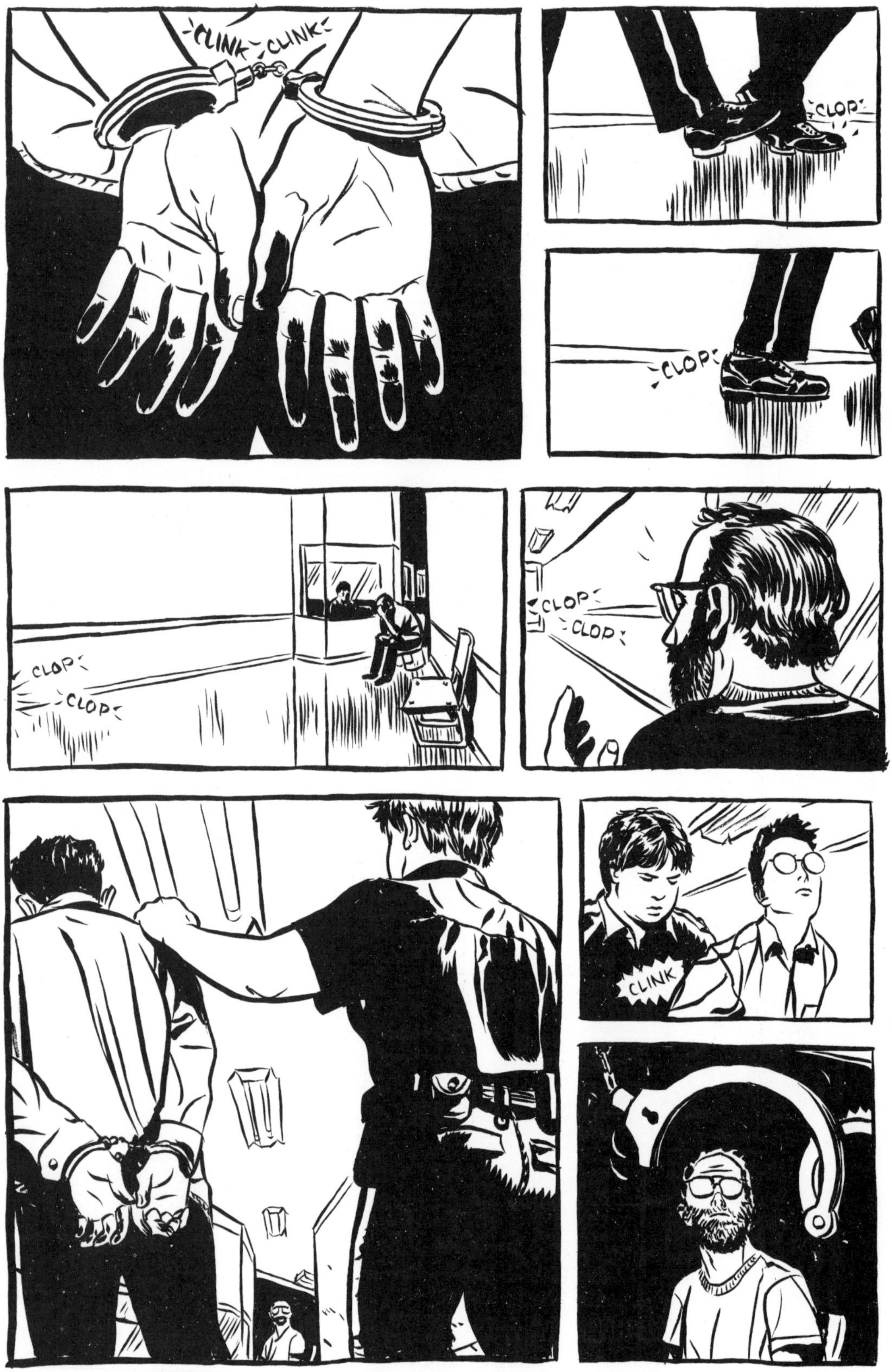
CLINK
CLINK
CLOP
CLOP
CLOP
CLOP
CLOP
CLOP
CLINK

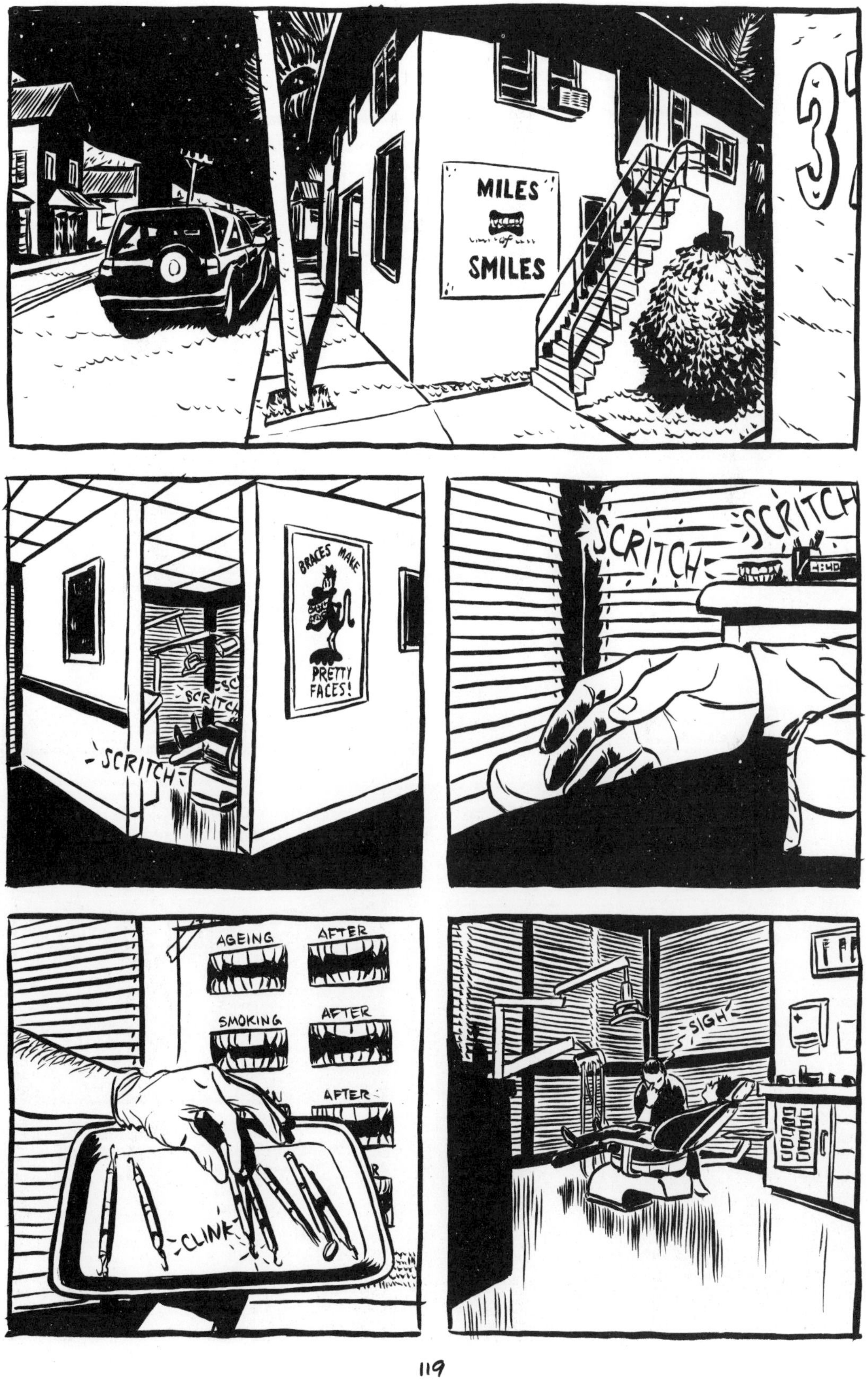

MILES of SMILES
BRACES MAKE PRETTY FACES!
SCRITCH
SCRITCH
SCRITCH
SCRITCH
AGEING
AFTER
SMOKING
AFTER
AFTER
CLINK
SIGH

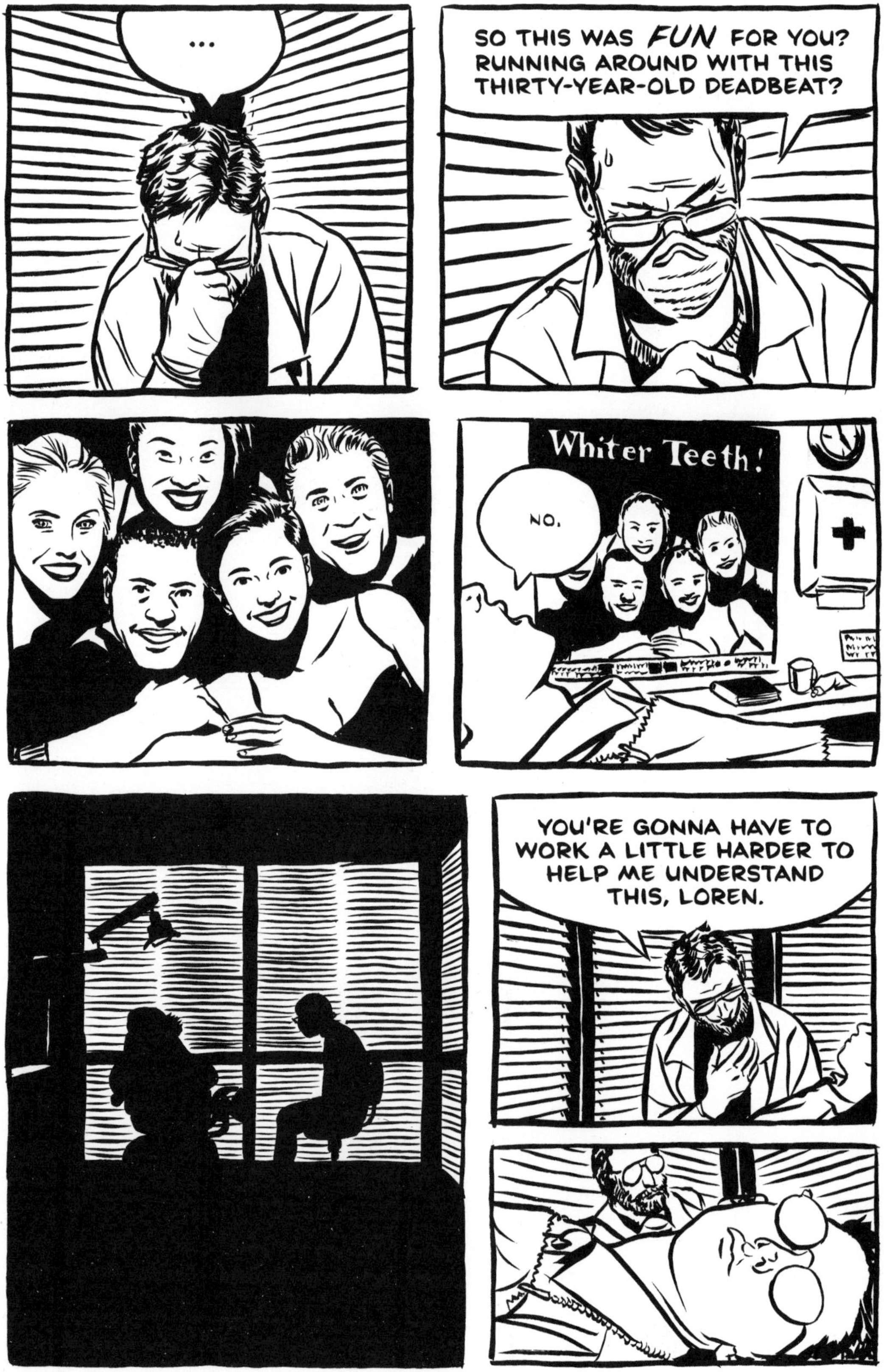
...
SO THIS WAS FUN FOR YOU? RUNNING AROUND WITH THIS THIRTY-YEAR-OLD DEADBEAT?
Whiter Teeth!
NO.
YOU'RE GONNA HAVE TO WORK A LITTLE HARDER TO HELP ME UNDERSTAND THIS, LOREN.

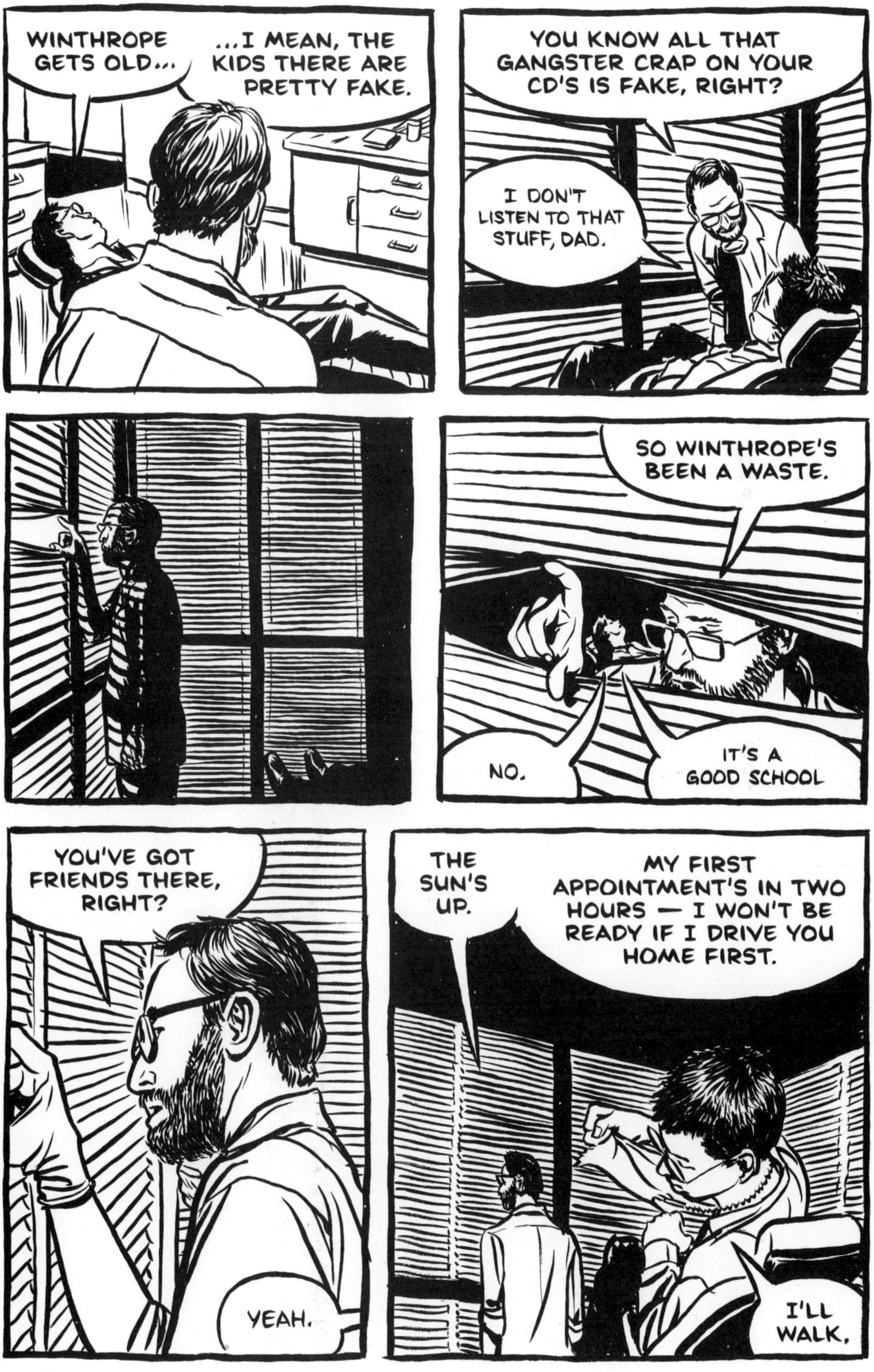
WINTHROPE GETS OLD...
...I MEAN, THE KIDS THERE ARE PRETTY FAKE.
YOU KNOW ALL THAT GANGSTER CRAP ON YOUR CD'S IS FAKE, RIGHT?
I DON'T LISTEN TO THAT STUFF, DAD.
SO WINTHROPE'S BEEN A WASTE.
NO.
IT'S A GOOD SCHOOL
YOU'VE GOT FRIENDS THERE, RIGHT?
YEAH.
THE SUN'S UP.
MY FIRST APPOINTMENT'S IN TWO HOURS — I WON'T BE READY IF I DRIVE YOU HOME FIRST.
I'LL WALK.

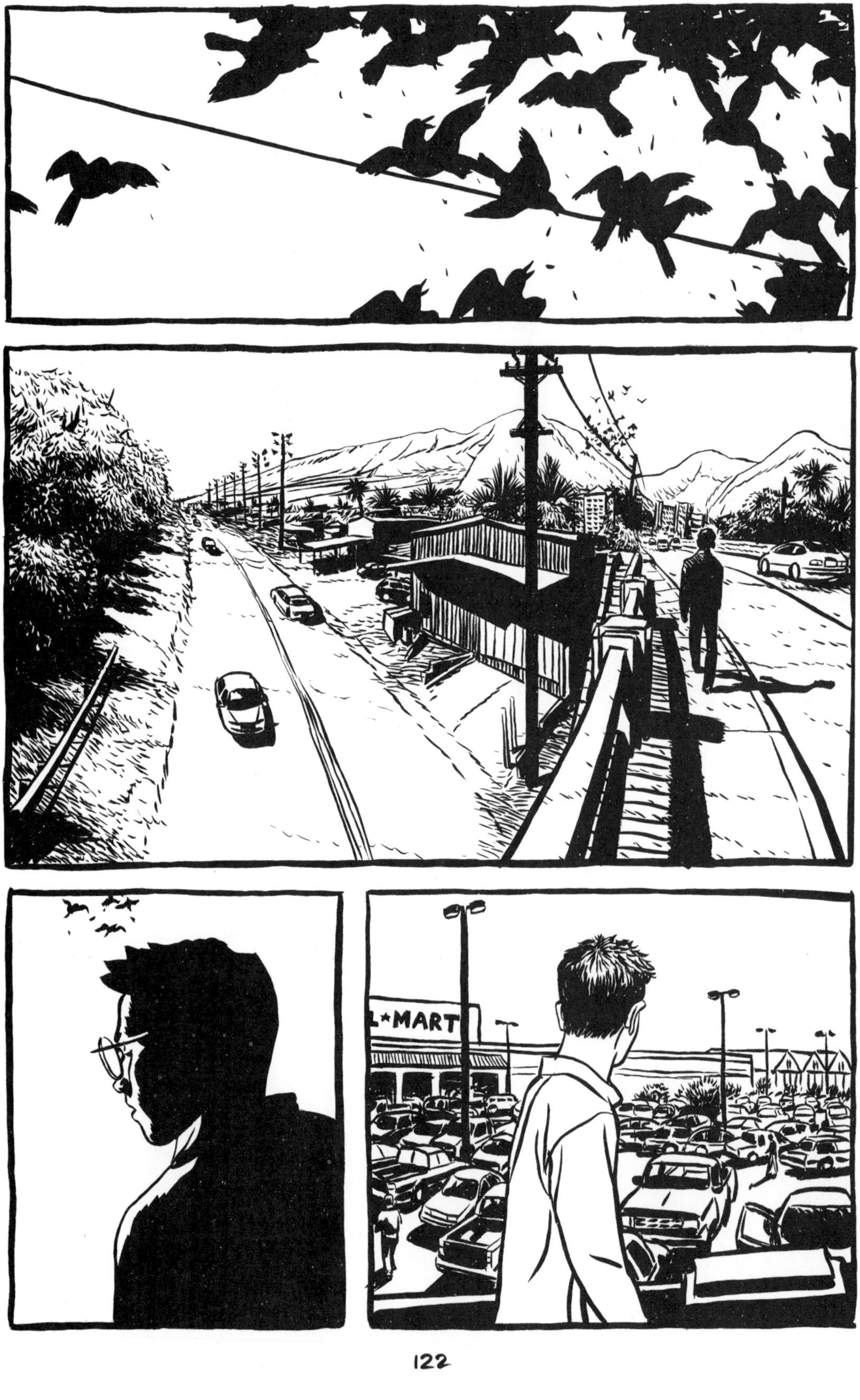
L★MART

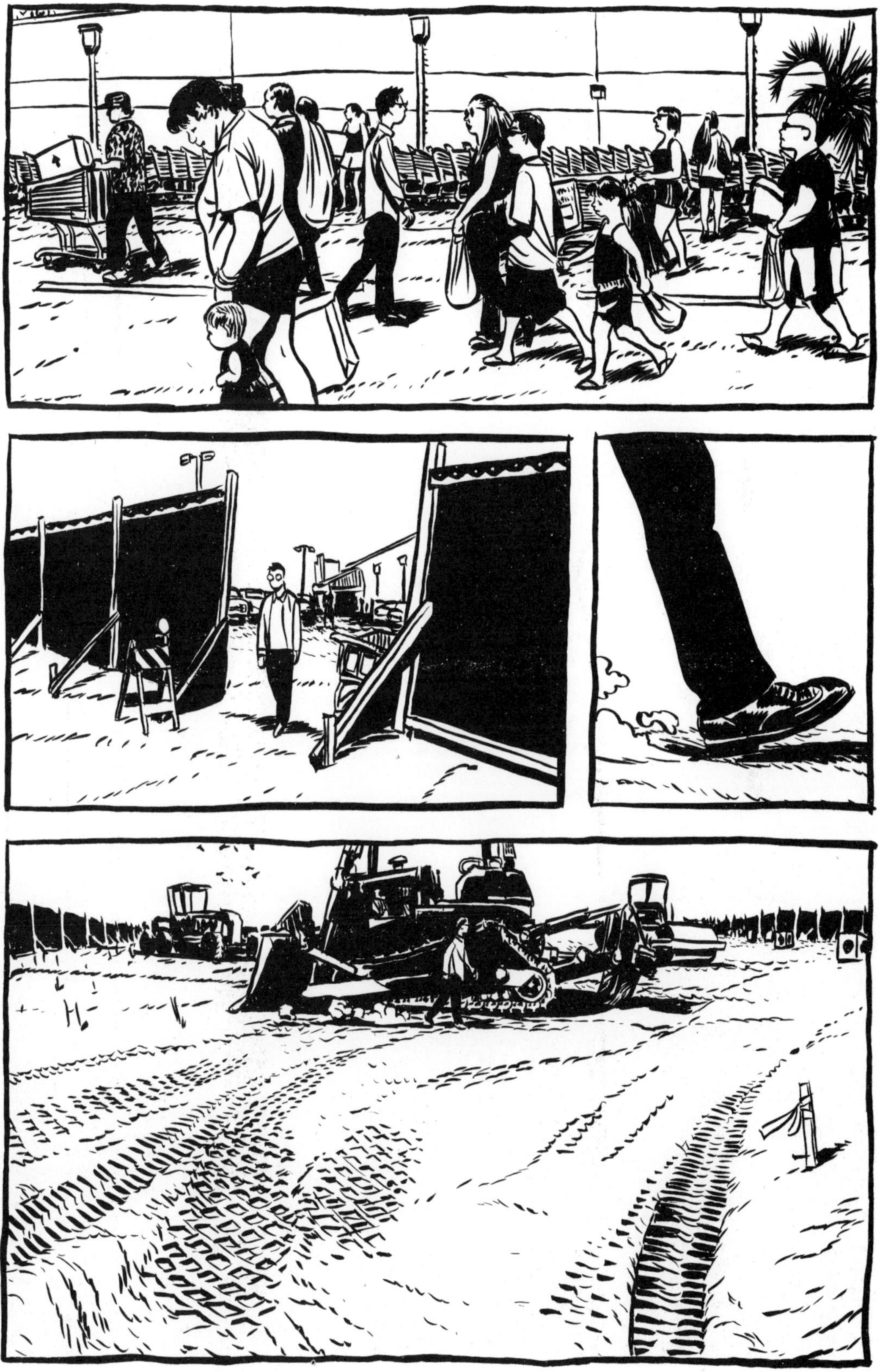

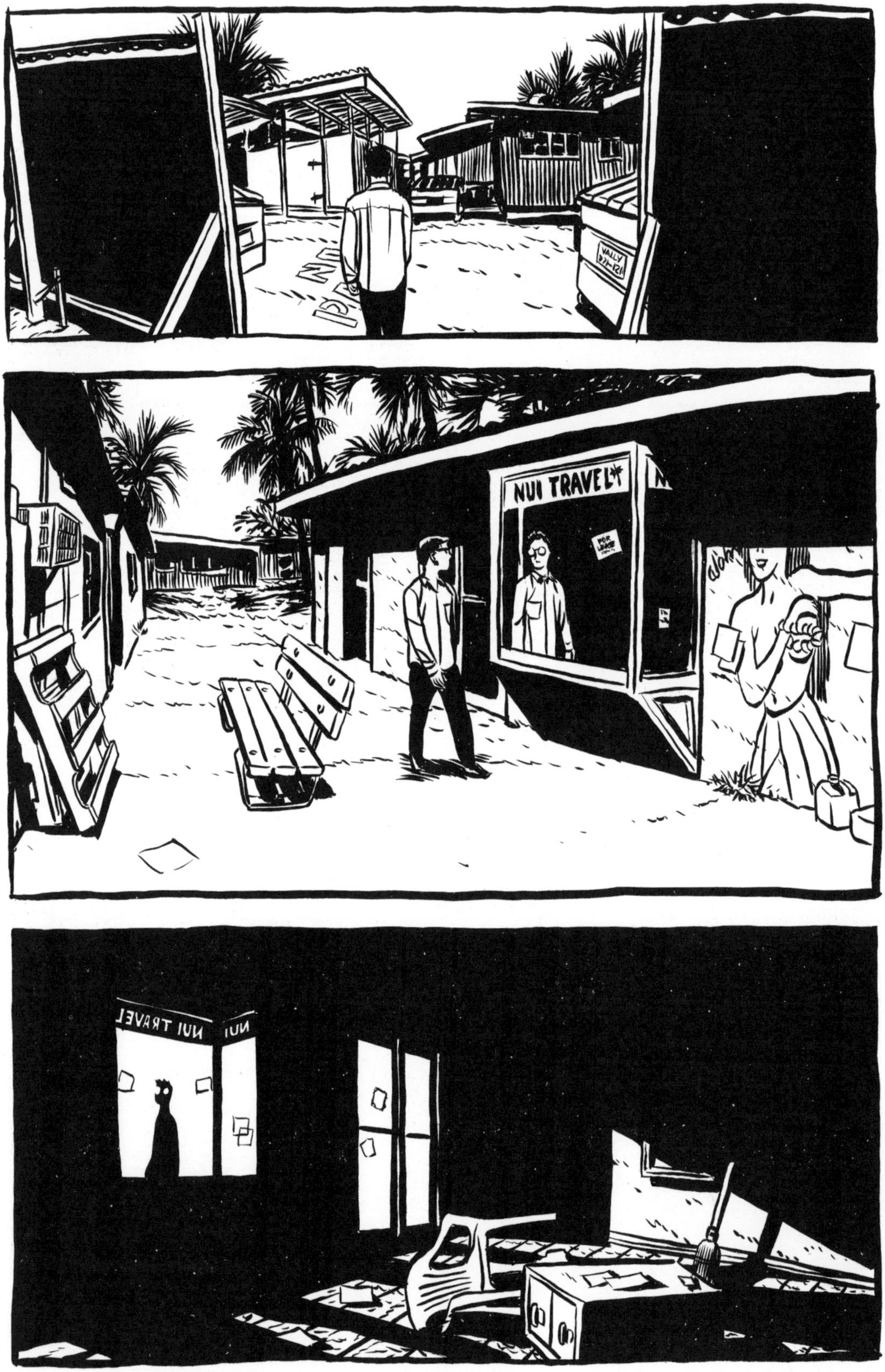
NUI TRAVEL

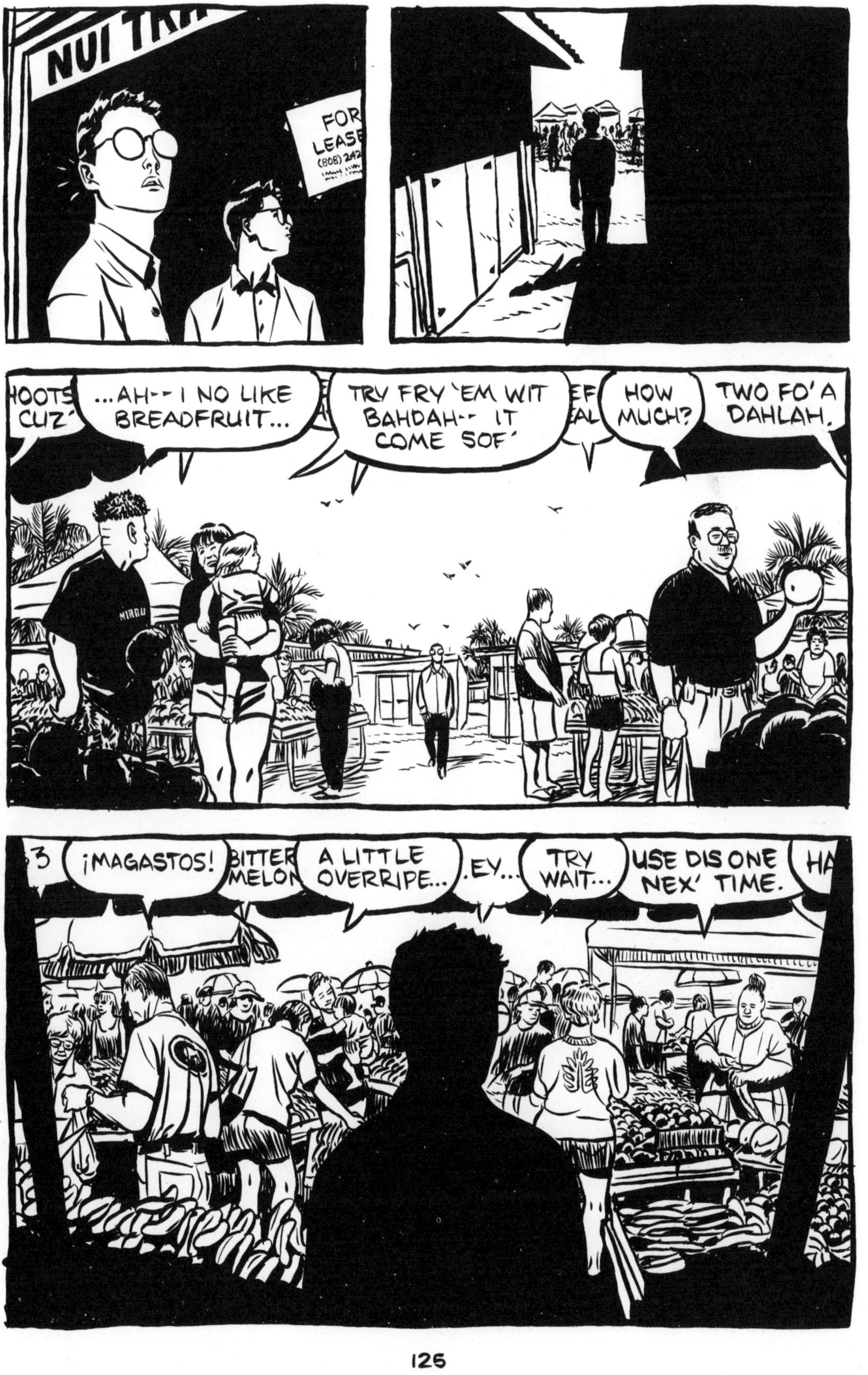
FOR LEASE
...AH-- I NO LIKE BREADFRUIT...
TRY FRY 'EM WIT BAHDAH-- IT COME SOF'
HOW MUCH?
TWO FO' A DAHLAH.
¡MAGASTOS!
BITTER MELON
A LITTLE OVERRIPE...
TRY WAIT...
USE DIS ONE NEX' TIME.

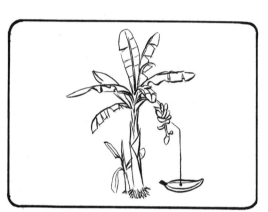

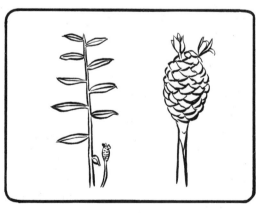

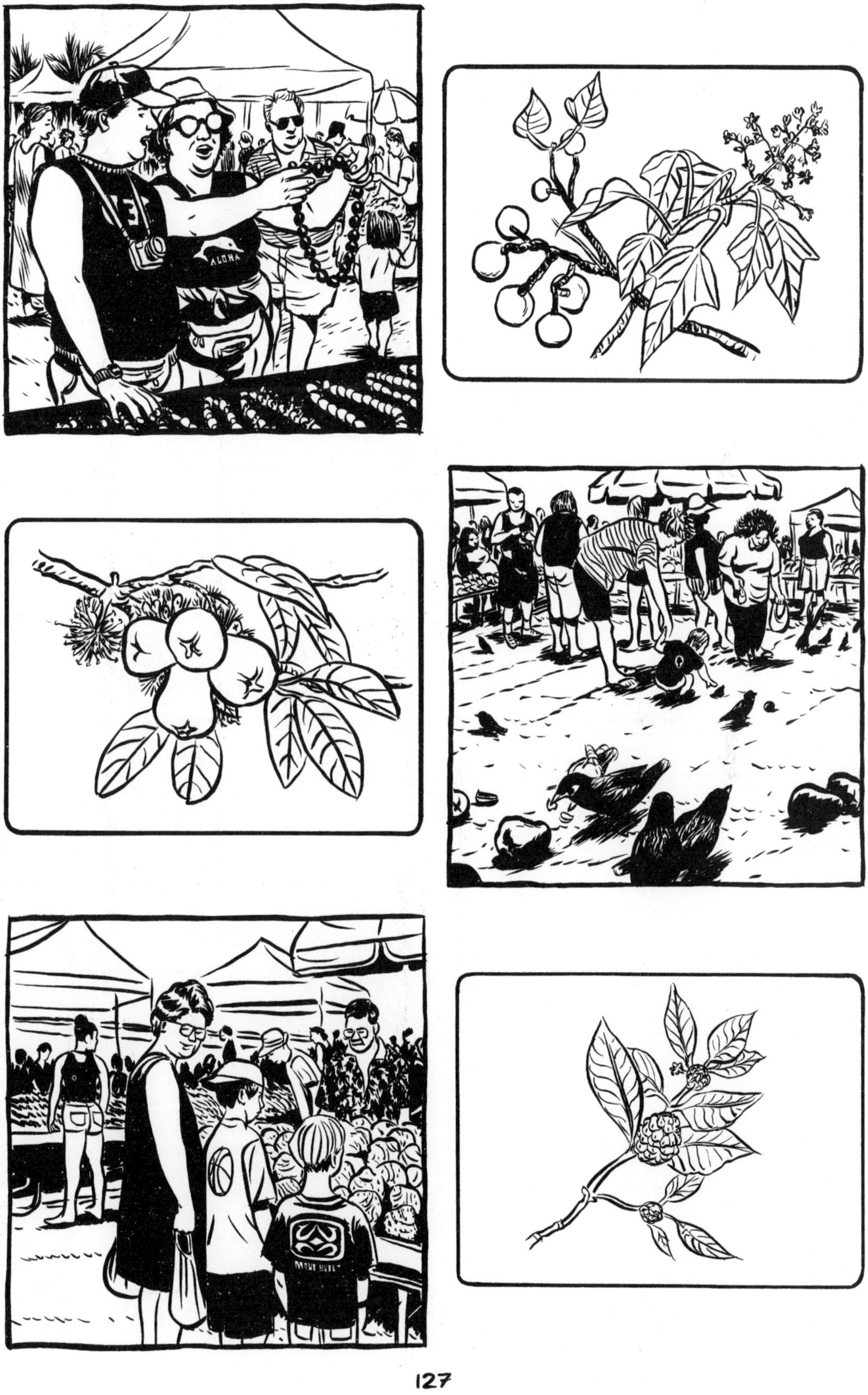
ALOHA

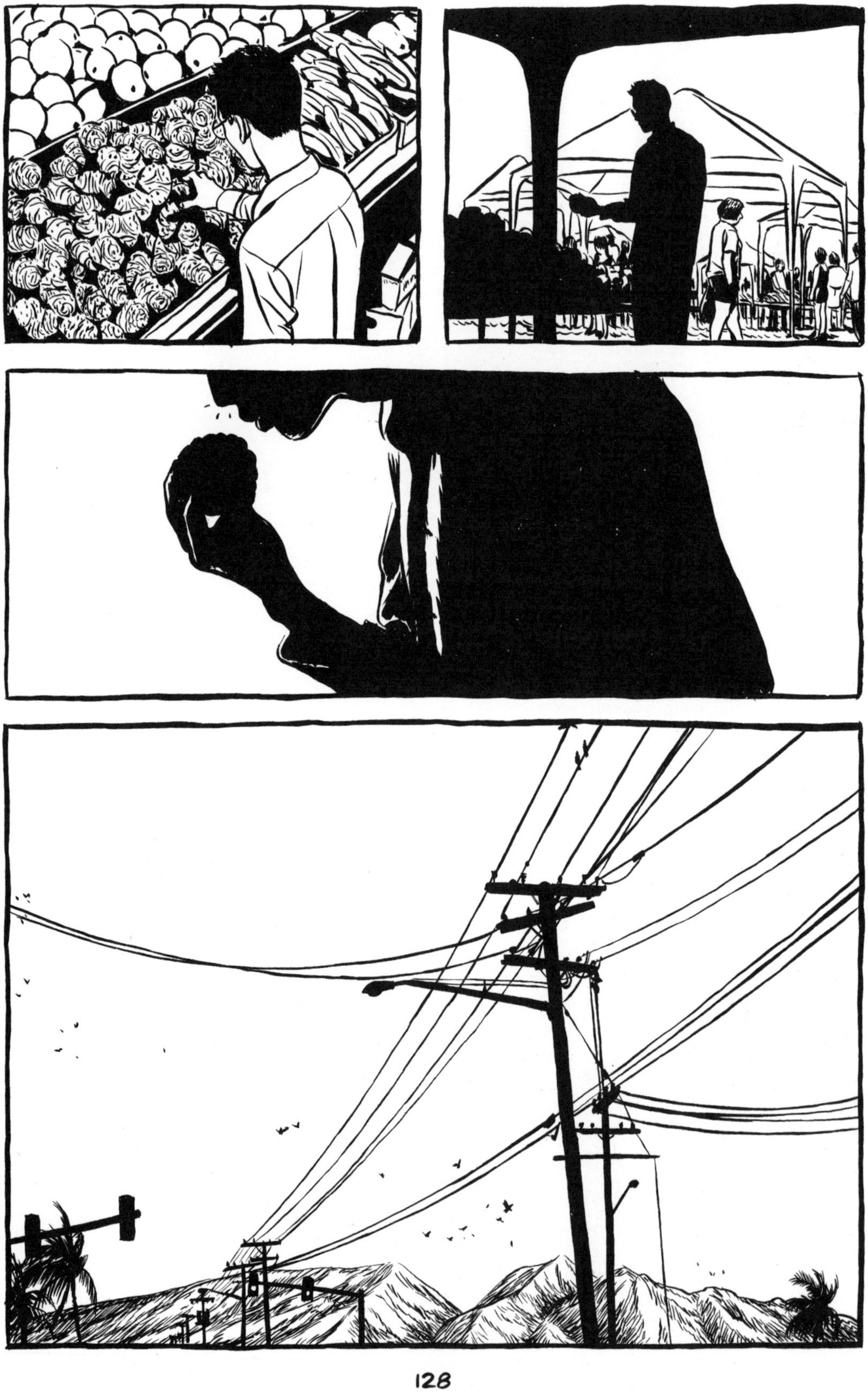

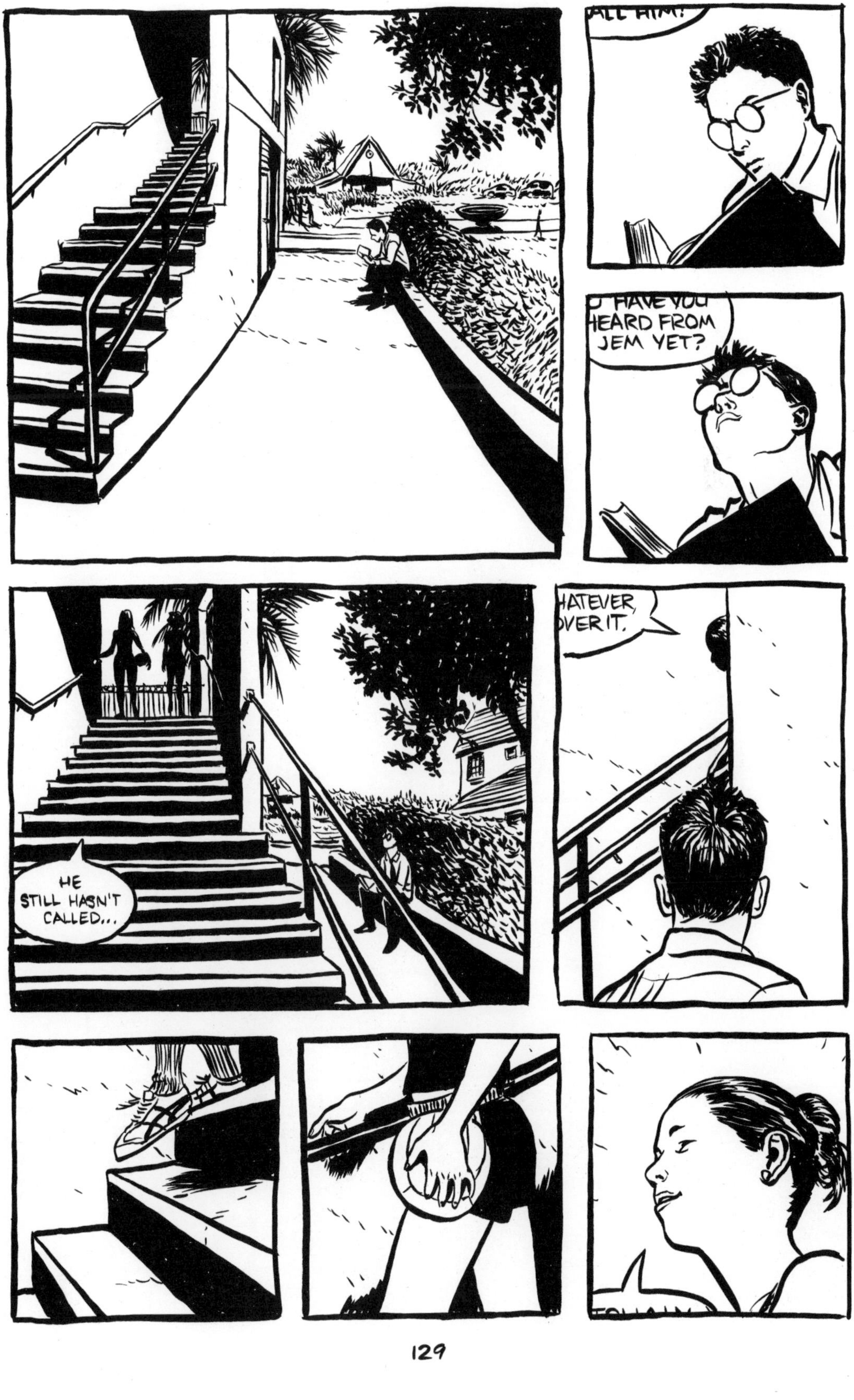
ALL HIM!
HAVE YOU HEARD FROM JEM YET?
HE STILL HASN'T CALLED...
HATEVER, OVER IT.

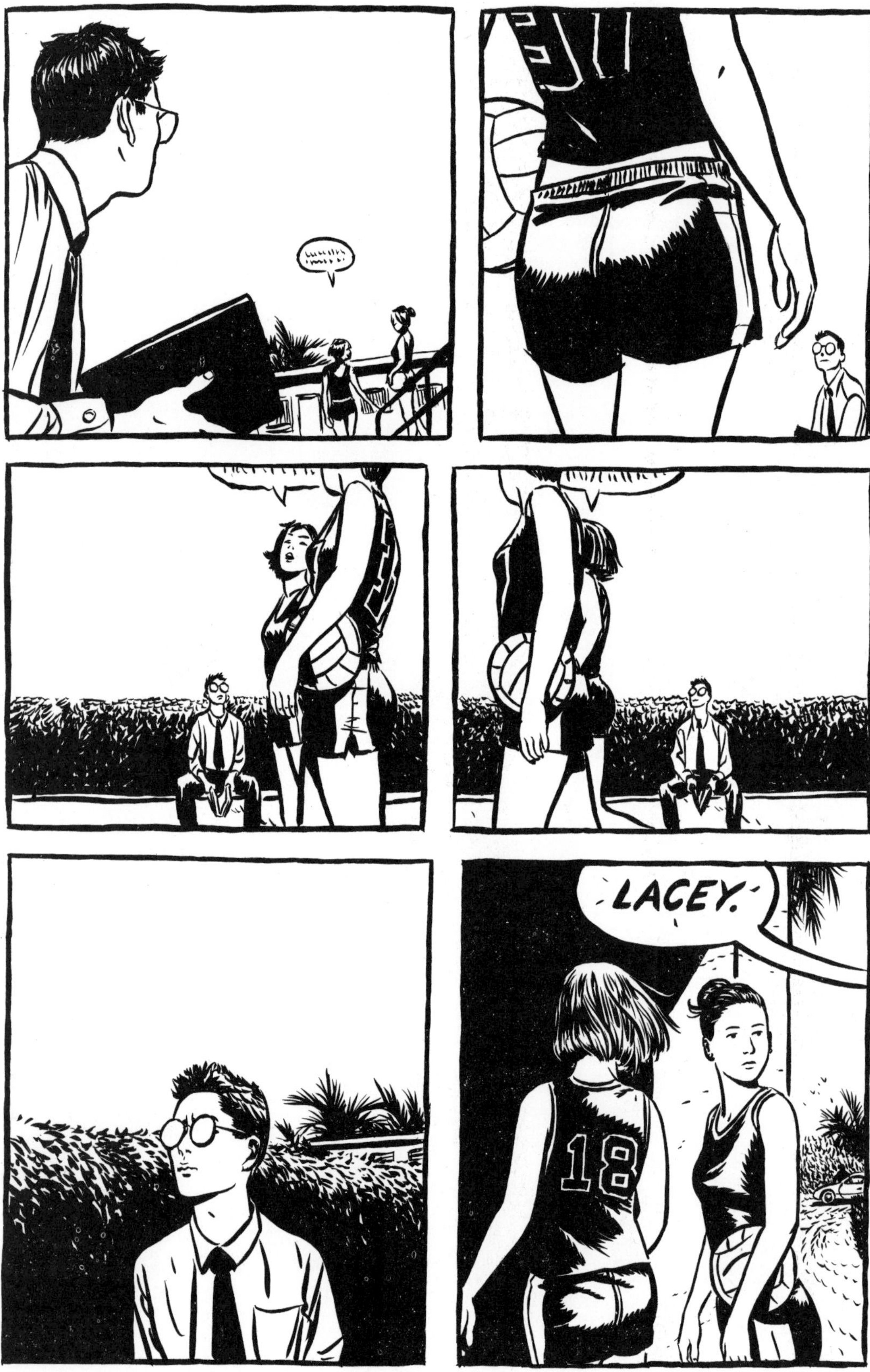
LACEY.

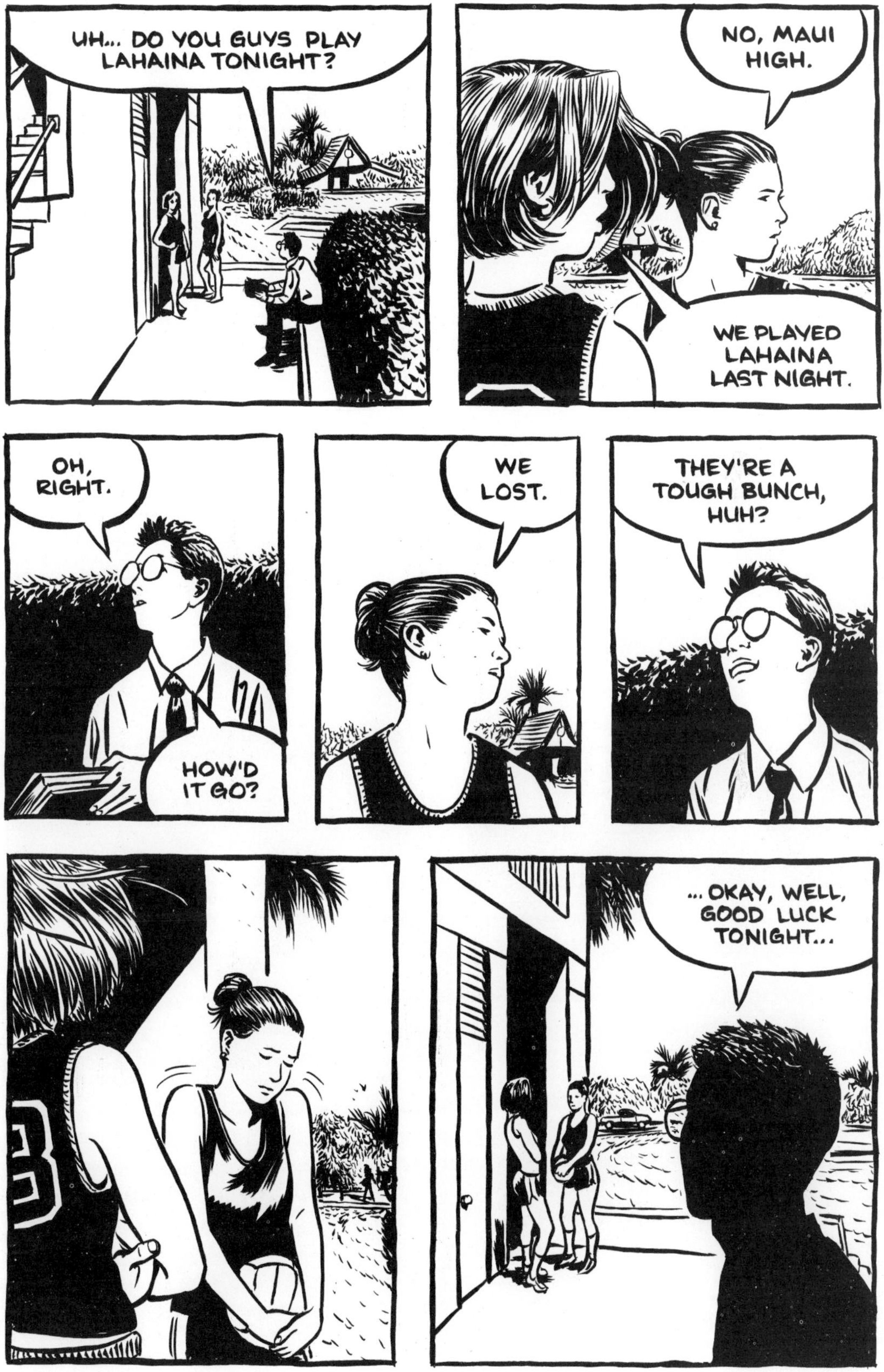
UH... DO YOU GUYS PLAY LAHAINA TONIGHT?
NO, MAUI HIGH.
WE PLAYED LAHAINA LAST NIGHT.
OH, RIGHT.
HOW'D IT GO?
WE LOST.
THEY'RE A TOUGH BUNCH, HUH?
...OKAY, WELL, GOOD LUCK TONIGHT...

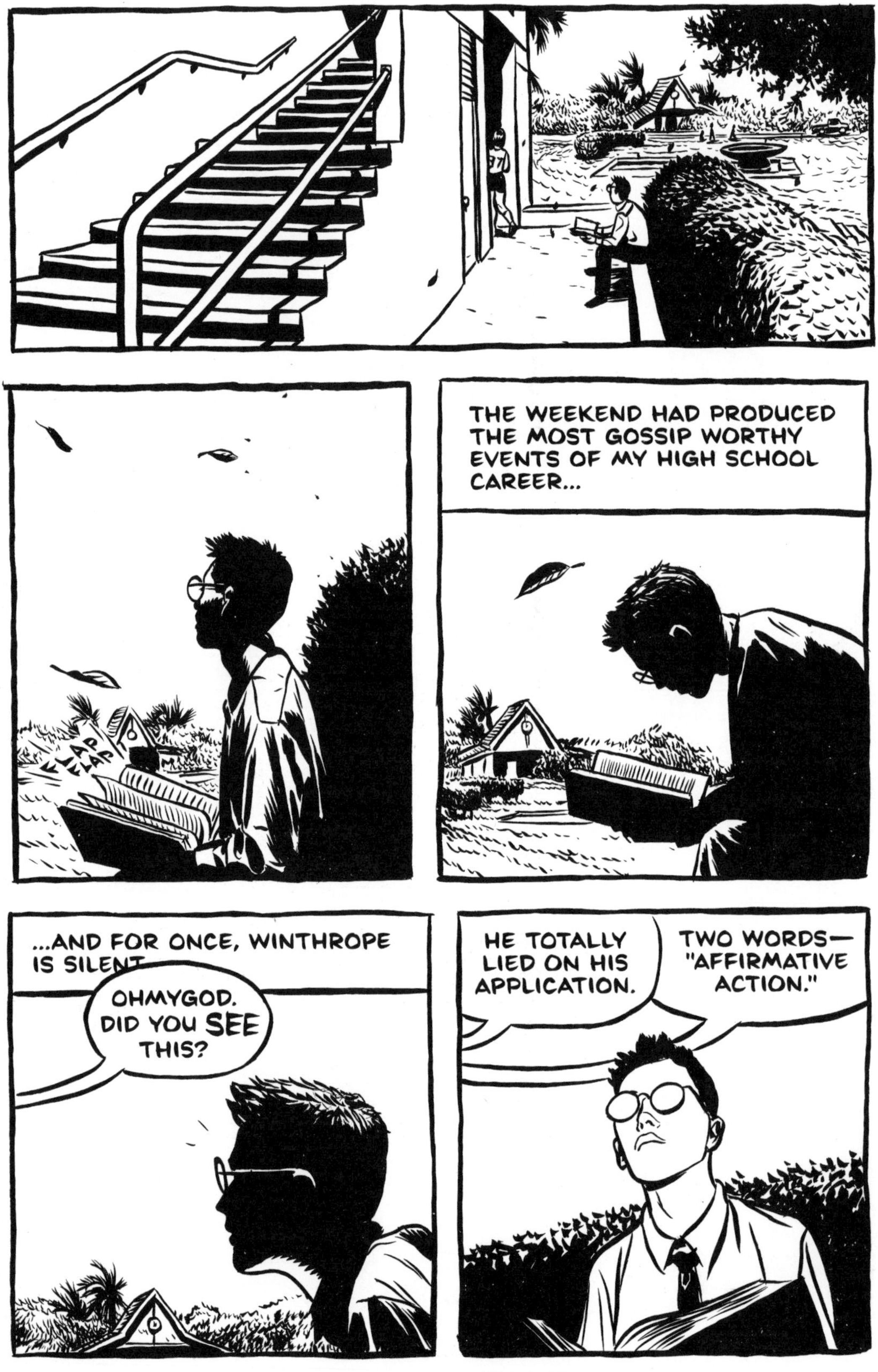
FLAP FLAP
THE WEEKEND HAD PRODUCED THE MOST GOSSIP WORTHY EVENTS OF MY HIGH SCHOOL CAREER...
...AND FOR ONCE, WINTHROPE IS SILENT.
OHMYGOD. DID YOU SEE THIS?
HE TOTALLY LIED ON HIS APPLICATION.
TWO WORDS— "AFFIRMATIVE ACTION."

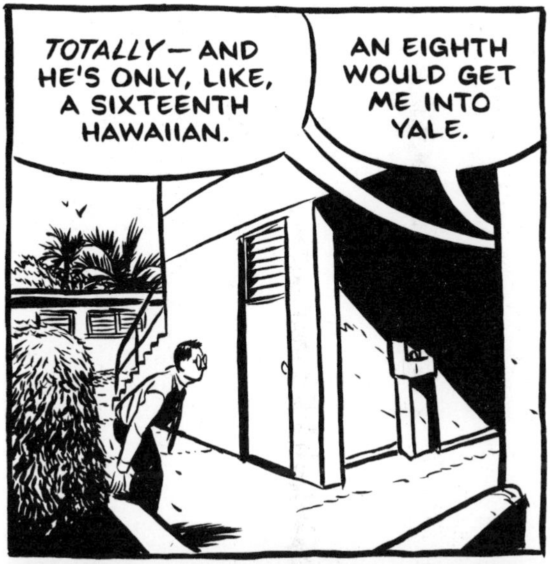
TOTALLY— AND HE'S ONLY, LIKE, A SIXTEENTH HAWAIIAN.
AN EIGHTH WOULD GET ME INTO YALE.

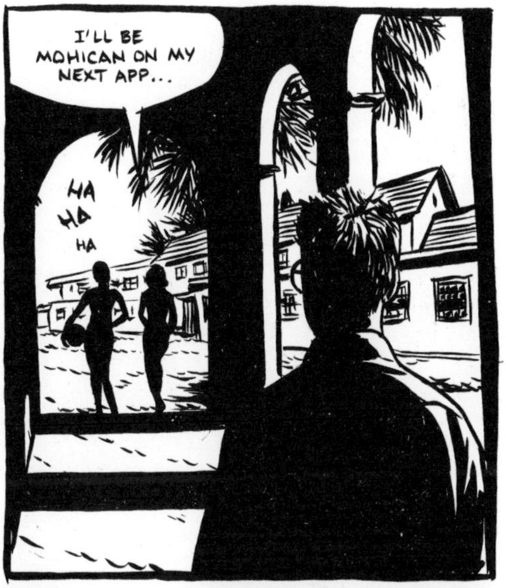
I'LL BE MOHICAN ON MY NEXT APP...
HA
HA
HA

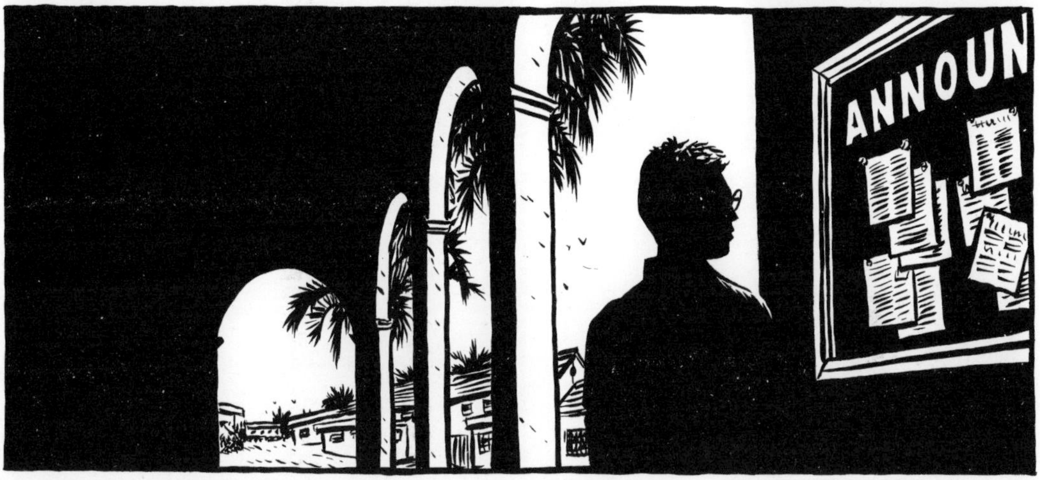
ANNOUN

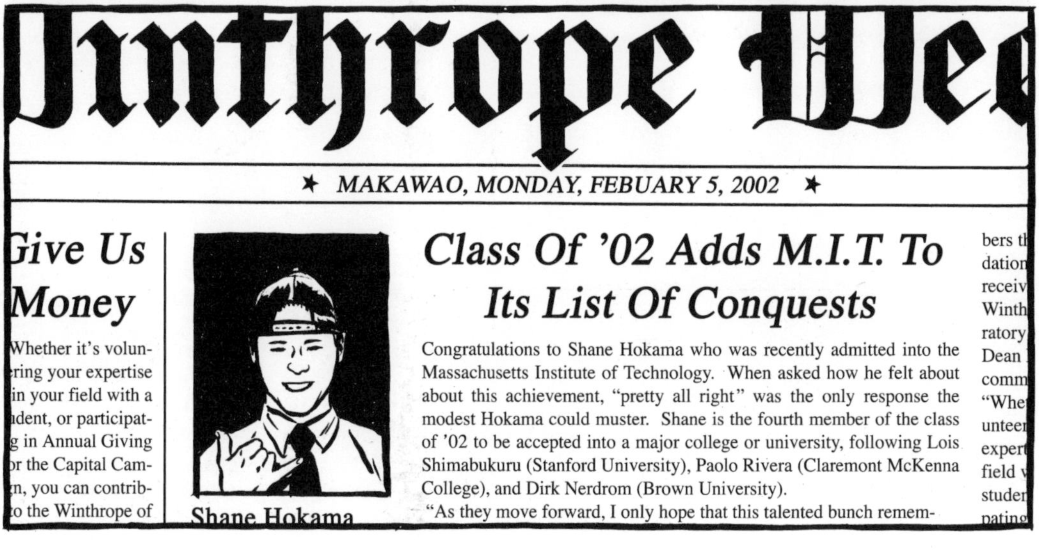

Vinthrope We

★ *MAKAWAO, MONDAY, FEBUARY 5, 2002* ★

Give Us Money

Whether it's volun-
ering your expertise
in your field with a
ident, or participat-
g in Annual Giving
or the Capital Cam-
n, you can contrib-
o the Winthrope of

Shane Hokama

Class Of '02 Adds M.I.T. To Its List Of Conquests

Congratulations to Shane Hokama who was recently admitted into the Massachusetts Institute of Technology. When asked how he felt about about this achievement, "pretty all right" was the only response the modest Hokama could muster. Shane is the fourth member of the class of '02 to be accepted into a major college or university, following Lois Shimabukuru (Stanford University), Paolo Rivera (Claremont McKenna College), and Dirk Nerdrom (Brown University).

"As they move forward, I only hope that this talented bunch remem-

bers t
datio
receiv
Winth
ratory
Dean
comm
"Whe
untee
exper
field
studer
pating

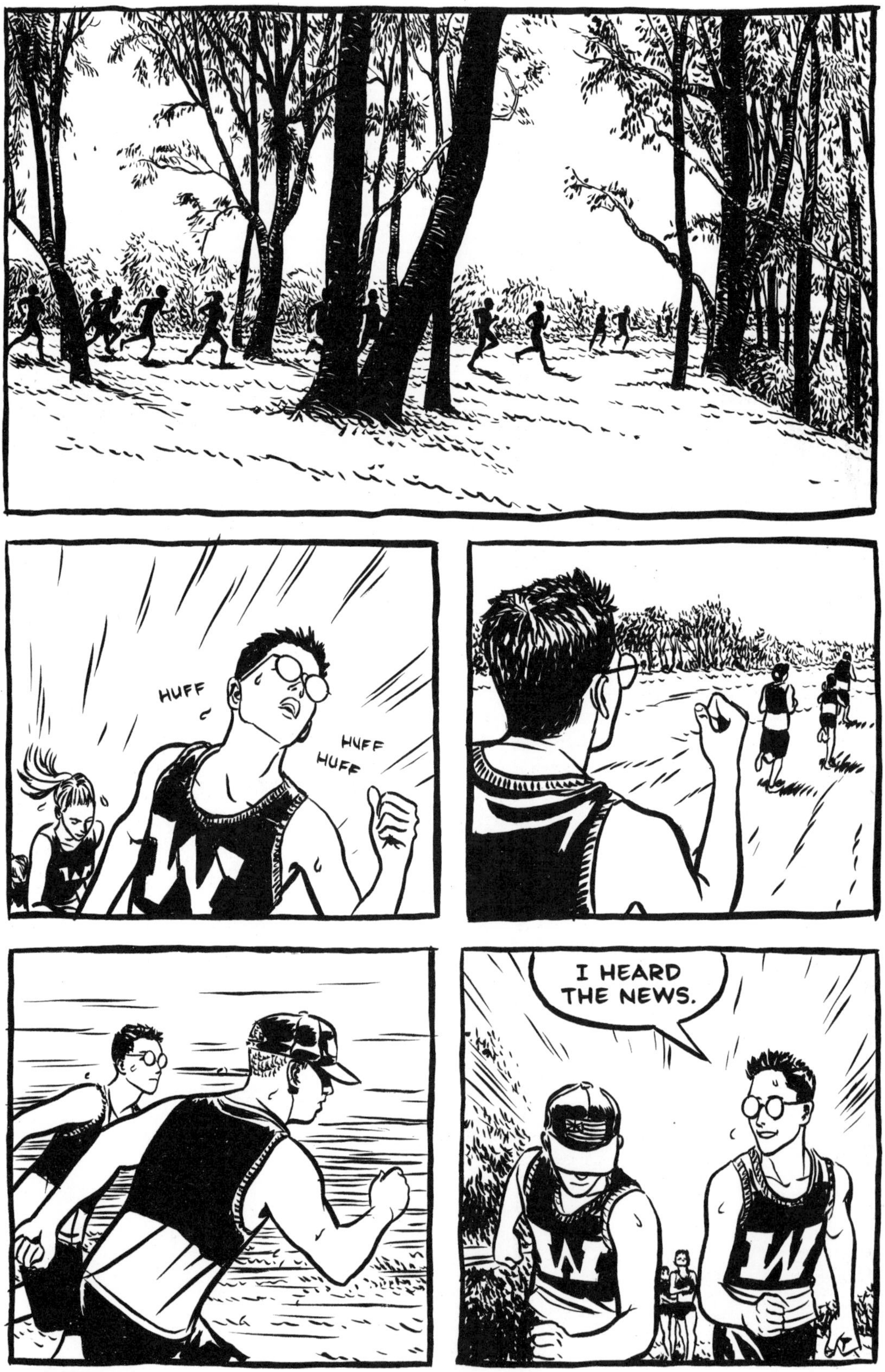
HUFF
HUFF
HUFF
I HEARD THE NEWS.

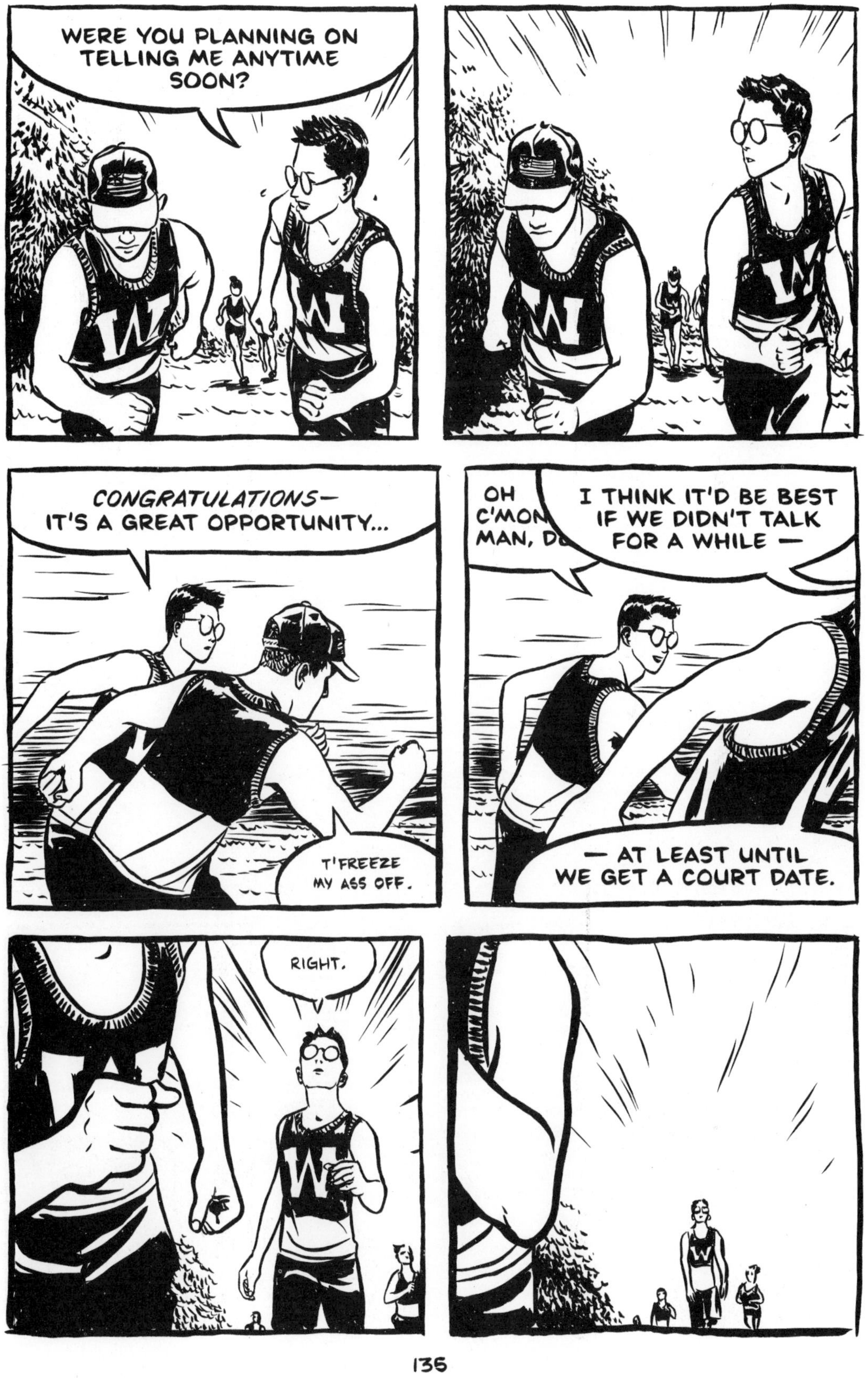
WERE YOU PLANNING ON TELLING ME ANYTIME SOON?
CONGRATULATIONS— IT'S A GREAT OPPORTUNITY...
T'FREEZE MY ASS OFF.
OH C'MON MAN, D
I THINK IT'D BE BEST IF WE DIDN'T TALK FOR A WHILE —
— AT LEAST UNTIL WE GET A COURT DATE.
RIGHT.

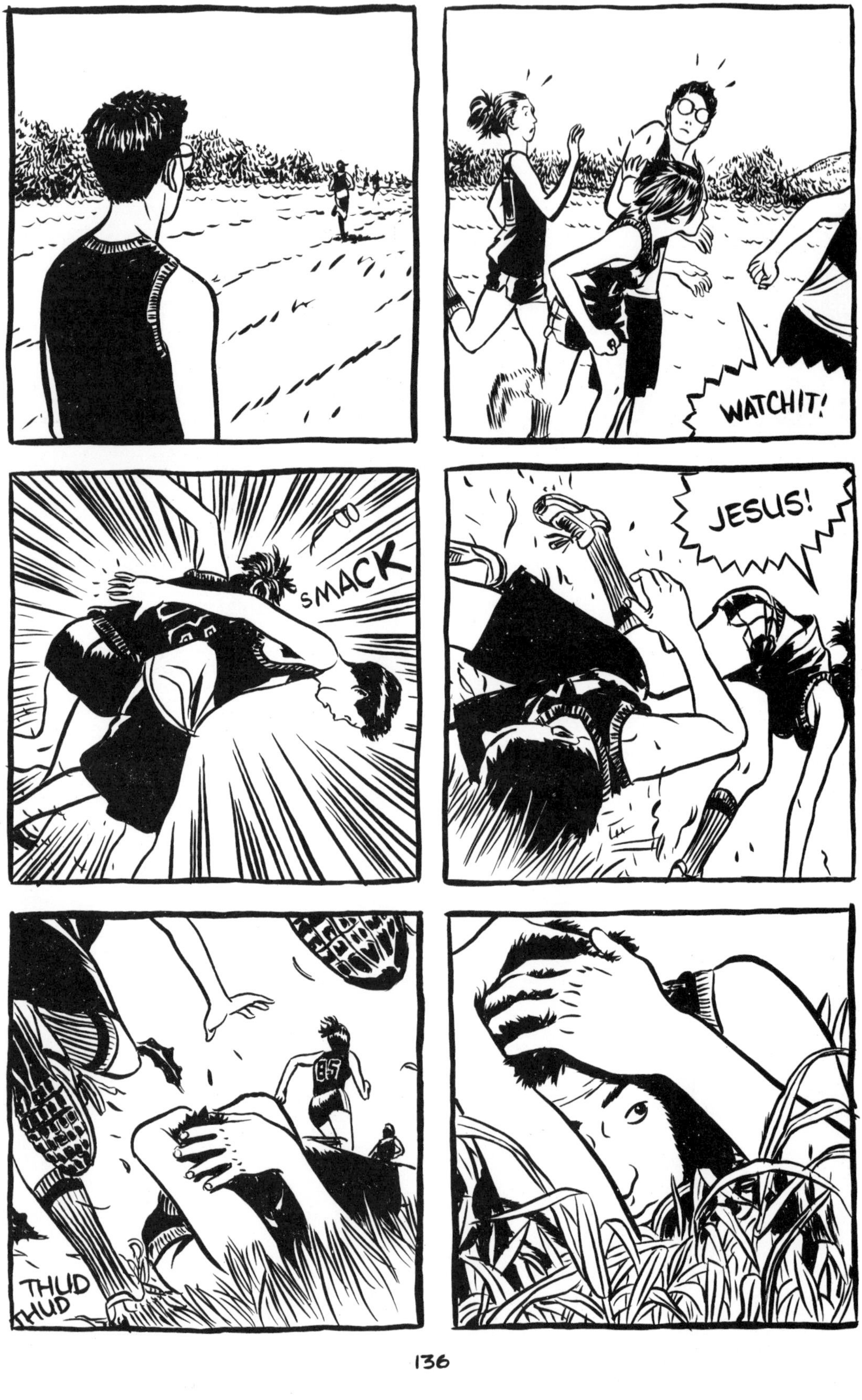
WATCHIT!
SMACK
JESUS!
THUD
THUD

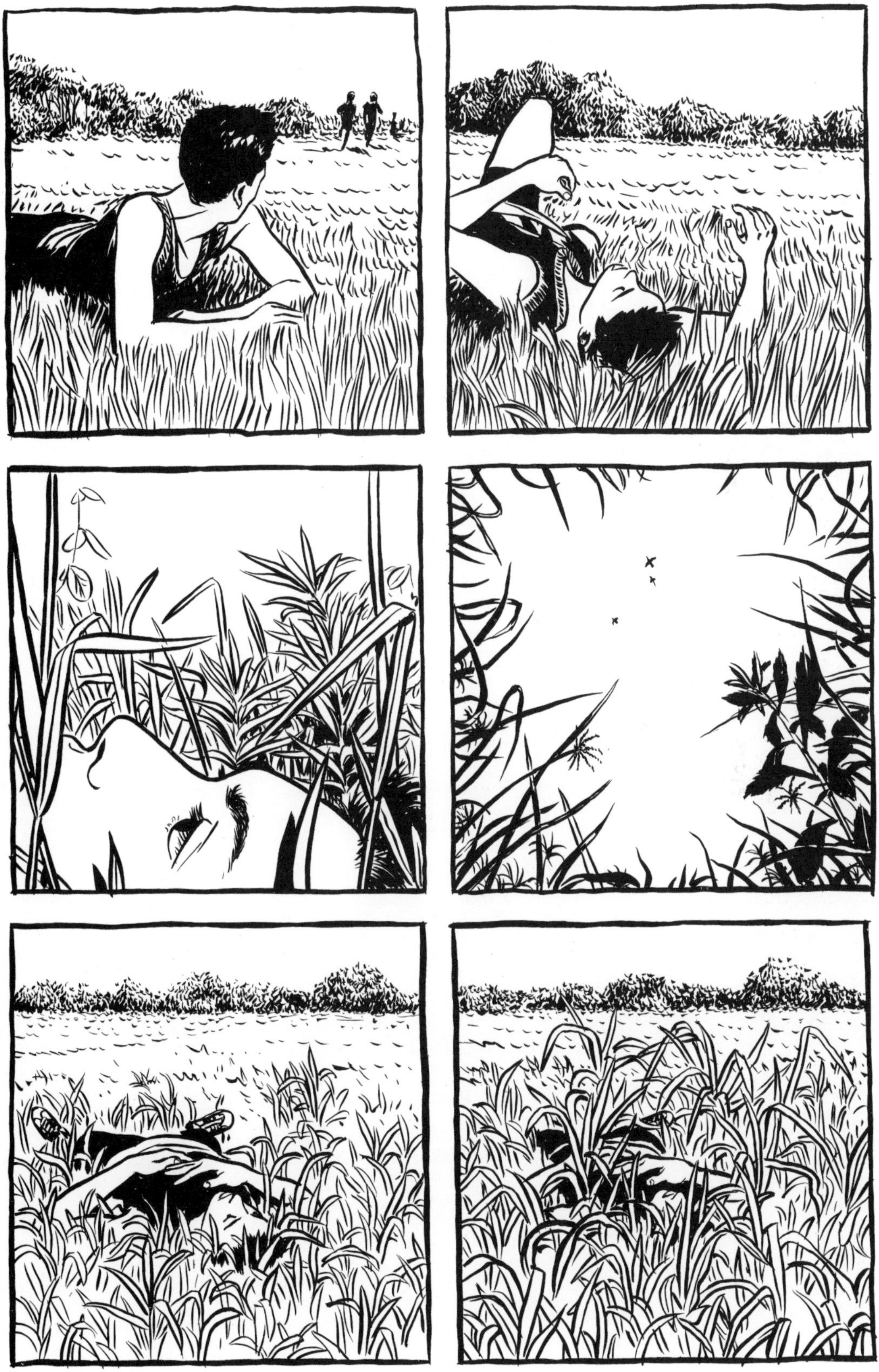

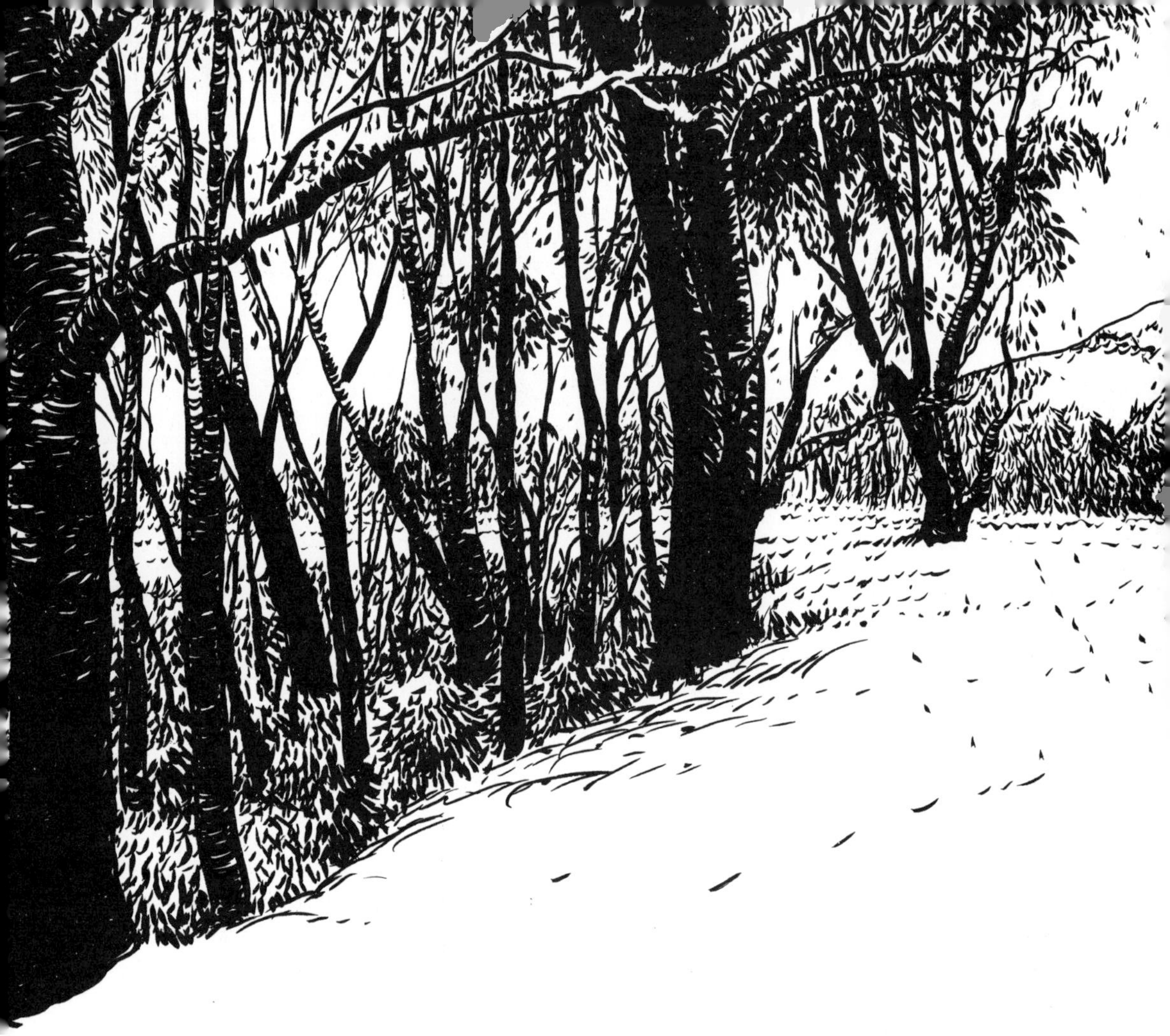

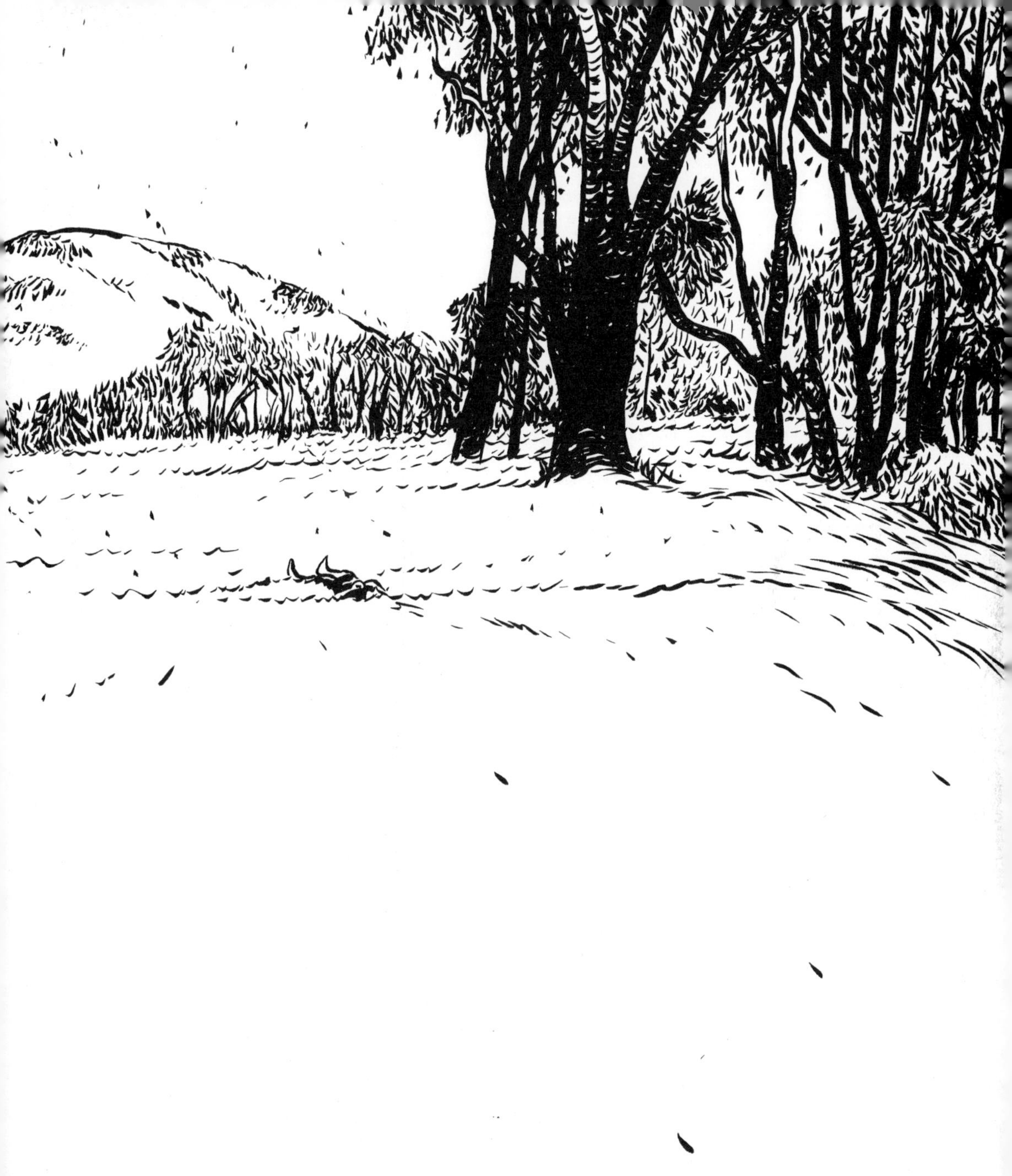

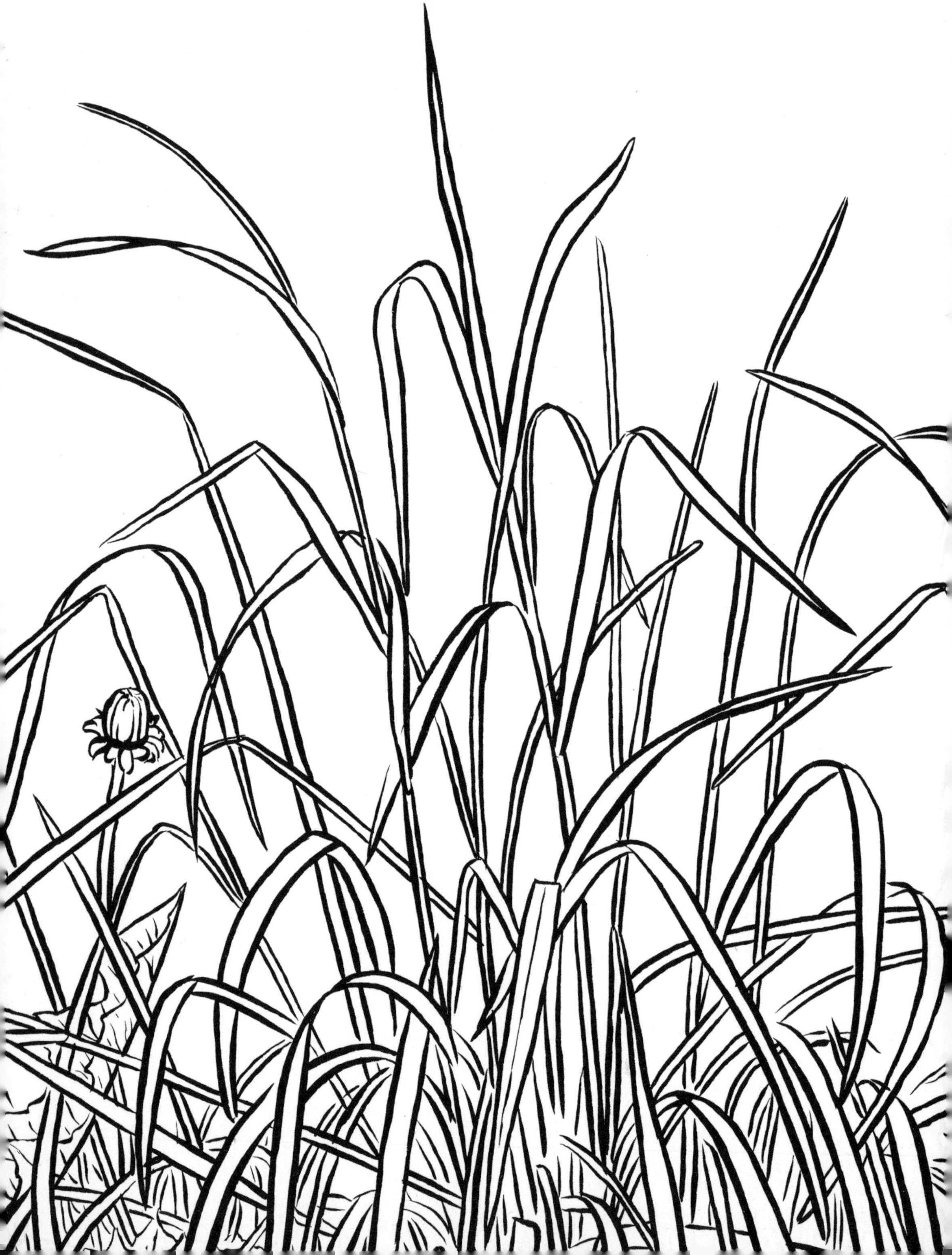

Special thanks to: Bryce Thayer, Gary Groth,
Eric Reynolds, Kim Thompson, David Mazzucchelli,
Paolo Rivera, Ryan Dunn, Steve Oh, and Lacey Browne.

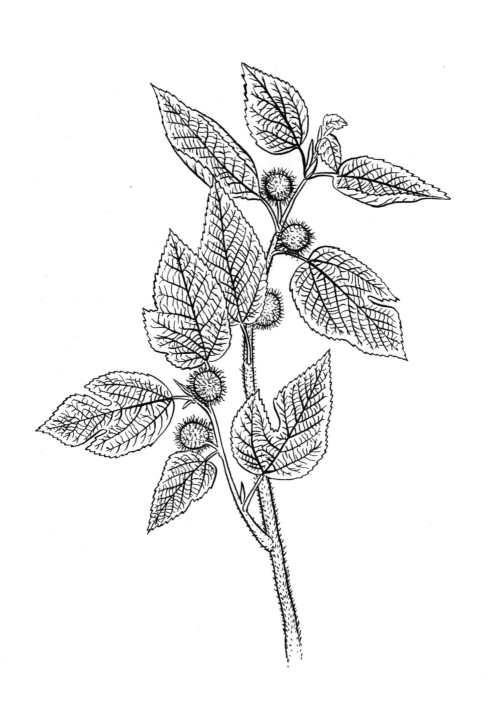

NOTES

2-5   Maps based on drawings by cartographer James Y. Nitta.

        Stearns, Harold T. *Geology of Hawaii*. Pacific Books, Publishers, 1966.

41   *Batu* [bah-**too**] Hawaiian slang for crystal methamphetamine, a narcotic that took a stronghold in Hawaii years before the mainland U.S. In 2004, Hawaii recorded the highest meth use per capita in the country, and in 2018, fatal poisonings associated with methamphetamine use continue to far outnumber those of opioids and other drugs.

        Avendaño, Eleni. "Meth Deaths Soar in Hawaii Even As Opioids Grab Public Attention." *Honolulu Civil Beat*, 12 November 2019.

51   Chinen, Jon J. *The Great Mahele*. University of Hawaii Press, 1958.

63   *Haole* [**hao**-ley] commonly used slang most frequently used to mean "of European ancestry." Formally, the word is Hawaiian for "foreigner."

79   60,000 Hawaiian residents have relocated to Las Vegas according to *Las Vegas Weekly Magazine*. That figure is 30,000 according to the *Honolulu Advertiser*, and 100,000 according to the Las Vegas Hawaiian Civic Club.

        Toole, Michael T. "Neon Honolulu: Hawaiian Culture Guide to Las Vegas." *Las Vegas Weekly* 13 May, 2004.

        Hurley, Timothy. "Pacific islander influx to Nevada 'extremely high.'" *Honolulu Advertiser* 31 October, 2003.

82-83   Kepler, Angela Kay. *Hawaiian Heritage Plants*. The Oriental Publishing Co., 1983.

83   The introduction of disruptive alien species such as the feral pig is one of many factors which lead to the decimation of Hawaii's dry land forests. Wildfires and land clearing by early human settlers also contributed.

83   Cameos of the endemic Hawaiian honeycreepers based on a painting by Douglas Pratt.

CHAPTER BREAKS, FACING PAGE   *Wauke* (paper mulberry) a species used in old Hawaii to make, among other things, *kapa*, a bark cloth often printed with fine patterns.

ENDPAPERS   Hawaiian wildflowers. Front: *pua kala*, an increasing scarce poppy endemic to the islands. Back: common thistle, an invasive weed rapidly gaining ground in Hawaii.

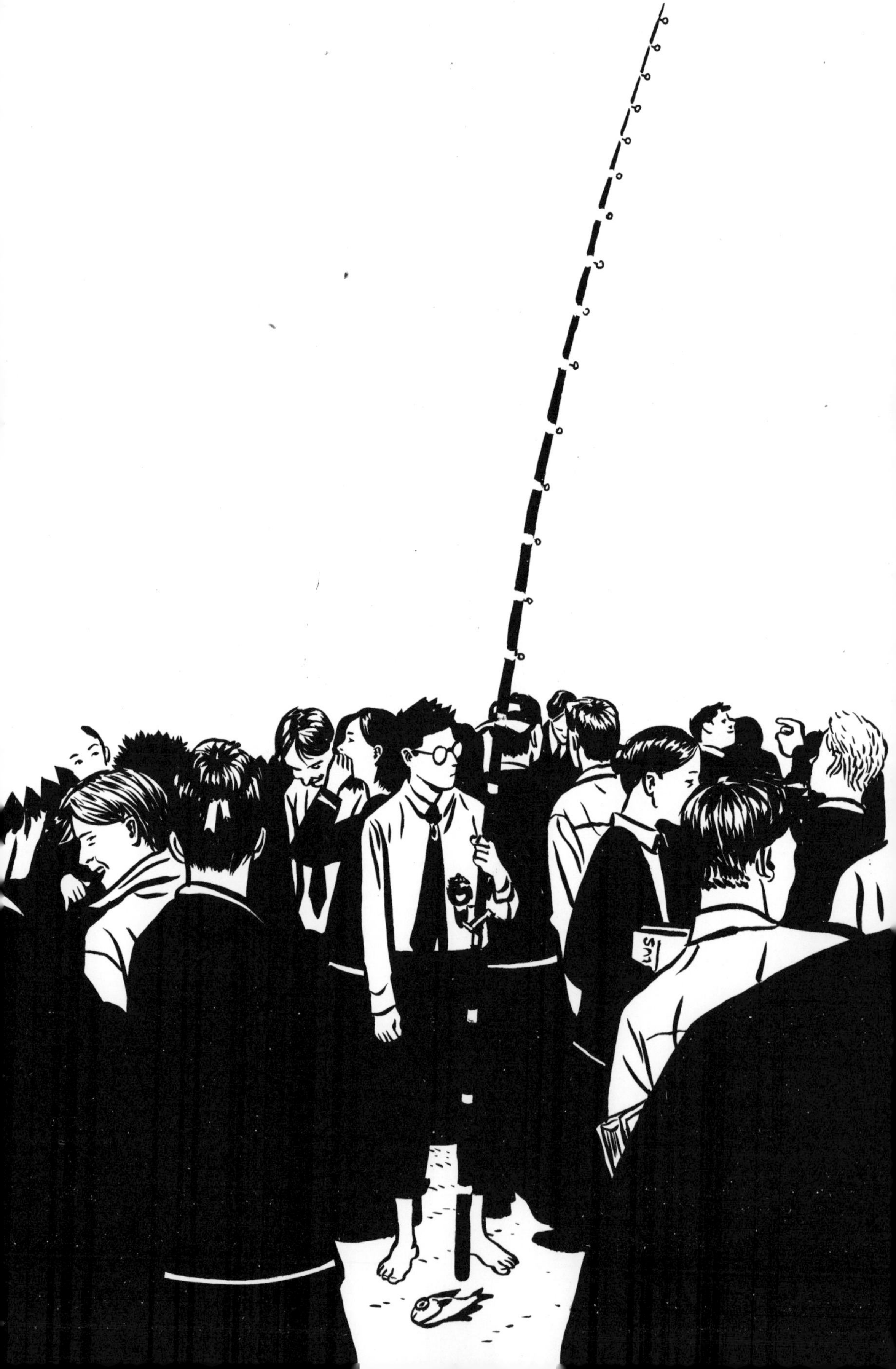

AFTERWORD

I began what would eventually become *Night Fisher* in 2002 as a junior in college studying abroad in Rome. It was my first time in a foreign country, and I never felt more out of place. I spent a lot of time there reflecting on the culture in which I grew up, and late one night, a story loosely based on my high school years on Maui poured out onto a yellow legal pad in words and drawings.

Over the next three years, the project ballooned as I graduated from art school and moved to Brooklyn, New York. I worked nights as a waiter and spent my days at a drawing table crammed beneath my lofted bed. I had no publisher, but I convinced myself that my story was worth telling. Hawaii was the backdrop for countless films and novels, but the place they depicted was never one I recognized. I thought I could honor Maui by showing it truthfully.

In January of 2005, I sent a photocopied manuscript to Fantagraphics as a blind submission, and *Night Fisher* was published later that year. Its release unexpectedly kicked off a career in illustration, and I put making comics on the back burner. By the time I was approached to repackage the book for its tenth anniversary, I could only see its faults, and I passed on its reissue. In 2019, I returned to making comics and took a fresh look at those faults. I retouched almost every page, redrew faces, and refined dialogue. Some of these revisions sharpened story beats, while others strictly indulged a nagging perfectionism. As I write this, *Night Fisher* is as old as its protagonist. I'm not sure this last draft finally achieves what I intended in 2002, but more than ever, I recognize the place and time it depicts.

—R. Kikuo Johnson, 2021

Facing page: cover illustration for a self-published edition of Night Fisher
sent as a submission to Fantagraphics in 2005.

FANTAGRAPHICS BOOKS INC.
7563 Lake City Way NE
Seattle, Washington, 98115
www.fantagraphics.com

Editor and Associate Publisher: Eric Reynolds
Book Design: R. Kikuo Johnson
Additional Design: McCarthy & Covey
Production: Paul Baresh
Publisher: Gary Groth

ISBN 978-1-68396-470-4

Library of Congress Control Number 0123456789

First printing: October 2021
Printed in China

R. Kikuo Johnson, Wailuku, Maui ca. 2003

R. KIKUO JOHNSON was born on Maui in 1981. His other
books include the graphic novel *No One Else* and the all-ages tale
The Shark King, both of which are set in Hawaii. Since 2006, his
comics and illustrations have regularly appeared on the cover and
in the pages of *The New Yorker*. He divides his time living and
working in Brooklyn, NY, teaching at the Rhode Island School
of Design, and playing the ukulele with his family on Maui.